KU-474-893

Critical Thinking in Human Resource Development

Human Resource Development is an emerging profession and is of increasing importance in the workplace. This collection of articles is a response to the fast changing socio-political backdrop against which HRD scholars and practitioners are seeking to understand and interpret the field, and find new courses of action.

Critical Thinking in Human Resource Development offers a radical alternative to mainstream thinking about developing people in the workplace. Traditionally, HRD literature has been based around functionalist and performativity perspectives with little attention paid to the wider social, economic and political contexts in which HRD operates. The chapters in this collection suggest new and cutting edge research agendas for the field and introduce the use of critical theory into the study of HRD. The book contains original chapters by some of the world's leading thinkers in the field and their work opens up the study of HRD, raising methodological questions and problematising current HRD practice.

The book will be of interest to students of human resource development, human resource management and organisation and management studies. It will also appeal to critically reflexive human resource practitioners seeking alternative ways to conceptualise their profession, and to interpret the challenges they are facing in today's organisations.

Carole Elliott is a Lecturer in the Department of Management Learning at Lancaster University Management School.

Sharon Turnbull is Deputy Director at the Research Centre for Leadership Studies, The Leadership Trust Foundation in Ross-on-Wye.

Routledge Studies in Human Resource Development
Edited by Monica Lee
Lancaster University, UK

HRD theory is changing rapidly. Recent advances in theory and practice, how we conceive of organisations and of the world of knowledge, have led to the need to reinterpret the field. This series aims to reflect and foster the development of HRD as an emergent discipline. Encompassing a range of different international, organisational, methodological and theoretical perspectives, the series promotes theoretical controversy and reflective practice.

Critical Thinking in Human Resource Development

Edited by
Carole Elliott and
Sharon Turnbull

Routledge
Taylor & Francis Group

LONDON AND NEW YORK

First published 2005
by Routledge
2 Park Square, Milton Park, Abingdon, Oxon OX14 4RN

Simultaneously published in the USA and Canada
by Routledge
270 Madison Ave, New York, NY 10016

Routledge is an imprint of the Taylor & Francis Group

Transferred to Digital Printing 2008

© 2005 Editorial matter and selection, Carole Elliott and Sharon Turnbull;
individual chapters, the contributors

Typeset in Garamond by
Newgen Imaging Systems (P) Ltd, Chennai, India

British Library Cataloguing in Publication Data
A catalogue record for this book is available from the British Library

Library of Congress Cataloging in Publication Data
A catalog record for this book has been requested

ISBN10: 0–415–32917–5 (hbk)
ISBN10: 0–415–48799–4 (pbk)

ISBN13: 978–0–415–32917–0 (hbk)
ISBN13: 978–0–415–48799–3 (hbk)

Contents

Illustrations

Figures

Table

Contributors

Finian Buckley is a Senior Lecturer in Organizational Psychology and Director of the MSc in Work and Organisational Psychology at Dublin City University Business School, Ireland. His research interests include diversity in organizations, trust development, communities of practice and life domain tensions. His work has been published in a variety of books and journals in Ireland, UK and USA.

John M. Dirkx is Associate Professor of Higher, Adult and Lifelong Education and Co-Director of the Michigan Center for Career and Technical Education at Michigan State University. He teaches courses in adult learning, teaching strategies for adults, programme planning, training and professional development, collaborative learning, group dynamics and research methods. He received his Doctor of Philosophy degree in Continuing and Vocational Education in 1987 from the University of Wisconsin – Madison. Prior to his appointment at MSU in 1996, Dr Dirkx taught adult education at the University of Nebraska – Lincoln for eight years. He has both practised and conducted research in professional education and continuing education, including the fields of medicine, nursing and the allied health professions. Over the last fifteen years, he has focused on the education, training and professional development of persons who work with adult learners in various settings. Dirkx has published scholarly articles and chapters on education and work, workplace learning, group dynamics, the psychosocial aspects of teaching and learning and the ways in which teachers and learners make sense of their experiences in adult and post-secondary education contexts. He is the author of *A Guide to Planning and Implementing Instruction for Adults: A Theme-based Approach*, published in 1997 by Jossey-Bass. Among his current research projects is the continuing study of student experiences in online, collaborative problem-based learning.

Carole Elliott is a Lecturer in the Department of Management Learning at Lancaster University Management School. Her PhD study was concerned with the impact of pedagogical practices on individual students following a part-time MBA programme. She has published in the *Journal of Management Education*, *Management Learning*, *Human Resource Development International* and *Human Resource Development Quarterly*. Broadly, her research interests focus on the development of the self for work, and she is exploring this in a number of empirical sites, including management education and professional networks and more recently within the BPO industry in India.

Ginny Hardy is a Visiting Fellow at the Department of Management Learning, Lancaster University and a freelance educator and writer, a position that allows her to work beyond the 'boundaries'. She has a strong interest in learning and how this is related to the concept of place. She now runs workshops for individuals and organisations, raising awareness of the links between place, environment and their work, learning and creativity. She is also involved in designing outdoor spaces that support learning.

Heather Höpfl is a Professor of Management in the Department of Accounting, Finance and Management at the University of Essex. She is a Visiting Professor of the University for Humanistics in Utrecht and the University of South Australia. Her research interests are primarily in the humanisation of organisations. Recent publications include articles in *Body and Society*, *Journal of Management Studies* and the *Journal of Organisational Change Management*.

Christina Hughes is a Senior Lecturer in the Department of Sociology and Co-Director of the Interdisciplinary Centre for the Study of Women and Gender, University of Warwick. Since completing her PhD she has taught and researched in the fields of social policy, lifelong learning and human resource development. Her research interests focus in two main areas. First, they are concerned with the development of feminist theory and feminist politics. Here, she has been working on how to understand the meanings of employment, education and family in women's lives. Second, they are concerned with the development of qualitative methodologies. She is founding co-chair of the Gender and Education Association and serves on the boards of the journals *Gender, Work and Organisation* and *Gender and Education*. Her recent publications include *Women's Contemporary Lives: Within and Beyond the Mirror* (2002, London, Routledge); *Key Concepts in Feminist Theory and Research* (2002, London, Sage) and *Disseminating Qualitative Research* (2003, Buckingham, Open University Press).

K. Peter Kuchinke, PhD is an Associate Professor of Human Resource Development at the University of Illinois at Champaign-Urbana. His current research interests focus on the philosophical foundations of HRD and on alternative approaches to leadership development. A native German with residence in the US for the past 25 years, much of his work is country and culture-level comparative in nature. He has served on the Board of Directors of the Academy of Human Resource Development from 1999–2003 and is presently General Editor of *Human Resource Development International*.

Monica Lee is a visiting Professor at Northumbria University, and is based at Lancaster University, UK. She is a Chartered Psychologist, and is a Fellow of CIPD, and associate Fellow of the British Psychological Society. She is the Founder Editor-in-Chief of *Human Resource Development International* (1998–2002) and Editor of the Routledge monograph series Studies in HRD. She came to academe from the business world where she was Managing Director of a development consultancy. She has worked extensively in Central Europe, CIS and the USA coordinating and collaborating in research and teaching initiatives. She is now concentrating on mentoring senior managers. She is intrigued by the dynamics around individuals and organisations, and most of her work is about trying to make sense of these. This can be seen in recent publications in *Human Relations*, *Human Resource Development International*, *Management Learning* and *Personnel Review*.

Kathy Monks is Director of the Centre for Research in Management Learning and Development at Dublin City University. She also manages the MBS in Human Resource Strategies. Her research interests include human resource practices and management education and development and she has published extensively in these areas. She is currently Chair of the Irish Academy of Management.

Colin Newsham was a dairy, beef and sheep farmer until 8 years ago on a 70 hectare family farm in North West England. He still lives on the farm but has diversified out of food production and now manages the land: for leisure – golf and fly fishing; for learning; wooden lodges and outdoor areas for management development and training; and for business – office space that is attracting complimentary organisations and creating a rural business community. He is also interested in the concept of place and how it relates to learning, particularly in his own life and business, and together with Ginny Hardy, runs workshops and gives presentations on this theme. He sees himself as working on the boundaries and values the advantage this position can give, particularly in thinking about policies and practices in agricultural development.

Linda Perriton has worked for a number of years as a management development and human resources consultant for a major UK financial services company. She is currently a Senior Lecturer within the Department of Management Studies at the University of York. She researches primarily in the field of management development and her work draws on various forms of feminist theory as the basis of critique of development and educational discourses used in the education of UK managers. This interest has led to further work in the field of gender and management – especially an interest in how women managers construct their workplace identities through training and development.

Rob F. Poell is Associate Professor of Human Resource Development in the Tilburg University HR Studies Department, The Netherlands. As a second-term elected Board Member for the Academy of Human Resource Development, he is currently liaison officer for its European Chapter and he chaired its Scholarship and Leadership Development Committee for two years. Rob serves as General Editor for *Human Resource Development International*. His 1998 PhD dissertation, entitled 'Organizing work-related learning projects: a network approach', was granted the Malcolm S. Knowles Dissertation of the Year Award by the Academy of HRD. His research interests include workplace learning, action learning, organisational change and learning, organisation development, learning in social networks, as well as the roles and strategies of HRD practitioners, managers and employees. He publishes in *Human Resource Development Quarterly*, *Human Resource Development International*,

Adult Education Quarterly, Applied Psychology International Review and *Management Learning,* amongst others.

Clare Rigg is Lecturer in Public Leadership and Organisation Change at the School of Public Policy at the University of Birmingham. She is currently involved in a range of projects and programmes across the public sector designed to facilitate leadership and organisation development. She is particularly interested in the use of action inquiry approaches to development, and in researching the question of links between individual learning and organisational/systemic impacts.

Sally Sambrook is a Lecturer in the Faculty of Health, University of Wales Bangor. Her main research interests are HRD in large and small organisations, and particularly in the health service, focusing on the changing role of HRD practitioners and integration of HRD activities in this complex organisation.

Jim Stewart is Professor of HRD at Nottingham Business School. He established one of the first Masters degrees in HRD in the UK at the School and for the last five years has been Joint Course Leader of its Doctorate in Business Administration programme. An active researcher and writer, Jim is the author or editor/co-editor of nine books including three of the other titles in the Routledge Studies in HRD Series, as well as numerous research reports, journal articles and conference papers. He holds three national appointed positions with the Chartered Institute of Personnel and Development and is the elected Chair of the University Forum for HRD. Before becoming an academic, Jim had a career in management and HRD in retail and in the public sector.

Kiran Trehan is Head of Department of Management at the University of Central England where she undertakes research, teaching and consultancy with a variety of public and private sector organisations in the area of human resource/ organisational development. Her fields of interest include critical approaches to human resource development, management learning, power and emotions in organisational development. Her current research interests include critical thinking in human resource development and critical reflection with particular reference to power, knowledge and group process.

Sharon Turnbull is Deputy Director at the Research Centre for Leadership Studies, The Leadership Trust Foundation in Ross-on-Wye. She is also a visiting Senior Research Fellow in the Department of Management Learning at Lancaster University Management School in the UK. She has worked on many corporate programmes, and has directed a number of Masters programmes. Her research interests are focused on leaders' work, identities and discourses of leadership; management fads and fashions and the social construction of emotions in organisations. Her PhD was entitled *Corporate Ideology and its Influences on Middle Management. A Study of Middle Managers' Responses to an Organizational Values Programme.* Her book with Caroline Gatrell *Your MBA with Distinction: Developing a Systematic Approach to Succeeding in Your Business Degree* was published in 2003 by Pearson Education.

Russ Vince is Professor of Organizational Behaviour and Human Resource Management at the Business School, the University of Hull, UK. His research interests cover: management and organisational learning, human resource development and organisational change. Russ is Editor-in-Chief of Management Learning. He is an International Advisor to the Doctoral School of Organizational Learning, Denmark; Associate Director, the Leading Consultation programme, Paris, France; Member of the Management Research Forum, the National College for School Leadership and Chair of the Knowledge and Learning Special Interest Group, the British Academy of Management. He is a member of several International Editorial Boards: Academy of Management Learning and Education, Human Resource Development International, Organizational and Social Dynamics and Action Learning: Research and Practice.

1 Critical thinking in Human Resource Development

An introduction

Carole Elliott and Sharon Turnbull

Over recent years there has been a growing interest by a number of researchers regarding the aims and purpose of HRD theory and practice. Many of these researchers have practical and theoretical roots in other areas, and have demonstrated a concern to challenge traditional notions of HRD practice, particularly that which is characterised by the performance metaphor. To confine HRD theory and practice to the strictures imposed by a particular financial management framework is, critical researchers would argue, to condemn HRD to a minor functional role whose specificity renders it incapable of moving beyond the boundaries of any one organisation. Many authors now argue that HRD must become more strategic (Walton, 1999; Grieves, 2003), that it is not a 'sub-set' of HRM (Stewart and McGoldrick, 1996) and that it must reflect more critically on, for example, its emotional (e.g. Turnbull, 1999) and ethical (e.g. Hatcher and Lee, 2003) impact, as well as its broader political (e.g. Vince, 2003), historical–cultural (e.g. Stead and Lee, 1996) and historical–political (e.g. Hamblett and Thursfield, 2003) contexts.

There is, therefore, now the development of a significant body of work within HRD that might broadly be described as critical. In relation to its disciplinary status, certainly in the UK context, obvious links can be made to the 'critical turn' in management studies. Due to UK HRD's location in business and management schools many HRD authors, whom we would describe as critical, also work within the critical management studies area. We are examples of this ourselves, oscillating between HRD and management studies conferences and texts. However, despite the influence of the critical turn in management studies on HRD in the UK, HRD has nevertheless neither been subject to the same degree of critical scrutiny as management and organisation studies, nor has it gathered together a significant mass of followers that might constitute it as a 'movement' in its own right.

With this observation in mind, we ran an 'Innovative Session' at the 2002 annual Academy of HRD (AHRD) conference called 'Critical Thinking in HRD'. This began with presentations from an international panel of researchers who each gave their individual perspective on the characteristics and attributes of critically informed HRD research, and was followed by a lively and creative discussion involving panellists and session participants. Many of the presenters and participants in that session are contributors to this edited collection, which we believe, constitutes the first collection of critical HRD texts.

Being critical in HRD

The chapters forming this book draw on a number of theoretical perspectives to inform their examination of concerns that have both a practical and theoretical interest. The variety of perspectives drawn upon by the authors reflects the critical turn's refusal to search for theoretical commensurability, and range from post-sructuralism to depth psychology, from critical theory to theology. Within the broader setting of critical approaches to management and organisation studies can be found researchers influenced by numerous epistemological positions such as postmodern, post-structuralist, post-Marxist, feminist and postcolonial as well as those whose critiques are predominantly influenced by the Frankfurt school of Critical Theory. Inevitably, ontological differences exist between researchers working from within such a range of perspectives, but what the chapters here have in common is a concern to question HRD's 'taken-for-granteds'. A critical perspective on HRD therefore does not assume that HRD's raison d'être consists solely to provide tools and methods principally designed to improve organisational performance. Taking a critical perspective involves researchers in the questioning and examination of HRD practices that are generally regarded as a 'good thing'. As Linda Perriton notes, organisations that provide training and development are automatically perceived as virtuous because learning is seen as intrinsically good. Little consideration, however, is given either to the ethical position that ensues for HRD, or to constructions of the learner that emerge from such a philosophical positioning. Similarly, Finian Buckley and Kathy Monks critique many organisations' use of training and development as a 'fix-it' solution for what is often entrenched organisation dysfunction. A high level of staff turnover may not be due to employees lacking necessary skills, which can be 'rectified' by re-training or re-education. Rather, employee dissatisfaction may lie within implicit or explicit organisational structures, policies and strategies.

For us, being critical emphasises the necessity for continuous examination of HRD's received wisdoms. This book stems from our concerns that the methodological traditions of the majority of HRD research does not allow researchers to engage in studies that challenge its predominantly performative and learning-outcome focus. We see evidence for this in leading publications and journals, as well as the content of AHRD conference proceedings. This book seeks to unpick the assumptions behind the performative orientation that dominates much HRD research by exploring whether this tradition is conducive to what we perceive is the greatest tension in HRD, the struggle to reconcile the needs of the individual with the needs of the employing organisation, the tension between autonomy and community (Elliott and Turnbull, 2003). For example, the emancipatory ideal, sometimes touched upon by those interested in individuals' aspirations to find spirituality and meaning at work (e.g. Chalofsky, 2001), challenges the performative view. If we are indeed witnessing a turn towards the sacralisation of work by organisations keen to co-opt the creativity and commitment of individual employees to an even greater degree, how does HRD respond to this? The traditional methodological frameworks utilised by HRD scholars, we argue, cannot adequately assess the impact of these moves upon the self. HRD theory, we suggest, subsequently needs to open itself up to, and equip itself with, a broader range of methodological perspectives and theoretical interpretations.

The structure of the book

We have divided the chapters that follow into two sections: theoretical debates and debates on practice. The division is in many ways a forced one, and we discussed at length the positioning of many of the chapters, which could quite comfortably sit in either section. By structuring the book in this way we do not intend to suggest that theory is divorced from practice and vice versa. Inherent to our notion of critical is the recognition that any practice engages a particular form of knowledge, and that theory derives from observations of practice(s). As such, the structure of the book is not intended to support the (artificial) division between objectivism and subjectivism. Rather, critical thinking in HRD seeks to examine the experience of practice, and requires that the theoretical presuppositions taken in these examinations be critically examined themselves.

Debates on practice

The overarching theme of this section, and one that preoccupies many of the writers whose work is included here is the set of issues around reflective practice in HRD and learning. For example, Kiran Trehan and Clare Rigg examine the notion of reflection that has primarily been employed in order to work towards the resolution of organisational problems, and compare this to critical reflection. They introduce the unspoken aspects of critical self-reflection through an analysis of the student experiences of critical reflection whilst undertaking a Masters programme in HRD. In suggesting that reflective practice has been unquestioningly appropriated within HRD, they argue for the examination of political and cultural processes affecting learning and development. They reflect on their concerns as educators about the powerful impact of introducing critical reflection to a post-experience programme, and the potential dissonance that this may unleash. Despite their examination of these concerns they suggest that the emancipatory objective of this approach is at least partially fulfilled, and conclude that the theoretical speculations on the hazards of critical reflection are overly pessimistic.

Russ Vince also examines critical reflection but from the perspective of critical practice and critical practitioners. His ideas are the outcome of what he calls a 'temporary community' of ten academics and practitioners, who came together for a two-day period, in order to discuss the future practice of HRD. These critical practitioners see themselves as playing an important role in challenging and examining the way HRD is configured in specific organisation settings. They often find themselves acting in a negotiating capacity, as the interface between powerful interest groups at all organisation levels. They seek to understand how organising avoids and excludes learning, and see HRD as speculative – as creating opportunities rather than seeking to control and regulate.

Clare Rigg develops further these debates by working to understand the relationship between these forms of critical pedagogies and their impact on managers' practice. Focussing on management education in particular, she concludes that there is not an inevitable link between critical pedagogy and critical management practice. Transformatory learning, whilst often producing individual feelings of empowerment and personal emancipation may not always lead to the broader change at an organisational or societal level to which it often aspires.

Finian Buckley's and Kathy Monks' chapter enquires about the implications of adopting management education as a panacea for all organisational ills. Based on a case study of a customised management education programme that took place over one academic year they found that the organisation ascribed problems to individuals, such as the lack of participation by women at senior levels, to women's perceived competency gaps. However, as Buckley and Monks discovered, the management education intervention was founded on false premises since the problem lay within the organisation's patriarchal culture, climate and the corresponding structures created and supported by top management.

Sally Sambrook and Jim Stewart draw on a pan-European research project set across seven European countries to form the basis of their chapter. They critically reflect on their experiences of researching in a cross-cultural context, as well as examining the concepts of HRD, learning organisations and lifelong learning. The chapter provides reflections on the possibilities of researching HRD, particularly in collaborative and comparative research projects. They highlight issues of interest and relevance to others wishing to adopt critical approaches to the study of HRD.

The chapter by Rob Poell questions the accepted notion of the roles and responsibilities of the HRD function, and suggests instead that HRD is about how workers learn and organisations work. He, therefore, places workers and learners at the heart of the HRD process. In his chapter he proposes an alternative framework for HRD, based on everyday learning and development activities often occurring informally and on an *ad hoc* basis. This proposed model aims to contribute to debates on critical HRD, by providing a means to discuss learning in organisational contexts as a contested domain heavy with often ignored power issues and conflicts of interest.

Ginny Hardy and Colin Newsham focus on the concept of 'place' as a departing point for learning, in order to work towards an alternative critical perspective to HRD practice. Adopting place as a central theme they suggest that connection to place both from an individual and organisational perspective may be a more power-ful approach to thinking critically about issues. Highlighting the dangers of tackling organisational contexts as separate from us, and the organisations in which we work, they advocate the immediate connection between our experience of our own place and the immediate connection to the wider environment.

Debates on practice concludes with Monica Lee's chapter, which draws on personal experiences to critique the role of codes of ethics as a constituent part of the HRD role. She challenges the notion that codes of ethics are problem free and neutral, sug-gesting that they are inevitably culturally bound, reflecting the values of current society. As a collective statement of responsible behaviour, they are susceptible to reification, are time dependent, and unable to respond to the emotions that are inevitably generated by questions of ethical decisions. She argues for the incorpora-tion of individual difference and flexibility in such codes in order to enable them to develop as ethical practice itself develops.

Theoretical debates

From the chapters forming this section emerges a concern to engage with the self, to examine how it is conceived in organisational constructs and to consider alternative more complex conceptualisations. The chapter by Heather Höpfl argues that conventional patriarchal representations of the organisation reduce the notion of 'organisation' to abstract relationships, rational actions and purposive behaviour. These inevitably present themselves as a quest for the good. In this context, she argues, regulation and control are achieved primarily via definition and location. Administration then functions in a very specific sense to establish a notion of 'good' order, to establish what is 'ordinary' in administrative and managerial practice. In contrast, Höpfl seeks to explore ways in which it is possible to restore the (m)other to the text of organisation, to restore the body. To work towards this, the chapter considers the possibility of a discourse of maternity and moves from this position to examine concepts of matrix reproduction and conditions of exile.

Christina Hughes's chapter that begins this section questions the assumptions associated with specific concepts, in this case with the perception of human resource development as egalitarian and gender neutral. She suggests that this has happened because the term 'human' has replaced more sexist terms such as manpower planning. However, rather than being gender neutral, she argues that major conceptualisations of human resource development are gender blind. In demonstrating that the concept of the human at the centre of discourses of human resource development privileges the masculine subject, she addresses a number of issues. These include an examination of Enlightenment and Cartesian rationality in the development of the humanist subject, and of the concept of the person in humanist discourses. The chapter goes on to present an alternative, post-structuralist understanding of the subject, as one who is constructed through discourse. One consequence of this understanding of the subject as multiply located is that the strive towards more egalitarian workplaces and HRD practices requires practitioners to engage in the tasks of critical literacy.

Peter Kuchinke's chapter continues the examination of the conceptualisation of the self, its relationship to work, and the subsequent implications this holds for HRD. How the self is constructed is, he argues, of key importance. In the literatures on HRD, HR and management, an instrumental view of personhood predominates and alternative discourses are foreclosed and ignored. This limits understanding, theorising and practical application. To begin to counter this, Kuchinke explores alternative theories of the self through an examination of developments in classic and postmodern philosophy and social science. He then goes on to address the implications this holds for HRD in both theory and practice. A more philosophically informed understanding of the subject he concludes has the potential to broaden HRD's range of options. This might include the possibility to create more humane workplaces, and a conception of HRD in line with the notion of the German idea of *Bildung* whose ideal encompasses a more general goal of education or self-development in the context of social institutions.

John Dirkx also problematises modernist assumptions present within the discourses of workplace learning such as rationality, and the progressive accumulation of knowledge and skill. He challenges these notions through reference to work informed by depth psychology, theology and postmodern thought, proposing an alternative 'discourse of desire'. This discourse allows a conceptualisation of our sense of self that acknowledges the ways in which it is bound up in the process of making meaning in work, and that it is a process fraught with uncertainty, contradiction and paradox. Dirkx observes that individuals' search for meaning in work is not served well by workplace learning programmes that continue to conceptualise their efforts within functional, performance-based and instrumental frameworks. He concludes by suggesting some implications for HRD practice, including the development of more constructivist perspectives on workplace learning, that engage workers more fully in determining their learning needs.

Linda Perriton's chapter concludes this section and challenges the idea that development should necessarily be considered a 'good thing'. Coupled with the adage that 'you can never have enough of a good thing' this has, she argues, been reflected in the lack of engagement with questions surrounding the moral and ethical boundaries of development. Her concern is to redress some of the neglect shown to these issues, and she does so by exploring eighteenth century ideas of sensibility and their applicability to some of the approaches to HRD in the twenty-first century. With reference to examples of HRD interventions, she questions whether HRD hasn't abandoned sense for sensibility in some contemporary and development practices and philosophies.

We conclude the book with a discussion of the socio-political implications of the processes and content of HRD interventions in different contexts. We conclude that programmes designed to empower and transform may lead to unintended outcomes relating to identity and participants' political responses, as a result of a lack of reflexivity in respect of pedagogic methods.

The chapters in this book have provoked a number of important issues for HRD practice and have provided a challenge to mainstream HRD theory. By drawing on a broad range of disciplines we have been able to re-conceptualise some of the age-old debates in HRD, and this has opened up further questions for future critical researchers. These might include, for example, further critical study of our HRD interventions, our understanding of work and the nature of organisations, the values inherent in organisational structures and practices and the meaning of 'emancipation', 'motivation' and 'self-actualisation'. This also suggests the need for a wider variety of methodological frameworks such as critical discourse analysis, post-structural or narrative analysis. Within this new research agenda we also propose a greater recognition of the socio-political and economic conditions within which HRD must necessarily operate.

References

Chalofsky, N. (2001) (interviewed by Callahan, J. and Ward, D.) 'A search for meaning: revializing the "human" in human resource development', *Human Resource Development International*, 4, 2: 235–42.

Elliott, C. and Turnbull, S. (2003) 'Reconciling autonomy and community: the paradoxical role of HRD', *Human Resource Development International*, 6, 4: 457–74.

Grieves, J. (2003) *Strategic Human Resource Development*, London: Sage.

Hamblett, J. and Thursfield, D. (2003) 'Other voices: a short case for the development of an historical dimension to the study of workplace and lifelong learning', *Human Resource Development International*, 6, 2: 167–86.

Hatcher, T. and Lee, M. (2003) 'Ethics and HRD: a new approach to leading responsible organizations', *AHRD International Research Conference*, Minneapolis, MN, 27 February–1 March, 2003.

Stead, V. and Lee, M. (1996) 'Inter-cultural perspectives on HRD', in J. Stewart and J. McGoldrick (eds) *Human Resource Development. Perspectives, Strategies and Practice*, London: Pitman.

Stewart, J. and McGoldrick, J. (eds) (1996) *Human Resource Development. Perspectives, Strategies and Practice*, London: Pitman.

Turnbull, S. (1999) 'Emotional labour in corporate change programmes: the effects of organizational feeling rules on middle managers', *Human Resource Development International*, 2, 2: 125–46.

Vince, R. (2003) 'The future practice of HRD', *Human Resource Development International*, 6, 4: 559–63.

Walton, J. (1999) *Strategic Human Resource Development*, Harlow, Essex: Pearson Education.

Part I

Debates on practice

2 Beware the unbottled genie

Unspoken aspects of critical self-reflection

Kiran Trehan and Clare Rigg

Introduction

Reflective practice has become almost obligatory within HRD but the instrumental reflections of what did I do, what did I learn, what would I do differently have been found to be limited. In a search for more challenging self-development tools, critical self-reflection has seen considerable recent growth. The field of critical reflection is imbued with hopes of transformational flow from individual learning and development to changes in HRD practice. Critical reflection has been central to definitions of critical management as epitomised, for example, by Reynolds' (1997) distinction between content radical and process radical pedagogies. Content radicals disseminate radical material, in the sense of critical theories and concepts and alternatives to technocratic management education. Process radicals attempt to address power asymmetries of the traditional teacher/learner relationship, for example, taking a critical reflective approach, using action learning, critical reflection, the conception of tutors and participants as co-learners in a learning community or action learning set and negotiated curricula. Brookfield (1995) argues critical reflection is not just a process of exploring assumptions of power and hegemony by viewing what we do through different lenses, but also involves the examination of political and cultural processes affecting learning and development. Critical reflection should be part of both formal and informal learning processes. As Nord and Jermier highlight, a critical perspective offers

> an intellectual framework for resisting domination by traditional science and technology, institutionally distorted communication, owners of capital, and patriarchal forces.
>
> (1992: 203)

Within this chapter we first review the origins, rationale, hopes and hazards of critical reflection. We then describe how critical reflection is expedited on a Postgraduate Masters Programme in HRD at the University of Central England (UCE). From this we present an analysis of students' views on the outcomes and impacts of critical reflection on their learning and development. The final section examines the unspoken aspects of critical reflection as a backdrop to exploring the contradictions and complexities of engaging in critical self-reflection.

Reflection: a critical interpretation

The concept of reflecting, particularly reflecting on experience, is central to the theories of learning which have come to inform thinking and practice in HRD education and development. The concept of critical reflection on the other hand, as described in critical theory and critical pedagogy, is very different and seldom reaches the domain of HRD. Much greater interest in critical reflection is shown in the realm of adult education, at least in the theoretical work of academics.

Put simply, whereas *critical reflection* is the cornerstone of emancipatory approaches to education, *reflection* as an HRD concept is expressed primarily as a key element of problem-solving. In both domains reflection is placed at the core of the learning process, especially in relation to learning as 'development' and not merely the acquisition of information (Usher, 1985; Garrison, 1991). The crucial distinction in usage is in terms of the questioning of contextual taken-for-granteds – social, cultural and political – which is the hallmark of critical reflection and its methodological foundation in critical theory.

Critical reflection has emerged as a field that goes beyond ideas of HRD education. Burgoyne and Reynolds (1997) see as central to it an emphasis on 'understanding the whole person as mediated through experience', thus paying attention to

> more connectedness to daily personal and professional life and, in avoiding that passivity thought to be associated with more conventional educational methods, as offering managers more opportunity for development than seemed possible in focusing exclusively on the acquisition of knowledge and skills.

This fits with Watson and Harris' (1999) concept of the individual as an emergent entity, a concept which also sits well with the influential writing, on experiential learning and reflective practice in management and professional contexts, by Kolb (1984) and Schon (1983). Watson and Harris say:

> the process of how people enter managerial work and 'learn to manage' has to be understood in the light of the individual's life, identity and biography as a whole. There is a clear continuity between the management of one's personal life and the formal managerial work done in the organisation.

Similarly Trehan (2003) argues HRD education is an educational domain where critical reflection might be expected, given increasing concern amongst HRD educators for introducing a more critical perspective into their practice. However, whilst illustrations are emerging that apply to the curriculum (Nord and Jermier, 1992); or to the introduction of critical analysis through the materials used (Thompson and McGivern, 1996); or through the selection of analytical frameworks (Summers *et al.*, 1997) and through encouraging students to apply critical ideas to their professional experience (Grey *et al.*, 1996), critical reflection is notable for its absence.

Critical reflection and learning has perhaps always been an aspiration of scholarly activity, as understood to be 'an activity engaged in by the wise scholar and the wise man and woman of action' (Watson, 1999: 4). A traditional view is that to be critical is to evaluate what is good and bad, to be 'concerned with giving reasons for one's beliefs and actions, analysing and evaluating one's own and other people's reasoning, devising and constructing better reasoning' (Thompson and McGivern, 1996: 2). Watson uses the term critical again to describe how

> *Critical commonsense* analysis tends to start from a consideration of the most obvious or likely explanation of what is going on; the everyday commonsense explanation in fact. But it then goes on to ask whether things are really as they at first seem. Alternative explanations are considered and attention is paid to available evidence in judging the serious rival explanations.
>
> (Watson, 2002)

He goes on 'being critical in the sense of constantly questioning taken-for-granted ideas and practices'. Here critical reflection is a process, the essence of questioning, the use of critique; 'the application of all the traditional scholarly criteria of rigour, challenge to taken-for-granted assumptions, debate, logical consistency and the setting of claims to valid generalisation and theories against the best evidence that can be mustered about what occurs in the world' (Watson, 2002).

Critical reflection and learning combines roots in radical adult education, influenced amongst others by Freire (1972), Giroux (1981) and Habermas (1972), and in critical theory, such as feminism, Marxism or post-structuralism. Some of the arenas in which critical reflection and learning have been most extensively written about and deployed include Paulo Freire's *Pedagogy of the Oppressed*, and feminist and postcolonialist pedagogies.

Critical reflection broadly, is described by Reynolds as manifesting such key principles as

> questioning the assumptions and taken-for-granteds embodied in both theory and professional practice;
> foregrounding the processes of power and ideology subsumed within the social fabric of institutional structures, procedures and practices;
> confronting spurious claims of rationality and revealing the sectional interests which can be concealed by them;
> working towards an emancipatory ideal – the realisation of a more just society based on fairness and democracy.
>
> (Reynolds, 1998a: 5)

Critical reflection, as a form of critical education, is also seen to embody these principles (Kemmis, 1985). As such it differs from the more instrumental reflection promoted by experiential learning advocates, such as Kolb (1984) or Schon (1983), which does not encourage such a fundamental critique, which Collins describes as the facility to

> put aside the natural attitude of their everyday life-world and adopt a sceptical approach towards taken-for-granted innovations 'necessary for progress', supposedly 'acceptable' impositions as the price of progress, and seemingly authoritative sources of information.
>
> (Collins, 1991: 94)

Processes of 'critical' thinking

Processes of critical thinking in practice are rooted in reflection, either in the form of self-reflection or as of the relationships between individuals, collectivities and society. For example, Carr and Kemmis suggest individuals 'reflect upon their own situations and change them through their own actions' (1986: 130). For Alvesson and Willmott

> Critical Theory seeks to highlight, nurture and promote the potential of human consciousness to reflect critically upon such oppressive practices, and thereby facilitate the extension of domains of autonomy and responsibility.
>
> (1996: 13)

Alongside the cognitive tools of analytical critique and application of Critical Theory, the methods of critical thinking borrow from psychoanalysis, using 'critical self-reflection as a means of bringing to consciousness those distortions in patients' self-formation processes which prevent a correct understanding of themselves and their actions' (Carr and Kemmis, 1986: 138).

A key rationale for encouraging HRD managers to be critically reflective lies in the realisation of how powerful managers now are in the world, yet how poorly traditional HRD education has prepared them for considering questions of power and responsibility. Alvesson and Willmott (1992a) argue that the practice of management has a dominant effect on the lives of an organisation's employees, its customers and wider society, extending even to the lives of unborn generations through the environmental impact of an organisation's processes.

Unveiling critical reflection

Clearly, given the rationales advanced for critical reflection, the hopes of its proponents have been concerned with transforming society and making it more democratic or emancipatory. Key to this has been that through education individuals become conscious of the oppression of or constrains on their lives and take action to change that for the better. It is clear that critical reflection is qualitatively different from the concept of reflection in experiential learning theory. While reflection focuses on the immediate, presenting details of a task or problem, critical reflection involves an analysis of power and control and an examination of the taken-for-granteds within which the issues are situated. The potential for critical reflection derives from the tensions, contradictions, emotions and power dynamics that inevitably exist in managers' lives. Critical reflection as a pedagogical approach emerges when these dynamics are treated centrally as a site of learning about managing and organising. McLaughlin and Thorpe argue

> At the level of their own expertise, managers undertaking critical reflection can come to know themselves and their organization much better. In particular, they can become aware of the primacy of politics, both macro and micro, and the influence of power on decision making and non-decision making, not to mention the 'mobilization of bias'.
>
> (McLaughlin and Thorpe, 1993: 25)

In Willmott's view

> To the extent that critical (reflection) learning engages with the struggles of individual students and practitioners, it may also open up an appreciation of, and sensitivity towards, 'darker' aspects of organizational life.
>
> (Willmott, 1997: 119)

For Vince critical reflection addresses the deficit in traditional reflection learning that offers little encouragement to or support in 'working with the emotional and power dynamics in learning processes' (Vince, 1996: 119).

The contribution of critical reflection to a critical management practice is epitomised by Willmott

> Critical action learning explores how the comparatively abstract ideas of critical theory can be mobilized and applied in the process of understanding and changing interpersonal and institutional practices. By combining a pedagogy that focuses upon management as a lived experience with theory that debunks conventional wisdom, managers can be enabled to develop 'habits of critical thinking...that prepare them for responsible citizenship and personally and socially rewarding lives and careers'.
>
> (Willmott, 1997: 173, citing Porter *et al.*, 1989: 71)

Other voices challenge this optimism both from theoretical perspectives and as a consequence of empirical experience of critical learning programmes, particularly in adult education. Reynolds (1998a) articulates one of the most comprehensive critical reviews, expounding three possible pitfalls or hazards. The first is the potential for management students to resist engagement in critical reflection, because to do so would be to question their profession and challenge their status quo. Reed and Anthony (1992) suggest managers would find the approach 'irrelevant, unreal and impractical' (1992: 607). Jackall (1988) implies managers would find it counter cultural to the pressures to conform to organisational ideologies. Reynolds (1998a) also suggests that, relevant or not, management students might simply find the language of much critical theory impenetrable. The second hazard outlined by Reynolds (1998a) is the potential for managers to merely assimilate critical ideas into their existing perspective, without really unpicking the underlying assumptions and ideologies. The third danger relates to the potential adverse psychological and social consequences for individuals of engaging in critical reflection, as Reynolds cautions, it

> can prove unsettling, mentally or emotionally and a source of disruption at home or at work. It carries the risk to employment and even – if we include stress related illness – to life itself.
>
> (1998a: 16)

Brookfield (1994) describes the dissonance produced by critical reflection, as the 'darker side' of such an approach and Reynolds (1998a) warns of the production of cultural misfits, facing 're-entry' problems on their return to work, feeling frustrated or powerless with their new awareness. Perhaps most pessimistic are Alvesson and Willmott (1992) in their concern that

> enhanced ecological consciousness and greater freedom and creativity at work – likely priorities emerging from emancipatory change – may result in bankruptcy and unemployment.
>
> (1992b: 448)

Willmott (1997) has described the inherently conflicting nature of organisations' social relations, in which managers may be both perpetrators of control systems at the same time as victims of those same systems. If critical reflection heightens awareness of deep flaws in the systems and values of their organisations, how do participants in our programme remain managers post critical reflection?

Critical reflection in practice

Drawing on the reflections of tutors and students on a masters programme for managers where a critical HRD perspective was adopted, this section presents an examination of the concrete experiences of advancing such an approach.

We found the course to be immensely powerful in its impact on participants, beyond what we had anticipated. Students were using terms like enlightened and transformed, in their conversations with us, yet we were also aware that the course had been an intensely emotional experience for many. Our interest focused on two questions in particular, which we explore in this section. First, how do managers cope with the dissonance that is generated by critical reflection? Second, what are the responsibilities of course tutors when initiating a process of critical reflection when the consequences of such an approach are potentially disturbing and 'unmanageable'?

The programme discussed here is a three year part-time post-graduate/post-experience Management Development Programme comprising Post-Graduate Certificate, Post-Graduate Diploma in Management Studies and MSc in Organisation Development and Management Learning. The subject areas follow external management standards, particularly those of the UK Association of Business Schools. However, pedagogically the entire programme takes an action learning approach where, supported by a small number of lecture inputs, students spend two thirds of their time working collectively in a specific action learning set (ALS) of 6–9 people, facilitated by a tutor. The ALS fulfils a number of functions for the course: they undertake group tasks on subjects from finance to marketing to human resource management; they provide a community for individuals to exchange work experiences; they are a source of support for individual work and they are a site of experiential learning about group process. In this sense students' experiences, feelings and interactions are fundamental to the pedagogical approach.

Pre-written case studies are not used and examinations have a minor role (10 per cent in the Diploma and none in the MSc). Reflective learning is promoted through assignments that are almost entirely based on student selected live organisational issues. These are not organisational puzzles or problems with ready technical solutions, but are 'situations', in the sense that Schon (1983) describes, characterised by uniqueness, uncertainty, instability, complexity and value conflict. Learning about managing and developing capacity to manage comes experientially from working on these 'situations'.

Many of the assignments require participants not only to demonstrate learning about content (e.g. organisational behaviour, performance management models etc.), but also to reflect on process issues they experienced in the course of undertaking the tasks, such as how they made decisions, what happened in their group, strategic exchanges that occurred in the course of doing their research or how they felt. The action learning set itself is seen as a source of learning about organisation dynamics, what Reynolds and Trehan (2001) have termed 'classroom as real world'. Because of the population in Birmingham, UK, the ALS is typically a source of gender, ethnic, age and occupational diversity, where issues mirror some of the patterns in organisations and society. Students are encouraged to reflect upon, act on and learn from their feelings and experiences of the ensuing value and power dynamics.

Reflexivity is seen as integral to learning and self-development in several fields; adult learning (Jarvis, 1987), work-based reflective practice (Argyris and Schon, 1974) and qualitative research (Blaxter *et al.*, 2001). A key principle of the programme is that through the combination of action learning sets, process facilitation and action research, not only do participants learn about others and about organisational dynamics, but they also learn about themselves. This is taken further on the MSc where participants write a critical self-reflection paper which is an autobiographical reflection on their development. They are encouraged to identify core assumptions and the contextual influences on them, as well as to understand some of their patterns. Depending on their particular focus, individuals may be introduced to critical concepts derived from such areas as feminism, post-colonial literature, Marxism, social constructionism or critical pedagogy.

The programme approach is informed by three key assumptions about learning. First, encouraging participants to become aware of their theories-in-use (Argyris and Schon, 1974), second, to think critically, as Carr and Kemmis say of action research 'a deliberate process for emancipating practitioners from the often unseen constrains of assumption, habit, precedent, coercion and ideology' (1986: 192). Third, informed by Bateson's (1973) and Belenky *et al.*'s theories on levels of learning (1986) tutors also encourage participants to value their own experience and insights; to make their own models, in other words, to create theory from practice.

In summary, we argue this programme can be construed as critical learning and reflection because of its foundation on principles of praxis, process, proactivity and reflexivity in the course of action learning.

Methodology

The research material is derived from an ethnographic approach, whereby the authors, as participant observers, recorded their accounts of events and verbatim quotes, and collected documents in the form of student reflective papers. The sense-making took the form of pair dialogue whereby the two authors shared their experiences and material, explored and questioned each others' interpretation and co-generated this account. As tutors and facilitators spending an average of 4–6 hours per week with 3 or 4 action learning sets each, and over a time period of 9 months a year, the authors were well placed to adopt an ethnographic approach to studying the question. Their context lends itself to ethnography because of the possibilities to collect accounts, to observe actions and processes and to explore the feelings, thoughts and meanings people attribute to situations as they happen. As Hammersley and Atkinson say of ethnography

> it involves the ethnographer participating, overtly or covertly, in people's daily lives for an extended period of time, watching what happens, listening to what is said, asking questions – in fact, collecting whatever data are available to shed light on the issues that are the focus of the research.
>
> (1995: 1)

The following illustrations present an interpretation of students' perspective on their experiences of critical reflection, based on discussions and analysis of their critical reflective papers. In the discussion that follows, the extracts are used as illustrations to illuminate a particular issue or issues within critical reflection. Interspersed with the extracts are commentary, reflection, theoretical insights and questions which portray the authors' sense-making of the issues raised. The issues have been divided under two sections

1   critical reflection and emotions
2   dissonance and the unspoken aspects of critical reflection.

Critical reflection and emotions

In this section the following extracts highlight that for some participants, engaging in critical reflection is often emotional, anxiety provoking and at times painful. As the extracts unfold, this section explores how emotions in critical reflection impact on the learning process. As emotional arenas, critical reflection provides valuable insights into individual feelings and emotions, be they of anger, confusion, vulnerability, uncertainty, fear, irritation, frustration or warmth, and provide opportunities for exploring how emotions shape the course and outcome of critical reflection. Critical reflection should, by its very nature, touch participants' emotions. The language used by students below conveys a picture where feelings during critical reflection were frequently intense, and at times painful, as Robert's account highlights.

> During the course there were moments when events began to spiral out of my control in my own mind, out of which there seemed no escape. Confusion quickly turned to anxiety and doubts. These demons began to destroy my confidence. I retreated into a defensive, dysfunctional shell, not confronting or understanding what had detonated such uncharacteristic behaviour. I was caught

in a frenzied accelerated learning cycle, avariciously devouring books, trying desperately to produce paper utopia by reaching some make believe learning terminus and destination that did not exist. My feet never came to rest on the neon flashing 'Welcome to the theory of everything' mat. My work always felt vulnerable and open to dreaded accusations of ignorance. The more I learnt the less I knew. I could not detach myself coolly from what was happening to me and open up peace talks with the protagonists of confusion and disorientation that were blocking the flow of learning and causing me emotional anguish, so I remained silent. However, as time went on, the experience of critical reflection provided many insights. I began questioning assumptions about the process that I had previously unexamined, it was immensely exciting, frustrating and humbling. I came to think of this serious condition as premature revelation. It had all been going on around me, and more poignantly, by me, and I hadn't even noticed. Today there is a very different voice inside my head. It is softer and less impetuous, it stays silent longer as it listens with more humility and understanding. It no longer looks for all the answers in books, but inside itself.

Robert's story exemplifies how fear and anxiety can interfere with critical reflection. Organisational psychoanalysts highlight the prevalence of unconscious fears concerning security and self worth that can shape people's behaviour and emotional responses in ways that seem anything but rational in terms of the objectives of the task.

Literature and practice on critical reflection often seems to ignore the expression of fear. Fulop and Rifkin (1997) highlight that some fears that individuals experience and reveal to others will propel collective learning, some will inhibit learning and some will have a mixed or an insignificant impact. Robert believes as a result of his fears he has learnt an important lesson 'nobody's knowledge is ever complete and discovery takes time'.

> As a result of critical reflection I have come to understand myself better through a greater understanding of my own behaviour and the forces that influence it.

This fear of exposure is discussed by Schein (1992) in terms of preservation of face and its effect on reflection in organisations. Schneider (1997) argues that exposure reveals the limits of the self, and talks of disruption, disorientation and painful self-consciousness which can create silence as a response to such fear. Robert believes that despite these fears it is important to overcome them.

> I began to confront rather than turn my back on this shadow of anxiety, the more you confront it, logic told me, the quicker and easier you will learn. I slowly began to see the confusion and fear as a natural, physical entity and friend rather than an enemy, that was part of me, a silhouette rather than a shadow. At this stage I felt myself not just learning but developing.

There is certainly dissonance in the above account, in the sense that the participant felt unsettled, had his perspectives disturbed and experienced uncertainty and anxiety.

However, combined in the same sentences is a co-incidence of pain and pleasure. Alongside the uncertainty and fear was elation, learning and a sense of empowerment. This resonates with ideas of Taylor (1986) and Mezirow (1981) that feelings of alienation, disorientation, struggle, are to be expected, are even necessary for transition. In our view, the idea of dissonance is not straightforward and is experienced in differing ways, as discussed in the following paragraphs.

Dissonance and the unspoken aspects of critical reflection

Many participants talked of the critical reflection process triggering far reaching changes and making them rethink about who they were and/or what they were doing with their lives. The reflective paper appeared to act as a catalyst, bringing into focus existing tensions and contradictions. Participants described new learning about themselves, other people and about being a manager.

On being a manager

Students wrote in their critical reflective papers of new insights into their role as a manager. A politicisation was not uncommon, as people described lowing their 'naivety', finding new ways to exert influence in their organisations; 'the sudden recognition' of how organisational changes were blocking their personal development, or were inconsistent with their values. These would seem to fulfil the emancipatory hopes of writers such as Fay (1987).

The politicisation can be described in two ways first, with an external focus, where people talk of the wider social or political implications of their work and the function and practice of managing (Watson, 1994); second, with an internal focus, where individuals' insights are into the inter-relationship between self and work, the expectations of being a manager and Mezirow's 'critique of the socio-political forces which constrain perceptions and choice' (McGill and Weil, 1989: 247).

Social and political implications of being a manager

For some critical reflection brought about a politicisation, bringing new understandings of the dynamics of their organizations; an awareness of different types of organisation politics; acquisition of 'a more critical view of the objective framework in which we as individuals operate' and a view of management 'in relation to its significance in terms of the structural inequalities of society'. Another contrasted the MSc with his view that on most business school courses 'there is never any question of examining the objectives or underpinning philosophies of management, everything takes place within the cosy managerialist discourse of efficiency ... I think that management is about engaging the whole "self" with the social and political world'.

For others the politicisation was more in terms of an awareness of their own power in relation to others at work, and a sense of responsibility over how to be; for example, 'I began to reflect on how inequalities and power differences within society can be mirrored in organizations, ... and the need for managers to address their personal role in perpetuating these inequalities'. Another, a fairly senior manager, said 'Surely it is better to move forward only one centimetre in organizational terms... rather than achieve one metre's growth with "costs" paid for by the personnel affected'.

However, there were also concerns raised on the power of critical reflection as well, which echo Brookfield's (1994) talk of the darker side of critical reflection. A number of students speculated that blissful ignorance might be preferable to impotent enlightenment, since 'the possibility exists also to create discontentment and frustration if the circumstances are not right' and the individual is unable to make changes to their situation. One individual argued that critical reflection raised questions for him, but did not provide any answers.

A further issue which a few participants raised was the potential for discord between a newly politicised employee and the organisation which wants conformity to cultural norms. The student concern was that employers do not want disillusioned, unsettled or demanding managers for their money, and that there could be adverse consequences for a manager who begins to challenge inappropriately, and perhaps naively.

Concluding reflections

We embarked on this research project, because of the unanticipated power of our critical reflection programme. We felt it was very positive, yet it led us to wonder if we had unleashed something beyond our control, and potentially dangerous, and it raised a number of questions in our minds which we have explored in this chapter.

First, how do managers cope with the dissonance that is generated by critical reflection? It was certainly true that participants on our course experienced dissonance, but our first conclusion is that this is an inevitable outcome of critical reflection and that it is by no means necessarily a negative experience. Could it be that our own fear, as tutors, of being in the midst of unleashed student emotions has been projected into a concern to protect students from disruptive feelings?

In our view it is more helpful to interpret the concept in three different forms: reconstruction or affirmation, as students formed new interpretations and reclaimed past selves from previously held images of failure; emancipatory, where revelations and transformed perspectives have brought a sense of widened horizons and expanded confidence, even if the process was painful; and unresolved dissonance, where new awareness of tensions and contradictions, has not been worked through into new actions. On our programme, unresolved dissonance was not widespread. This may be because the critical content resonated with the particular individuals involved because of the place they were within their lives, and the prior existence of tensions, such as between values and work, between family and job demands, or contradictions between self-image and employer perception. Despite the politicisation which a number experienced, there were no re-entry problems as described by other commentators (Reynolds, 1998b), and no voices describing a sense of powerlessness or disablisation. We would speculate that the integrated approach of the course was significant here, so that whilst participants might have become critical of the values and dynamics of their organisation, or of management practice, they were simultaneously learning how they could take action to make changes through their action research dissertation and their group consultancy project. Arguably, this combination enabled them to be what Meyerson and Scully term a 'tempered radical . . . struggling to act in ways that are appropriate professionally and authentic personally and politically' (1995: 587).

Our experiences suggest to us that the hope that critical reflection can be emancipatory is not misplaced, as our course participants talked of personal transformations, as well as new social and political perspectives. How far the emancipation moves beyond the individual into workplace practices is a question which needs further exploration.

We would also contend that the theoretical speculations on hazards of critical management reflection, outlined above, are overly pessimistic. None of the students within this piece of research expressed regret at undertaking the programme, or being asked to critically reflect, including those who had felt unsettled by the process, or still felt unresolved dissonance at the end. Although we might feel uneasy about the notion of an uncontrolled genie being let out of the bottle as a result of the critical approach, we are reassured by Mezirow's ideas of perspective transformation, 'New forms of being and relating emerge out of struggle. It is some time however, before we can feel a sense of integration between such learning and our actual transactions with the world' (quoted in McGill and Weil, 1989: 247).

It could be argued that even a small risk of unbalancing one individual or rewarding an employer with a 'soggy manager' is enough to justify sticking to non-critical teaching and learning approaches. However, we would counter this by maintaining that uncertainty and change are always uncomfortable, as is holding non-mainstream values and beliefs. If we think that insight and understanding of self, organisations and society is better than blissful ignorance, and we believe we have something positively powerful to offer, which we do, then perhaps the ethical justification is reversed. Maybe it would be ethically wrong to withhold it?

This is not to ignore a potential for serious adverse psychological or social consequences for managers engaging in critical reflection, and this relates to the second question our paper set out to address; what are the responsibilities of course tutors when initiating a process of critical reflection, when the consequences of such an approach are potentially disturbing and 'unmanageable'? We do not aim to offer a prescription, but some of the issues we conclude as important include the fundamental importance of facilitating the action learning set, tutors' reflexivity and students' informed choice.

Learning is a social process as well as an individual one (Jarvis, 1987). Brookfield (1994) talks of the value to students of a supportive peer community and we found the action learning set had high importance as a site of learning, a place for dialogue and a source of emotional support. Establishment and facilitation of the sets is therefore of great consequence, which demands skilled facilitators with good group work skills and insight into the social dynamics of diverse groups.

Our experience reminds us of the power that lecturers can have to influence students' lives which clearly indicates responsibilities we have for questioning our own intents, motives and practices, to be reflexive. Tutors have to be prepared for emotionality and conflict, and aware of their own needs and impetuses, perhaps to avoid it. It is also incumbent on us to be humble about the superiority of our perspectives, to try to practice critical principles such as democratic working and querying the roots of our own assumptions.

We have used managerialist language to talk about the 'product customers think they are buying' when managers engage in critical reflection. The students in our research generally had an experience very different from their initial instrumental expectations, despite our best attempts in course promotion material. The critical approach was usually a surprise, often a total shock, even though the outcome was welcomed. Just because we think there are emancipatory and perhaps performative rationales for being critical, if there are individuals who are determined to resist or who are vulnerable to seriously adverse outcomes, there are implications for how we communicate and justify critical reflection. Should we be more blunt in our descriptions of what the course could involve? Would that undermine its power? Perhaps we should be giving students the option not to critically reflect. These are questions we have no definitive answers to but are currently working through.

Implications

In the debates presented above we have reviewed and discussed the various perspectives on critical self-reflection and the challenges it presents in relation to HRD education and practice. A number of implications can be distilled from the discussions.

First, critical reflection engages participants in the process of drawing from critical perspectives to make connections between their learning and work experiences to understand and change interpersonal and organisational practices.

Second, the theoretical debates presented have sought to emphasise the distinctive nature of critical self-reflection and to argue for its place in the professional activity of HRD education and practice. Within HRD critical reflection can support people in an examination of the social and political processes within the workplace. Critical reflection is about social, political and ethical issues and, as Reed and Anthony (1992) argue, these are fundamentals upon which any organisational reality rests. It is also important for education and organisational practice to counter current preoccupations with instrumentalism and introduce methodologies which focus their attention to the moral, political and cultural aspects of HRD.

For HRD educators and HRD practitioners adopting critical reflective approaches is a choice and a responsibility. As Kemmis argues:

> in reflection we choose, implicitly or explicitly, what to take for granted and what to treat as problematic in the relationships between our thoughts and action and the social order we inhabit. In reflection, we have a choice about whether to think and act in conformity and the patterns of communication, decision making and action in our society, or whether we will intervene at this historical moment on behalf of more rational communications, more just decision making and more fulfilling human and social action.

(1985: 148)

References

Alvesson, M. and Willmott, H. (eds) (1992a) *Critical Management Studies*, London: Sage.

Alvesson, M. and Willmott, H. (1992b) 'On the idea of emancipation in management and organisation studies', *Academy of Management Review*, 17, 3: 432–64.

Alvesson, M. and Willmott, H. (1996) *Making Sense of Management*, London: Sage.

Argyris, C. and Schon, D. (1974) *Theories in Practice*, San Francisco, CA: Jossey-Bass.

Bateson, G. (1973) *Steps Towards an Ecology of the Mind*, London: Paladin.

Belenky, M. F., Clinchy, B. M., Golderger, N. R. and Tarube, J. M. (1986) *Women's Ways of Knowing: The Development of Self, Voice and Mind*, New York: Basic Books.

Blaxter, L., Hughes, C. and Tight, M. (2001) *How to Research*, Buckingham: Open University Press.

Brookfield, D. (1995) *Becoming a Critically Reflective Teacher*, San Francisco, CA: Jossey-Bass.

Brookfield, S. (1994) 'Tales from the dark side: a phenomenology of adult critical reflection', *International Journal of Lifelong Education*, 13, 3: 203–16.

Burgoyne, J. and Reynolds, M. (eds) (1997) *Management Learning: Integrating Perspectives in Theory and Practice*, London: Sage.

Carr, W. and Kemmis, S. (1986) *Becoming Critical: Education Knowledge and Action Research*, London: Falmer Press.

Collins, M. (1991) *Adult Education as Vocation: A Critical Role for the Adult Educator in Today's Society*, London: Routledge.

Fay, B. (1987) *Critical Social Science*, Cambridge: Polity Press.

Freire, P. (1972) *Pedagogy of the Oppressed*, Middlesex: Penguin.

Fulop and Rifkin (1997) 'Representing fear in learning organisations', *Management Learning*, 28, 1.

Garrison (1991) 'Critical thinking and adult education: a conceptual model for developing critical thinking in adult learners', *International Journal of Lifelong Learning*, 10, 4.

Giroux, H. A. (1981) *Ideology, Culture and the Process of Schooling*, Philadelphia, PA: Temple University Press.

Grey, C., Knights, D. and Willmott, H. (1996) 'Is a critical pedagogy of management possible?', in R. French and C. Grey (eds) *Rethinking Management Education*, London: Sage.

Habermas, J. (1972) *Knowledge and Human Interests*, London: Heinemann.

Hammersley, M. and Atkinson, P. (1995) *Ethnography Principles in Practice*, 2nd edn, London: Routledge.

Jackall, R. (1988) *The Moral Mazes: The World of Corporate Managers*, Oxford: OUP.

Jarvis, P. (1987) *Adult Learning in the Social Context*, London: Croom Helm.

Kemmis, S. (1985) 'Action research and the politics of reflection' in D. Boud, R. Keogh and D. Walker (eds) *Reflection: Turning Experience into Learning*, London: Kogan Page.

Kolb, D. A. (1984) *Experiential Learning*, Englewood Cliffs, NJ: Prentice Hall.

McGill, I. and Weil, S. (1989) 'Continuing the dialogue: new possibilities for experiential learning', in S. Weil and I. McGill (eds) *Making Sense of Experiential Learning*, Buckingham: OUP.

McLaughlin and Thorpe (1993) 'Action learning: the problems facing a challenge to traditional management education and development', *British Journal of Management*, 4, 1.

Meyerson, D. E. and Scully, M. A. (1995) 'Tempered radicalism and the politics of radicalism and change', *Organization Science*, 6, 5, September–October: 325–42.

Mezirow, J. (1981) 'A critical theory of adult learning and education', *Adult Education*, 32: 3–24.

Nord, W. R. and Jermier, J. M. (1992) 'Critical social science for managers? Promising and perverse possibilities', in M. Alvesson and H. Willmott (eds) *Critical Management Studies*, London: Sage.

Porter, J. L., Muller, H. J. and Rehder, R. R. (1989) 'The making of managers: an American perspective', *Journal of General Management*, 14, 4: 62–76.

Reed, M. and Anthony, P. (1992) 'Professionalizing management and managing professionalization: British managers in the 1980s', *Journal of Management Studies*, 29, September: 591–613.

Reynolds, M. (1997) 'Towards a critical pedagogy', in J. Burgoyne and M. Reynolds (eds) *Management Learning: Integrating Perspectives in Theory and Practice*, London: Sage.

Reynolds, M. (1998a) 'Grasping the nettle: possibilities and pitfalls of a critical management pedagogy', *British Journal of Management*, 10, 2: 171–84.

Reynolds, M. (1998b) 'Reflection and critical reflection in management learning', *Journal of Management Learning*, 29, 2: 183–200.

Reynolds, M. and Trehan, K. (2001) 'Classroom as real world: propositions for a pedagogy of difference', *Gender and Education*, 3, 4: 357–72.

Schein, E. (1992) *Process Consultation in Action*, Vol. 1, Reading, MA: Addison Wesley.

Schneider (1997) 'Representing fear in learning organisations', *Management Learning*, 28, 1.

Schon, D. (1983) *The Reflective Practitioner*, New York: Basic Books.

Summers, D. J., Beje, D. M. and Rosile, G. A. (1997) 'Deconstructing the organisational behaviour test', *Journal of Management Education*, 21: 343–60.

Taylor, M. (1986) 'Learning for self-direction: the pattern of a transition process', *Studies in Higher Education*, II, 1: 55–72.

Thompson, J. and McGivern, J. (1996) 'Parody, process and practice perspectives for management education', *Management Learning*, 27: 21–33.

Trehan, K. (2003) ' Who is not sleeping with whom: what's not being talked about in HRD', *International HRD Conference*, Toulouse.

Usher (1985) 'Experiences in adult education', *Journal of Philosophy of Education*, 26, 2.

Vince, R. (1996) 'Experiential management education as the practice of change', in R. French and C. Grey (eds) *Rethinking Management Education*, London: Sage.

Watson, T. (1994) *In Search of Management*, London: Routledge.

Watson, T. (1999) 'Beyond managism: negotiated narratives and critical management education in practice', *First International Conference on Critical Management Studies*, Univeristy of Manchester, 14–16 July.

Watson, Tony J. (2002) *Organising and Managing Work: Organisaional, Managerial and Strategic Behaviour in Theory and Practice*, Harlow: Financial Times/Prentice Hall.

Watson, T. and Harris, P. (1999) *The Emergent Manager*, London: Sage.

Willmott, H. (1997) 'Critical management learning', in M. Burgoyne and M. Reynolds (eds) *Management Learning*, London: Sage.

3   Ideas for critical practitioners

Russ Vince

Introduction

In this chapter I discuss various ideas and actions associated with critical practitioners. I should emphasise from the outset that I am not talking about 'the critical practitioner' (as in 'the reflective practitioner'). In fact, I am trying not to talk about the individual practitioner at all. There is plenty that has already been said about the HRD practitioner and his or her capabilities, behaviour, role and responsibilities for the development of people and performance. There has been plenty said about the techniques, instruments and approaches that the HRD practitioner can employ to develop, empower and stimulate the corporate citizen. In using the term critical practitioners, I am saying that HRD can also be appreciated as a collective endeavour, even where an individual occupies an explicit HRD role. To conceptualise and to act on HRD as a collective endeavour generates critique and insight about the relationship between HRD and organising. In this way, HRD is seen less as a combination of individual responsibility and professional technique, and more as a key part of ongoing, 'negotiated narratives' of learning and change (Watson, 2001). There are two related critiques of HRD implied in what I have said, and these emerge and develop throughout the chapter (although I do not draw firm conclusions on them). To summarise, the first concerns a shift in the practical emphasis of HRD away from effective development and towards *provisional knowing within a political context*. The second stems from the first, and concerns a transformation of the role of HRD within organising. HRD is not peripheral in the sense of implementing the development needs implied in strategic decisions, but pivotal in the sense of being the medium through which strategic learning takes place.

Critical practitioners are a group or groups of people concerned with strategic learning. To an extent, both of these concepts (critical practitioners and strategic learning) can be defined through reflection on the key ideas that motivate critical practitioners. First, it is likely that critical practitioners understand and undertake HRD as a central process in the negotiation of what learning and change mean and involve within organisations, they are continually aware that they are trying to make a political impact on organising and they also realise that this is not necessarily the impact that was intended. Critical practitioners may well be suspicious of a number of the assumptions that inform human resource development, but they see this suspicion as adding to the further development of HRD in practice, as well as the impact that it can make on organising. They see the job as promoting creativity and innovation but recognise that in doing this they are also making people compliant and placing restrictions on their ability to act. They share an understanding that HRD inevitably has and makes limitations. At present these limitations are constructed through a focus on people development and rational planning; through the reliance on standardised products and services; the obsession with competencies and the unimaginative leadership offered by professional bodies. HRD has been weak strategically, placing the emphasis on individuals to learn and change, and largely ignoring the wider politics of organising in which HRD exists and can have an impact. HRD managers have tended to ignore or avoid the various emotional, relational and political dynamics that underpin the organisation of learning and change. The fears and anxieties that are inevitably mobilised by attempts to learn and to change underpin and inform the choices that are made in the name of HRD. It seems important, therefore, to start to ask what function HRD has within the political systems of organising, how and why HRD provides mechanisms for the control and manipulation of organisational members and what role fear (or other such powerful emotion) plays in defining how HRD is and is not done. The role of HRD in organising can be to express a critical agenda, arguing for discussion of what is uncomfortable to address and beyond rational control.

Second, critical practitioners recognise that they are the intermediaries between different power interests in organisations, in the middle of competing or contested expectations, interpretations of events and desired outcomes. To organise is also to institutionalise. Organisation is a process driven by the twin desires for stability and coherence, which necessarily involves defining the boundaries of what can and cannot belong in the organisation. There are emotional boundaries – organisation is built from values and mission statements that give the impression that there is a coherent direction that all members (might/must) subscribe and adhere to. There are political boundaries – organisation reflects the outcomes of differential power relations and also the legitimacy of certain opinions and behaviours as well as the illegitimacy of others. Critical practitioners are, therefore, interested in understanding how an organisation has managed to become set in its ways, as well as how to organise opportunities for change that can challenge a tendency to resist change. Trying to make change happen inevitably means saying things about managing and organising that others, above and below, will not want to hear or acknowledge.

Third, critical practitioners try to make sense of, and to transform, the various practices that emerge within specific situations of learning and development. HRD is therefore about *what might be*, creating a space in the knowledge that something will happen, but without having to keep tight control on it. Critical practitioners, from their experience, are likely to know what other leaders need to know regarding development; that you can only create a process, you can't actually control it. Leadership is more about creating the conditions and enabling them to be put into place, than it is about trying to control a process once it has been set in motion. They, therefore, try to identify the possibilities and problems located in processes, practices and roles – including the roles of manager and leader. In addition, critical practitioners understand that defining capability or competence always serves a dual function, to provide an idea of desired performance and to define the limitations of performance within an organisation. Competencies create both a list of skills and behaviours to be achieved and they constitute a description of how employees are expected to be compliant. Critical practitioners recognise the HRD role as a focal point for the development of projects and projections in an organisation, as activity that inspires critique in order to create possibilities for learning and as attempt at organisation and organising that seek to create the ways employees will be thinking and acting.

I can summarise these as key points for an understanding of critical human resource development

- HRD is a pivotal process in negotiations over learning and change, especially in discovering what these words mean and involve in practice. Critical practitioners have an important role in questioning the assumptions that inform and undermine HRD in specific organisational contexts (as well as the rhetoric and discourses that accompany these assumptions).
- Critical practitioners are intermediaries between different power relations; they are often in the middle of competing expectations, interests and desires, from above and below. Such power relations inform and construct the relationship between learning and organising in context. The experience of attempting human resource development helps to identify how organising avoids and excludes learning as well as how it might seek and promote it.
- HRD is inherently speculative; it is about what might be. Critical practitioners are, therefore, more concerned with the creation of opportunities to organise knowledge and development than with attempts to control the impact of development within an organisation. In addition, what is imagined to be creative and empowering is also likely to be attached to compliance and control. This perspective has implications for the practice of key organising processes like leadership and reflection.

The ideas in this chapter are the product of discussions within a temporary community of ten academics and practitioners. This community of critical practitioners was a short-lived group that existed for and met over two days, the focus being 'the future practice of HRD'. The only point of further development after these two days was that our discussions (all the plenary discussions were recorded and transcribed) would be written up by myself and published in places where they might be able to make an impact on the further development of HRD. In addition to this chapter, variations on these views have been published in the 'Soap Box' section of *Human Resource Development International* (*HRDI*), a leading HRD journal (Vince, 2003). They also are part of an extended writing project by the author (Vince, 2004). Over time it should be possible to see the extent to which the collective opinions and ideas generated here do or do not contribute to the transformation of thinking about what is HRD, as well as the influence they have on practice.

The rest of this chapter is organised into five connected sections. These are

- Definitions and assumptions in HRD
- Why does HRD need to change?
- Useful knowledge for critical practitioners
- Further reflections on the HRD role
- Critical practitioners and HRD – a reality check.

Definitions and assumptions in HRD

There is no single or preferred way to understand or to do HRD. Definitions of HRD are always likely to be *working* definitions, emerging from the experience of attempts to do HRD. The idea of a working definition is useful because it implies that definitions can and will change in line with everyday perceptions and perspectives on how to do human resource development. A working definition reflects the current understanding of what it is that HRD practitioners aim to do. This might include changing the organisation, creating a collaborative work environment, making a difference to performance, developing core capabilities, making interventions, putting systems into place and being involved in organisation design and development. The question of why HRD practitioners aim to do this is linked to the function of HRD within organisations, which involves shaping and responding to the business agenda and informing and providing 'added value'. Change is therefore the underlying theme. However, the desire for change inevitably interweaves with the complexity of attempting to make change happen.

Part of the role (of critical practitioners) in relation to HRD is to express a critical agenda, arguing for continuous discussion of what is undiscussable and uncomfortable in organisations – the impact of emotion and politics on HRD in practice. HRD is important because its practice provides many examples concerning the impact of emotion and politics in strategic attempts at learning and change. Change is unlikely to be sustained without a consideration of the various emotional, relational and political dynamics that underpin the organisation of learning and change within specific organisational contexts. The fears and anxieties that are inevitably mobilised by attempts to learn and to change underpin and inform the choices that are made in the name of HRD. I am not saying that individuals have to be aware of their fears and anxieties; I am not talking about self-awareness. I am saying that I think it is important that internal groups and communities attempt to understand how fears and anxieties (or other emotions) have contributed to the emergence of particular 'ways of doing things here'. One risk that HRD practitioners may be able to take is to create processes for reflection on how inaction or constraint is being produced collectively.

Politics (in addition to emotion) is also integral to HRD. Having responsibilities for HRD means being aware of the various interests that HRD practitioners serve within a hierarchy. As I said in the introduction, HRD practitioners are often the intermediaries between different power interests in organisations; they are in the middle of learning. Practitioners are often expected to create processes that reveal what people think, to empower collective voices and to mobilise participation in change. In addition, when senior managers have ignored or filed away all of this consultation, the role is also to deal with the disappointment of undermined and unfulfilled expectations. This is not a passive role. Instead of waiting for the outcome of established power relations to become apparent, critical practitioners want to be direct about the likely impact of power relations on organisational processes of learning and change. Making this clear from the outset is a powerful contribution to understanding the possibilities and limitations of change within specific organisational contexts, as well as contributing to increased reflection on the political element of HRD.

In addition to reflection on politics there is also the politics of reflection. A Local Government Chief Executive recently told me that reflection was not always a good idea since it might undermine the strategic decisions that senior managers had spent so long making. Such a view places the emphasis on critical practitioners to make the business case for reflection. This involves, at the very least, a transformation from the idea that reflection is the province of the individual practitioner. Reflection is an under-developed organising process, which could provide information about the *organisation* of learning and change (Reynolds and Vince, 2004). For example, project-based initiatives are currently popular in organisations. Project-based work, driven by business imperatives, is aimed at using diverse combinations of existing individuals' knowledge to find creative solutions to key issues within the organisation. Despite the impact that such projects have on key issues, there has often been little reflection on the ways in which project intervention has changed or re-enforced the system dynamics of the organisation in which they were built and whether the knowledge they generated could be usefully transferred across boundaries within and outside the organisation. Much of the collective knowledge that organising generates is not being used.

There is one other issue that has an impact on definition in HRD, the continuing debate about differences between training, management development and organisation development. HRD in organisations can carry an implicit hierarchy, from the work of 'chalk and talk trainers' and instrumental skills programmes at one level, to intervention, consultancy and organisation development at the other. Increasingly, the focus of HRD is organisation development, which involves being an integral part of the business, and organising interventions aimed at helping the business move forward. Within some organisations HRD is seen as organisation development. In other organisations, training, management development and organisation development blur. These differences raise many questions about the HRD role. For example: who exactly has an HRD role in organisations? Is HRD something to be done by trained professionals or does everyone need to integrate perspectives from HRD into their role? How is HRD linked to tacit and explicit structures of managing and organising? What does HRD mean in practice and how do development practices need to change?

Why does HRD need to change?

Currently, the practice of HRD in the UK is rooted in standardised products and services, driven by competencies, defined by professional bodies and focussed on predictability and consistency. There are too many organisations whose approaches require staff members to learn mechanistically, and only a very small number of models of development that are used and that make any lasting impact (the top three are the training cycle, Kirkpatrick's evaluation ladder and Kolb's learning cycle). Current training standards are not sufficiently strategic and are weak in relation to organisation development, particularly in terms of a failure to establish links between people management development and business performance. There aren't many senior levels in HRD and there is no consistent commitment to HRD from senior levels. The focus of HRD is on the development of people in teams in organisations, and such development is often seen as separate from the social, political, emotional and economic pressures on business. HRD, which has a central concern with change, has demonstrated a persistent inability to change itself. Approaches to change management have been based on rational planning and people development, more often than not failing to make the desired impact on organising processes, practices and strategies. This reinforces the already compelling evidence that change initiatives are more likely to fail than to succeed (Palmer and Hardy, 2000).

HRD is currently driven by a need to respond to a narrow set of market perceptions. If this is the way that HRD is to be conceived, then ultimately it is not going to be able to contribute to organisational change. Training people as HR practitioners simply to respond to market perceptions is tempting but short sighted. It is tempting because the development of individual skills and knowledge is important, it can reinforce confidence, help to broaden action and improve capability. It is short sighted because it places the emphasis on individuals to learn and to change, and largely ignores the wider contexts of organising in which HRD exists and can have an impact. HRD practice can and should make a discriminating contribution to organising. HRD is an intervention within a political system, a practice of management and leadership, with all the difficulties that attempts to manage and to lead are likely to contain and reveal.

There is currently a need for HRD to construct itself critically, as an integral part of continuous attempts to change. At the same time, HRD has to provide approaches to knowledge generation, provide ways of organising for knowledge and highlight the issues that arise from attempts to give and to share knowledge. HRD is no longer easily seen as a function within a single organisation, rather it is responsible for supporting moves beyond 'the organisation', not only into configurations like supply chains and networks but also into wider contexts involving stakeholders, communities and customers. Organising is now as much about shifting form and transience as it is about stability and coherence (although shifting organisational forms do not necessarily imply changes in assumptions), and the actions of HRD practitioners will have eventually to reflect this. HRD can take a lead in creating the designs and developments for future business; this means a focus on how change is avoided as well as planned, on the different forms and approaches to leadership required and on consulting for organisation development. The focus of HRD is on action, on developing the capacity to act, on generating credibility through action, influencing and working with others. HRD practitioners may have to make a significant contribution alongside other people who have a monopoly on resource use or power.

Useful knowledge for critical practitioners

People try and create something solid and bounded when we organise – we seek that kind of certainty. It allows us to delineate relationships, to manage meaning and to make sense of the complexities generated through interaction. The difficulty and the challenge facing us is to break through the dependencies we have created on those particular designs and forms of organising. The institutionalising or stabilising forces that inform and construct organisation necessarily make change more difficult. Change is usually justified by stability – 'I want to change this in order to keep this steady' (or, less overtly, 'I want you to change to allow me to stay the same'). Such forces are inherently about the organisation of clarity, of knowing what is involved and included. This also means that, in a complex and incomprehensible world of globalisation, discontinuity, policy change and intervention fatigue (to name but a few) some organisational members will have to try to intervene or interfere in order to make change happen. The role of critical practitioners is, therefore, both complicated and interesting. It implies discovering how an organisation has managed to become set in its ways, to organise opportunities for change that can challenge a tendency to resist change and to imagine and deliver processes that can underpin organisational development and transformation. Given the emotions and politics that inevitably surround any attempts at change, this means that critical practitioners have to think about *transforming leadership*, both as a defining characteristic of their roles and as an organisational imperative.

Trying to change the ways in which leadership is done (e.g. by shifting the emphasis from individual to collective leadership) can be anxiety provoking, but also intriguing and stimulating, it reflects the idea that underlying the roles of leader and manager is the ability to take risks, to challenge existing ways of working and to find new practices, approaches and solutions. Critical practitioners, therefore, from their position in the middle of organising (between strategic and operational staff, between competing interests and functions, between different agendas and interpretations of change), take political risks. Given the difficulty of holding this most important aspect of organising it is not surprising that HRD has tended to institutionalise itself into the smaller space of training and personal development. Because of the politics that are integral to organising, critical practitioners are likely to be aware that there is a time and a place to say what they think. Critical practitioners place themselves in the middle of an enduring and ever-present dynamic between experiences at different hierarchical levels of an organisation. Their role involves both generating intelligence (in the sense of information and knowledge obtained from others that is of political value) for their superiors, and helping to make subordinate voices heard. Attempting to generate both intelligence and voice means being in the middle of something political.

This also raises the issue of the tools and techniques that might be needed to thrive in this role. In HRD, techniques are necessarily unclear, which is ironic since it is techniques that are most often sought. It is not very useful to ask the question 'how do you do it', when the success or failure of development interventions depends more on why you do it, who you are doing it with, how they feel about you, what you represent, and how you feel about them – none of which is actually to do with technique. Techniques can impose themselves on complex situations in order to simplify them, thereby undermining emotions, relations and knowledge that might lead towards learning and change. The leap of faith that critical practitioners have made is that learning and development are less about what is known or even knowable and more about what is *mutually discoverable*. The danger in doing HRD is that practitioners have to engage with each other collectively in order to change things. Critical practitioners try to make this happen. However, it is also necessary to be aware that giving voice to people who don't normally have it and providing intelligence to people who don't normally get it (and actually may not want it) is not something that can be engineered or planned, and it is always something that can backfire.

Further reflections on the HRD role

Intervention is paradoxical because it implies both some kind of purposive activity to make something happen, at the same time as creating and/or entering situations with no clear idea or agenda about what is to happen. It is the importance of this paradox that makes HRD a necessary and integral aspect of organising. Critical practitioners carry the insight that the knowledge we lack is as important as the knowledge we have. Not knowing is an HRD strategy, it is an acknowledgement that the things we have done in the past, and the previous knowledge and experience emerging from it, may get in the way as much as they may help. We may also defend against what we know because it is sometimes dangerous in organisations to speak out. People know more about the emotions and power relations that characterise the organisation than they are prepared to let on. Commonly avoided knowledge, therefore, is as potent an organisational force as common knowledge. Critical practitioners are aware of a developmental dilemma that is at the heart of organising – the continuous and competing dynamics between trying to promote both stability *and* change.

On a day-to-day basis critical practitioners have to hold back from implementing what they know, and occasionally have to profess not knowing as a strategy for getting things to happen. This skill – not knowing – is troublesome both for critical practitioners and for the groups and people they work with. The point of doing it is to undermine the role of (expert) facilitator, and consequently all the anti-developmental expectations, dependencies and restrictions that accompany this role. It is to encourage a 'critical mass' of shared experience and knowledge in the hope and expectation that this will produce what is needed to support and encourage learning and change.

HRD people in organisations attract the idea that 'in HRD they have the solution' – a fallacy that may originally have been initiated by an HRD practitioner. As a result of not wanting to appear incompetent or useless, practitioners can be dogged by a sense that they have to *protect* themselves in some way against feeling a fool, seeming to know nothing, not doing what is wanted or not providing value for money. However, this means that critical practitioners are in a unique position to understand a particularly powerful and useful form of authority in organisations. This is often the authority that senior managers need but don't have (or avoid), as well as being the authority that less senior managers might want but are afraid to take up. It is the authority that comes from experiencing and understanding the complexity and circularity of a development role within organisations.

While critical practitioners are likely to be aware of tools and analytic techniques that support learning and change, they also know that it is not the tools and techniques that make the most difference to organisational members. This is made as a result of experience, the type of experience that tells you that the silence in the room is all right, that it doesn't intimidate you into saying something or into taking over. The importance is not in the solution, but in the sense-making – being able to reflect on experience in a way that transforms it. Critical practitioners are not interested in attempts to mechanistically recreate organising processes that occur naturally, for example, communities of practice, mentoring relationships and informal patterns of coaching. It rarely works that organising that occurs naturally, by chance, or because of the specific situation or variables, can be recreated as a technique.

The difference between change programmes that do and don't work is often more about the quality of relations than the techniques used. However, such relations are also inevitably part of the emotions and politics that are mobilised through intervention. Critical practitioners are trying to contribute to processes of change within organisations where change is paradoxically both sought and feared. There is much that is not out on the table. There is much that would not be recognised, accepted or wanted by other people if it was. It is part of the role of critical practitioners to bring difficult things to the forefront so that they become part of the debate. It is the role of critical practitioners to ask risky questions, to get further into the emotions and politics that surround attempts at learning and change. Critical practitioners have to juggle the twin pressures of safety and risk, creating processes and 'spaces' within which the personal and political risks that underpin development can be taken. There are several dilemmas. Much HRD is concerned more with filling spaces rather than creating them, learning environments always contain anxiety (in both senses of the word 'contain'), what seems to be safe sometimes isn't and public and open discussion is often avoided. Creating learning spaces means running risks, not least the risk that they will be taken over by the usual people who take them over. To create learning environments that are free from anxiety and risk creates the danger of making them invisible or self-indulgent. Participants might well be happy with that but it doesn't change the organisation.

HRD can be very prescriptive, based on attempts to devise systems and processes and to rationalise why we are doing it. The emphasis of HRD, therefore, needs to be learning not prescription, and while the starting point may be the same for many organisations, the actual journey is likely to be very different. HRD has to move away from prescribed competencies, both in relation to the HRD profession and to the managers and leaders that practitioners serve. In moving away from prescribed competencies for individuals, critical practitioners are also necessarily abandoning the idea of 'good' or 'best' practice, since practice is always situated within different organisational or inter-organisational contexts. HRD is reductive when it seeks to identify practice that works in one context and apply it into a different context. Part of the HRD role, therefore, is to help reinvent the wheel of practice in the search for innovation. Critical practitioners will lead the idea that changes can be determined lower down in the organisation and that there are likely to be benefits from decentralisation and democracy. Leading such a political change can be a frightening thought, and it requires a good understanding of key power relationships, as well as what the politics are and how one might work with and through those politics. Such leadership is more about creating the conditions and enabling them to be put into place than it is trying to control a process once it has been set in motion. An outcome of this idea is the explicit desire to create processes and procedures for collective or public reflection and action (rather than individual reflection and action). Critical practitioners will be responsible for the development of new perspectives on and approaches to reflection (see Reynolds and Vince, 2004).

Critical practitioners and HRD – a reality check

In this chapter I have expressed a variety of opinions about HRD in order to promote discussion and dialogue within groups of people with responsibility for human resource development. It may be that these ideas for critical practitioners are at best impractical, hypothetical and a minority vision. It is likely that the ideas outlined here would be completely alien to many practitioners, that very few practitioners would look at HRD as this complex and that they would see it as focussed on *effective development practice within organisations* – which is to say how involved people are in development processes. This certainly fits with one mainstream assumption that drives HRD; that development is everyone's business and everyone's right, it supports the development of all the people in the organisation and it is about widening access to learning opportunities, in whatever form that takes.

One danger in imagining that those who are interested in HRD might combine as 'critical practitioners' – a group whose function is to mobilise critique as well as learning – is that the idea romances at the frontiers of HRD while ignoring its important core. Ultimately, HRD comprises a lot of basic but quite important development work, such as Health and Safety Training, which is often required by law. It is important that such development work is done well, and it matters that it is done on a big enough scale. It is possible that this core work of HRD is the most important in terms of reaching the bulk of staff, particularly support or front line workers who make a big difference to the way services are delivered. Perhaps, in general, I have not thought enough about basic training of a kind that actually helps the widest constituency of people. In making the suggestions I have made I may have neglected to understand that core training is part of the overall 'value chain', and also I may have reinforced how it can be devalued within organisations.

It is also possible that it is not the function of HRD people to engage with the power relations mobilised by organising, to take risks, to lead collective approaches to reflection and leadership, to support democracy, or to engage with the paradox within organisations that managers both want and want to avoid learning and change. It is probably unrealistic to imagine being able to have such a role, especially without being sufficiently well paid to take these risks. It may be that the majority of practitioners are not seeking new ideas or ways in which HRD can have increased impact, but rather a couple of good ideas to get them through their next instructional session. The notion of practitioners informed by critical thinking is perhaps too idealistic, especially if we are at the same time aware that in practice HRD is not going to change much from its current emphasis.

I do not think it necessary to resolve the various issues and complexities of debate that are represented here, either in terms of further detail on the ideas for critical practitioners or in terms of the critique that undermines these ideas. The value of ending with critique is exactly that it leaves all these assumptions, thoughts and questions open. It is a provocation, one that might give rise to many other opinions and ideas about the roles of HRD practitioners. There are many different assumptions about what HRD is and why HRD is an important activity, as well as concerns about the processes and practices associated with HRD. The ideas for critical practitioners that I have outlined imply that HRD is a pivotal process in organising for the future since its primary concerns are learning and change. HRD, therefore, has implications for future ways of behaving, structuring and organising across organisations and organisational domains. HRD can be characterised as evolving practice, as activity that inspires critique in order to create possibilities for learning, as attempts at organisation and organising that seek to create the ways we will be thinking and acting, as well as (and alongside) the inevitable problems and possibilities mobilised by actions.

Acknowledgements

I would like to acknowledge John Burgoyne, Heather Chisholme, Philip Lenz, Mike Pedler, Julie Reader, Michael Reynolds, John Stevens, Kiran Trehan and Jean Woodall for their contributions to the discussions that informed this chapter.

References

Palmer, I. and Hardy, C. (2000) *Thinking about Management*, London: Sage.

Reynolds, M. and Vince, R. (eds) (2004) *Organizing Reflection*, London: Ashgate.

Vince, R. (2003) 'The future practice of HRD', *Human Resource Development International*, 6, 4: 559–63.

Vince, R. (2004) *Rethinking Strategic Learning*, London: Routledge.

Watson, T. J. (2001) 'Beyond managism: negotiated narratives and critical management education in practice', *British Journal of Management*, 12, 4: 385–96.

4   Becoming critical

Can critical management learning develop critical managers?

Clare Rigg

Introduction

Many practitioners in the 'management and human resource development business' have long felt our role was dubious if we merely operated in a technocratic way – refining individual skills and developing organisational capabilities to continue operating in ways that have serious human and ecological consequences. Corporate scandals such as Enron,[1] Arthur Andersen,[2] WorldCom,[3] ImClone Systems[4] and endowment mis-selling,[5] have focused attention on the ethics of managing and provided additional impetus for those who argue for management education and development to integrate consideration of social and environmental terms of business. This is so, not least, in the field of critical management learning, which is imbued with optimistic assumptions of a transformational flow from individual learning to changes in managerial practice. However, the crucial question is does critical management learning make any difference to management practice? Does it actually bring about critical management practice? The aspirations of critical management learning literature certainly depend on it, yet there is a paucity of recorded empirical investigation into the subject (Reynolds, 1997) and a dearth of accounts of the consequences of critical management learning for participants' managing. Where experience of critical learning has been recorded it is drawn from research on participants during their educational programme (e.g. Belenky *et al.*, 1986; Brookfield, 1994), and consequently focuses on impacts on individuals, not on organisational collectivities.

This chapter is based on a study into the comparative influences of critical management and technicist management learning on managers' practice at work. It illuminates how a discourse perspective on learning, managing and organising enables an exploration of how managers talk about and perform their management practice. This is explored both as a way of understanding learning as an encounter with new discourse, and as providing, through discourse analysis, a methodological approach to studying the influence of formal learning on management practice by researching micro-processes of managing through everyday social interactions that company members engage in as they undertake their work.

A discursive view of managing and organisation

Figure 4.1 summarises the conceptual framework used in the study reported in this chapter, in which the notion of discourse is central to a processual perspective on organisation, management, the making of managers and learning.

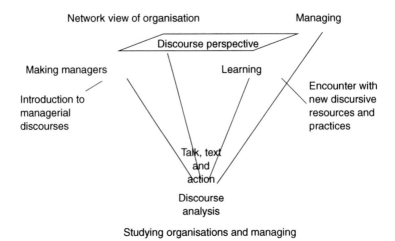

Figure 4.1 A discourse perspective on managing, organising and learning.

The conceptual framework for this research was based on the concept of discourse deployed in four ways. First, taking a network perspective on organisations, 'talk' was seen as essential to the conception of organisation. Talk was also taken to be integral to the process of managing, the second application of discourse. Third, learning was understood as an encounter with new discourse, and fourth, critical management learning was conceived as introducing a particular management discourse, which challenges and differs from functionalist and technicist management discourses.

Whilst discourse often refers simply to spoken dialogue (Sinclair and Coulthard, 1975), or to written and spoken text (e.g. Gilbert and Mulkay, 1984; Potter and Wetherell, 1987), in this study a broad understanding was taken, defining discourse more broadly, as discursive practices – not only language, but also ideas and philosophies (Van Dijk, 1997). If discourse is understood in this way, discursive practices 'do not just describe things, they *do* things' (Potter and Wetherell, 1987: 6), that is talk is intended to shape practices; discourse is 'a piece of language in action' (Watson, 1999: 4).

The study reported here deployed Sambrook and Stewart's (1998) distinction between discourse as noun and as verb to define discourse as a coherent, but not watertight, system of meanings encompassing discursive resources – individual ideas and language coalesced together with apparent logic and coherence, and communicated through discursive practices – and the communicative acts deployed to express dominant values, beliefs and ideas.

I define 'an' organisation as a network of shared meanings which are created, perpetuated and modified through discursive practices, but in so-doing I use the idea of network not as a reification but as a dynamic process. Working with a discourse perspective of managing, I define this as an activity of creating direction by meaning-making, in which talk is central. The role of talk is fundamental to a discourse perspective of organisations. Grant *et al.* argue: ' "organization" can be seen as a continuous process of social accomplishment which, in both senses of the term, is *articulated* by and through the deployment of discursive resources' (1998: 12). They maintain discourse is essential to 'constructing, situating, facilitating and communicating the diverse cultural, institutional, political and socio-economic parameters of "organizational being" ' (1998: 12).

Management learning as encounter with management discourse

The mystical processes of 'learning' are rarely articulated in literature on management learning or organisation change. Learning theory suggests that learning at higher levels, what Bateson (1973) terms Level III or Belenky *et al.* (1986) refer to as Level 5[6] is concerned with people challenging dominant discourses and discovering or creating others in which they have reframed themselves, and, with different discursive practices are able to engage in different actions. This constant interplay between talk, meaning and action, at an individual level and collectively within relationships, resonates with Watson and Harris's concept of the 'emergent manager', drawing on Chia's (1996) 'ontology of becoming' in which 'people engaged in *managing* as a kind of work are seen as *making their worlds at the same time as their worlds are making them.* Managers are seen as involved in "emergence" both in shaping their personal sense of "self" and in shaping organisational work activities through "organising" ' (Watson and Harris, 1999: 238).

I want to argue that a discourse perspective on managing provides a way of conceiving of management learning as encounter with new discourse or an engagement with new discursive resources and practices – put simply, new ways of thinking about, talking about and doing work. This offers insight into how management learning may, but may not, influence management practice, and may, but may not, influence the wider organisational discourse of a manager's work organisation.

Hopes of change within critical management learning discourse

Critical management learning can be understood in terms of what is described as 'critical pedagogy' in that it

> not only offers a challenging view of management as a social, political and economic practice, but does so in a way that stimulates student involvement of a kind that is rare in other forms of management education.
>
> (Grey *et al.*, 1996: 109)

A key rationale within the literature on critical management learning for encouraging managers to be critical, lies in the realisation of how powerful managers now are in the world, yet how poorly traditional management education has prepared them for considering questions of power and responsibility. Porter *et al.* suggest that the purpose of critical management thinking is to develop in managers 'habits of critical thinking... that prepare them for responsible citizenship and personally and socially rewarding lives and careers' (1989: 71). For Willmott the challenge for critical management learning is

> to envision and advance the development of discourses and practices that can facilitate the development of 'management' from a divisive technology of control into a collective means of emancipation.
>
> (1997: 175)

A critical management discourse is grounded in 'an appreciation of the pressures that lead managerial work to become so deeply implicated in the unremitting exploitation of nature and human beings, national and international extremes of wealth and poverty, the creation of global pollution, the promotion of "needs" for consumer products etc.' (Alvesson and Willmott, 1996: 39).

In contrast, a technicist management discourse presents managing as a value-neutral activity that strives for rationality, seeking to control, predict, and search for efficiency. The social relations of managing and the emotional (Fineman, 1999) and psychosocial dynamics of organisations have no place. Questions of business standards or the role of business in society receive no priority. As Alvesson and Willmott argue 'the functional rhetoric of technical rationality' denies or mystifies the moral basis of management practice (1996: 17).

Reynolds (1997) distinguishes between content radical and process radical pedagogies. Content radicals disseminate radical material, in the sense of critical theories and concepts which are alternatives to technocratic management education. Process radicals attempt to address power asymmetries of the traditional teacher/learner relationship, for example, taking an experiential learning approach, using action research, critical reflection, the conception of tutors and participants as co-learners in a learning community or action learning set and negotiated curricula.

Inherent to much critical management learning literature is an optimism that if managers are guided to consider questions of power and responsibility and gain an appreciation of their influence in questions of global pollution, exploitation of nature and human beings or extremes of poverty and wealth, they will manage in more ethical ways. Fundamental to this question are implicit thought/action assumptions on the relationship between management learning and managerial action. This study was designed to explore whether managers who have encountered a critical management discourse make sense of their practice in ways that differ from those who have engaged in functionalist or technicist management development.

Studying management practice – an ethnographic approach

A discourse perspective on organisation and managing opens up the prospect of researching management practice through studying the talk/action in use, the 'network of action' or in other words, the discursive practices of a particular organisation and the language or discursive resources managers use. The distinction between discursive practice and discursive resource has methodological implications, in that a focus on resources is a focus on the content, whilst inclusion of discursive practices[7] encompasses a range of communicative acts, both verbal and non-verbal, that shape our sense of the world as much as the content of any communication. Such processes of communication (or textual production) might include stories, narratives, rituals such as making the tea or the format of meetings, rhetoric, language games such as names, conversations, sense-making, signs and architecture – the physical organisation of space and bodies.

This focus lends itself to an ethnographic approach because of the possibilities to collect accounts, to observe actions and processes and to explore the feelings, thoughts and meanings people attribute to situations as they happen.

The research from which this chapter draws involved a comparative study of managers from small organisations[8] who have participated in a critical management post-graduate course with others who participated in technicist management courses. The former was characterised as critical primarily through its process radical pedagogical approach, as described earlier. In each case these were part-time courses undertaken alongside participants' employment. Small organisations were deliberately selected on the assumption that organisation practices were more open to individual influence than in large organisations where many processes are prescribed.

The study explored the following questions:

1   How do managers talk about themselves, their managing and their organisations?
2   What sense do they make of their work and their organisations?
3   How do their colleagues talk about them?

The ethnographic approach adopted used 'micro-ethnography', which 'zeroes in on *particular* settings drawing on the ways that a cultural ethos is reflected in microcosm in selected aspects of every day life...' (Wolcott, 1995: 102). The specific methods deployed were shadowing (Czarniawska, 1998) combined with semistructured ethnographic or narrative interviews of them and their colleagues. Czarniawska describes her use of shadowing as allowing 'me to move with them and to move from one point in an action net to another because I am after not individual experience but a collective construction' (1998: 28). Shadowing was combined with two other ethnographic methods: narrative interviews and ethnographic interviews. In narrative interviews, using Czarniawska's definition of 'chronological relations of events that occurred under a specified period of time' (1998: 28), I explicitly asked for stories, for example, of organisation members' early impressions when they joined the company – for accounts of funny and difficult incidents. Ethnographic interviews (Spradley, 1979) I defined as generalised, of the moment, not necessarily collecting stories. An example would be taking the opportunity at a tea-break in the middle of a meeting, as we waited for the kettle to boil, of asking someone what they meant, felt or thought about a particular aspect of the meeting. In this study the aim of the shadowing was to observe key collective events, such as particular kinds of meetings, which could constitute Wolcott's cultural ethos in microcosm. In the case companies a core manager was shadowed; a non-participant observer accompanied them throughout a day at their workplace, observing them interacting with their work colleagues, interviewing them and several of their colleagues, talking to people opportunistically and observing organisation members going about their work. Eight managers were interviewed, 4 from a critical and 4 from a technicist management development programme, and 2 each of these and their small companies were studied in depth. A total of 17 people were interviewed.

This combination of methods offered the possibility of taking an ethnographic approach, with its benefits of depth, whilst not being an ethnography in the sense of studying one organisation through long-term immersion as a participant observer. This was neither feasible as a part-time researcher, nor would it have addressed the comparative research questions, which required study of more than one organisation. It could claim to be an ethnographic approach in the sense suggested by Watson when describing ethnography as an extension of the processes we use in everyday life: 'Ethnographic research involves feeling one's way in confusing circumstances, struggling to make sense of ambiguous messages, reading signals, looking around, listening all the time, coping with conflicts and struggling to achieve tasks through establishing and maintaining a network of relationships. But that is what we do all the time as human beings' (1994: 8).

This chapter presents a part of the research analysis drawn from two of these cases – one manager from each of a critical and a technicist management development programme.

Analysing discourse

The resultant research material was a mixture of tape recordings, which became transcribed texts; notes, sketches of building layout and people's interactions, documents such as complement slips, logos and project records from the key meetings. The material therefore combined research notes and verbatim records of language used in various interactions, and accounts of discursive practices employed. In analysing these, given the definition of discourse employed, it was imperative to move away from focusing on language, and to think in terms of discursive practices and resources: to keep focused on searching for examples of talk-as-action within the texts; and to keep asking what is being done in an inter-action. Ian Parker's framework for discourse analysis (1992) and Karl Weick's (1995) concept of sense-making were particularly helpful. For example, Parker provides a sorting category for analysing actions within particular settings, for instance, with questions such as in Step 2, 'what are the connotations evoked to me?'; in Step 5, 'what's the relationship between the text author and the addressee – what "role" are they being put in to receive the message?' or in Step 6, 'what right has the addressee to speak – what can they say?' The value in Weick's sense-making was his guidance to consider authoring, identity construction and what he calls ongoing reality-making through retrospective sense-making. This contributed themes such as 'who are you, who are we and who are they', which helped construction of an analytic framework.

Though this chapter cannot go in to depth, the framework was used to make a comparison of the focal managers and their companies, based on the analysis of discursive practices and discursive resources deployed in the following:

- Beliefs and identity
- When things go wrong
- Disagreeing with the boss
- Developing new practices – light touch meaning-making
- Defining/steering – forceful meaning-making
- Forging relationships
- Co-framing
- Organising.

For example, taking the theme of 'Beliefs and Identity' for each company, all instances which would help construct an account of how members talked about themselves and others were collated. This encompassed a range of discursive practices including logos, written signs, building layout, interactions within meetings, names of meetings and job roles, informal interactions, body language, conversations as well as narrative accounts given in formal interviews. So attention was paid not only to the specific language or discursive resources being deployed but also to the discursive acts and what meaning they might convey, conceiving of them as pragmatic acts (Mey, 1993). With the themes 'light-touch' and 'forceful meaning-making', I was interested in what discursive practices or resources managers drew on to encourage, persuade, cajole or coerce other members to adopt new working practices. In some instances they could be described as 'light-touch meaning-making' in the sense of subtle ways in which meanings were made; ways in which organisation members engaged interactively, co-framing new ways of thinking about and enacting their business. At other times there was a much stronger steerage where one or more people attempt to steer the definitions of what is happening – more a sense of 'it will be like this' or what I termed forceful meaning-making.

The underlying question explored through these themes was whether there was a coherent interconnection that could be attributed to either a critical or a technicist management discourse.

Discourses of management learning and organisation practice – a tale of two companies

The next part of the chapter presents an account of the relations between management learning and practice through two case studies of managers and their companies: Sam and Metal Tubes, and Jack and Market ReDesign. Both companies are UK based. The cases will be discussed in terms of two themes: individual change and managing critically.

Introducing the cases

Sam at Metal Tubes

Sam founded Metal Tubes with his co-Director, Don, in the early 1990s. Metal Tubes is a small company of ten people who work across the UK to project manage the design and instalment of air-conditioning systems. Sam completed a critical management Diploma in Management Studies (DMS) and MSc in Organisation Development at a UK University, studying part-time alongside his work.

Several features of DMS/MSc in Organisation Development combine to give it a critical management learning approach in terms of the definition advanced at the beginning of this chapter. Participants of the management development programme encounter critical learning predominantly in process, through action learning sets, process facilitation, action research and the idea of a learning community, but to a lesser extent in content. There are lecture inputs, but students spend two-thirds of their time working collectively in a specific action learning set (ALS) facilitated by a tutor. The ALS fulfils a number of functions: it undertakes group consultancy tasks, and in doing this participants are encouraged to reflect on how they work together and to confront process issues in some depth. Participants are also encouraged to exchange their experiences within the ALS, of doing their dissertations and preparing their individual papers. In this sense students' dialogue and social support are seen as fundamental to the course. The ALS is also frequently a source of diversity, where issues mirror some of the patterns of power and inequality within organisations and society. Students are encouraged, through reflective assignments and facilitator questioning, to work constructively with that diversity and to reflect on and learn from their feelings and experiences of doing so. An action research methodology is deployed for the Masters dissertation during which students are encouraged to explore the epistemological basis of action research. Action research has a long history of use for radical community action, and this leads many to engage with some of the critical theory that it implies (Carr and Kemmis, 1986). A further element of critical learning is a critical self-reflection paper, an autobiographical reflection on the manager's development, which each individual writes. In this participants are encouraged to identify core assumptions, to understand some of their patterns and the contextual influences on them. Depending on their particular focus, individuals may be introduced to critical concepts derived from such areas as feminism, marxism, social constructionism or critical pedagogy.

The key collective event observed at Metal Tubes was their Communications Forum, a monthly meeting of the following staff: Sam and Don – the two Directors – John, Martin and Andy, all Project Managers and Bethany, the Project Design and Sales Manager. Interviews were also conducted with Sam, John, Andy and Bethany.

Jack at Market ReDesign

Jack is Brand Consultant in the second company, Market ReDesign, a design agency created in the early 1990s which now employs around 30 people. He recently completed a post-graduate Diploma in Marketing, a technicist management development programme, at a UK university, studying part-time alongside his work.

The post-graduate Diploma in Marketing Jack undertook at a UK university was taught entirely through lectures, case study exercises and readings, and assessed through timed examinations. It was designed by the university to prepare participants for admission to the UK's Chartered Institute of Marketing. In terms of the definition of technicist management education outlined at the start of the chapter this course had no process radical features in the way participants learnt or interrelated with each other or their tutors and there was no content radical curriculum, for example, examining wider questions of the implications work on brands for employees or the environment, or exploring the marketing discourse of the primacy of customer needs. Marketing ideas were presented as value-neutral means of improving individual and organisational performance.

The key collective event observed in Market ReDesign was the Monday morning sales meeting, involving the following staff: Rowan, the Marketing Director, Ron the Managing Director, three Account Managers, Sue, Adrian and Catriona, Jack the Brand Consultant, Reanne, Creative Director, Anna the Finance Director and Nick the Operations Manager. Rowan, Catriona, Jack and Nick were also interviewed.

Individual change – new language or new discourse?

A thought-action perspective implies that introduction to new thought and language can contribute to an individual reconstituting themselves, which might be expected to produce changed managerial action. In exploring whether and when learning produced new discourse, the question was whether the focal managers' course-acquired language had become a language of action in their managing and organising.

Metal Tubes

When Sam was asked whether he thought the course influenced his practice, his narratives conveyed an interweaving between the company's development and his views of the course, that permeate his sense of thinking and managing. He described how he applied ideas from the course, such as a particular way of running key meetings which drew from his experience of exchange and critique through action learning:

> we have a Communications Forum which was designed from my DMS paper, funnily enough, that was one of the outputs of my paper . . . 'because we do try to do the good and the bad, and that is one way of sharing information'.

Some discursive practices encountered on his course appear to have become integral to the ways Sam thinks about his work, particularly the action research approach of his MSc:

> then from the DMS point of view, and certainly the Action Research MSc point of view, that is very much something you are doing in action research, you are

finding out a piece of information, applying it, checking it out and then going back to the literature or your peers or some other area to find out some more information and gradually rack it up, how you improve the company.... You can overlay action research on to the sort of company that we wanted to be, that was a company that knew very little to start with but wanted to improve ourselves through the methods that we were getting from the DMS and MSc.

Throughout discussions with other organisation members the idea of learning was a dominant theme of Metal Tubes' company discourse. All those interviewed referred to the term frequently, describing the emphasis on improvement, reviews of practice and on learning from mistakes without a blame culture. All were engaged in formal qualification-based courses and many discursive practices were imbued with notions of learning. For example, Sam described his direct application of some of his course work:

What we find (is) that individuals tend to learn themselves but don't pass that learning on to others and to the wider organization, and to change the systems that we use. So we have put certain things into play from the projects that Don and I did, to try to enable this company to do that.

Here it could be said the organising of Metal Tubes integrates a range of discursive resources and practices from action learning and action research.

Market ReDesign

In Market ReDesign, when Jack was asked whether he thought the course influenced his practice, he attributed new ways of thinking about and describing his work to his Diploma in Marketing. He said it gave him both a business language that helped him talk to clients as well as a new language of thought that gave him a different way of thinking about graphic design, and of enacting his role. He said,

I mean marketing is a consumer-friendly approach to business, and design has a critical part to play in that. It's meant that I've been able to filter business-talk into design language.

When he was asked how he made use of his course learning, he explained how it had affected his entire perception of his own role and of his company's business. He described what he and his colleagues aimed to do with clients, describing the *'customer journey'* that takes the customer through *a 'brand journey'*. He talked of *'creating a play'* and of *'choreographing the customer experience'* using *'visual language'* to build a brand. Since the course, he said he has reconstructed himself as a Brand Consultant, replacing his old titles of graphic designer and account manager.

He related how he drew from his course to conceptualise what he did:

my whole job is about building personalities around companies, so therefore the Porter's Forces things,...I use all the time to understand the environment in which the business operates, so I can actually define the right design visual language, the right visual tone to suit the personality that they need against their competitors, either future ones or current ones. So I'm designing something that's got a lot more longevity to it, than if, historically, whereas if I hadn't done the Marketing Diploma it would have been very much now-and-then, without a picture, a broader picture, the horizons of what was coming up...

Here he could be said to be drawing on a range of discursive resources from marketing to reframe the company discourse, as well as his own role.

Managing critically

As argued above, critical management writers suggest that managers with a critical awareness are not only conscious but are also concerned that their choices and actions have political consequences on the environment, on exploitation of people or on extremes of wealth and poverty (e.g. Guba and Lincoln, 1994; Alvesson and Willmott, 1996). The assumptions of critical management learning are that managers exposed to such, what is often termed liberatory discourse, will be influenced in the ways they work. In this sense there were differences between Sam and Jack's managing, and although one would need to be very cautious in attributing these to the influence of their management courses, there are consistent links between their management and their course discourses. The theme of co-framing is insightful in this respect.

Co-framing

Dialogical accounts of discourse were of interest – the extent to which different voices were encouraged or whether members were involved in co-framing conversations (Hardy *et al.*, 1998). Indications of this can be drawn from various interactions within the two companies, for example, in responses to mistakes and conflict, in challenges to the boss and in how talk was used to try to make meaning.

Metal Tubes

In Sam's discursive practice there were a number of elements of egalitarianism: he made the coffee; he shared a cramped open plan office; he espoused a desire for openness and honesty within the company Communications Forum and he had self-consciously tried to recruit and train women into a predominantly male industry. There were many ways in which members of Metal Tubes organised with considerable co-framing. Collaborative decision-making and exchanges of learning were part of the espoused organisation discourse. Whilst there were differences of opinion and Martin's accounts in particular appeared to have least influence, there were still many exchanges that included him as an insider and indicated he was seen to do valuable work. There were times when Sam was forceful and definitive in his framing, but there were examples where his own account could be rendered marginal. Perhaps a clear indication is to illustrate the patterns of interaction between members during the Communications Forum through Figure 4.2.

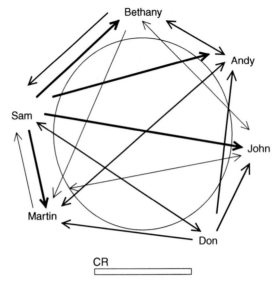

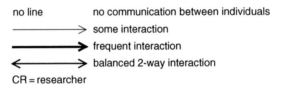

Frequency and direction of interactions is symbolised
by the arrows and thickness of lines:

no line   no communication between individuals

————————▷ some interaction

————————▶ frequent interaction

◀————————▶ balanced 2-way interaction

CR = researcher

Figure 4.2 Patterns of interaction between members during the Communications Forum.

Market ReDesign

In Market ReDesign Jack was critical in the sense of critique (Watson, 1999) in ways
he made use of content or discursive resource from his course. However, there was no
evidence of him being critical in the meaning of critical management outlined earlier.
For example, Jack recounted one of his projects, working with a nationalised company
to rebrand themselves '*that we got paid £1/2 million to do*'. In his view implementation
of these rebranding plans was that the company '*needed a new culture – new employee
behaviours, but the employees were a blockage*'. In his account he made no acknowledgement of any problematics in this situation. For example, there was no suggestion that
employees might have a perspective and Jack did not question his own role, accountability or power in framing strategy in this publicly owned company. It could be said
that this absence of critical management discourse reflects a similar absence in the
management discourse of his Marketing Diploma.

Co-framing was also notably absent from the dominant company discourse of
Market ReDesign. For example, interactions between members of the sales meeting

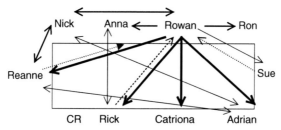

Frequency and direction of interactions is symbolised
by the arrows and thickness of lines:

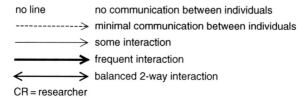

no line — no communication between individuals

`-------------->` minimal communication between individuals

`------------>` some interaction

`━━━━━━━►` frequent interaction

`◄━━━━━━━►` balanced 2-way interaction

CR = researcher

Figure 4.3 Patterns of interaction between Market ReDesign members during the sales meeting.

were strongly steered by Rowan the Marketing Director, again illustrated in Figure 4.3.

Many accounts and exchanges suggested minimal co-framing, even if the space were offered. For example, Catriona narrated how Rowan came in one Monday morning and said: 'I've been thinking about how we could make these meetings more friendly.' She said,

> we said to Rowan, well, a) we could move them and he said, no absolutely not, Monday, need to get ahead, start the week, and all that kind of stuff.... Basically the conversation spiralled round, it started here, what can we do to be more friendly in these meetings and it ended up back at the same point saying we can't be more friendly, the meetings are really hard and they have to be this way.

Rowan's tone of speaking to other members positioned them as recalcitrant children/pupils, with few rights to speak. His discourse appeared to be that everyone else is deficient, lazy, has the wrong view, doesn't care; a sense of 'I should be the one in charge and everyone else should work like me'. Within this, dialogical accounts were not tolerated. When we talked about collaborative decision-making, Rowan asked, without irony, *'you mean, pretend to ask them what they think?'*

When Jack was asked what sense he made of these interactions, his comments drew either on discursive resources of personality, 'That's just how Rowan is; it's because he's from the music industry.'

Or to explain why Rowan as Marketing Director was at such variance with the Designers, he called on his earlier occupational discourse as a graphic designer, saying,

'Design is part of you. Designers invest themselves in their work.... The culture here, a lot of people work long hours, it's their social life, they eat here.'

It appeared that his management course had provided him with no discursive resources to make sense of the pattern of interactions between organisation members, either in Market ReDesign or in the nationalised company.

Conclusions – can critical management learning develop critical managers?

The ethnographic case studies illustrate how course-acquired language had become a language of action in the managing and organising of the two focal managers. Their working practices and their definitions of what they did were developed through this language. They also gave the language meaning through their actions. Whilst the study is small it demonstrates the possibilities, if not the inevitability, for a relationship between discursive practices of managing and formal management learning. If this is so then can we be optimistic that critical management learning might lead to more critical management practice? One conclusion is that it may do, but that any expectation that critical management learning produces critical managers whilst technicist courses do not, is simplistic, for a number of reasons. Not only are managers emergent (Watson and Harris, 1999) in the sense that they weave resources from their learning into pre-existing values, it is also important to differentiate between the transformatory potential of critical management learning at individual, organisational and societal levels. At a societal level many claims for critical management learning seem very optimistic, in that there is no inherent link between an individual's critical learning which they might find personally transformatory, and how they might use that socially, regardless of the constraints they might face on their actions. At an organisation level individual transformation may have wider transformatory potential. For example, a critical discourse may 'empower' an individual to deploy critical management practices at work because it has provided an alternative to technicist management and perhaps legitimised pre-existing values. However, it could well be that a critical management awareness, in heightening the manager's awareness of power, merely enhances their ability to influence more effectively. The consequence may or may not be emancipatory for anyone. At the third level, that of the individual, the claims of critical management learning have perhaps most potential to be realised. However, a further conclusion from this study is that transformatory learning, as related, for example by Freire (1972), to people who are 'oppressed' is very different from managers in already relatively powerful positions with at least some degree of autonomy, who describe their learning as transformatory. Such a distinction seems little recognised in the literature on critical management learning, although it is by feminist writers such as Lather who has attacked what she sees as the current fashion for exalting empowerment as 'individual self-assertion, upward mobility and the psychological experience of feeling powerful' (1991: 3).

In conclusion, we can hang on to our hopes that critical management learning might result in more critical management practice, but with the awareness that there is no inevitable flow between individual transformatory learning and critical practice at an organisational or societal level.

Notes

1 Enron, the US energy company that collapsed amid scandal in late 2001, evaded billions of dollars in tax with the help of 'some of the nation's finest' accountants, investment banks and lawyers, as reported by Bateson report, February 2003, commissioned by US senate finance committee.
2 In 2002 a jury in the United States found accountancy firm Arthur Andersen guilty of obstructing justice by shredding documents relating to the failed energy giant Enron.
3 WorldCom, the telecom firm, filed for bankruptcy in 2002 after uncovering $11bn in alleged accounting fraud. In 2003 the company itself and six former employees including the ex-chief executive and former chief financial officer, were charged with 'executing a scheme to artificially inflate bond and stock prices by intentionally filing false information with the Securities & Exchange Commission' (Source: Accountancy Age.com 28-08-2003).
4 In 2002 the former president and founder of biotechnology firm ImClone Systems was indicted for fraud in an alleged insider trading scandal, accused of providing information to family members that enabled them to sell shares before the price fell.
5 Millions of people in the UK are thought to have been mis-sold mortgage endowment policies during the 1980s and 1990s, meaning that the policy was inappropriate for them and advisers who sold the product did not fully explain how the endowment worked, the market risks or its suitability for the individual's circumstances.
6 At Bateson's level III a person has an ability to step outside their previous worldview, has an awareness of their own subjectivity, has gained control over habitual ways and can take responsibility for making changes. Belenky *et al.*'s Level 5 is termed constructed knowledge: the learner comes to view knowledge as contextual and themselves as potential creators of knowledge, through both subjective and objective strategies.
7 Discursive act and discursive practice will be used interchangeably.
8 Using the European Commission's definitions of small: 0–49 employees; medium: 50–249; large: 250+ (Commission of the European Communities Recommendation of 3 April 1996).

References

Alvesson, M. and Willmott, H. (1996) *Making Sense of Management*, London: Sage.
Bateson, G. (1973) *Steps Towards an Ecology of the Mind*, London: Paladin.
Belenky, M.F., Clinchy, B. McVicker, Golderger, N.R. and Tarube, J.M. (1986) *Women's Ways of Knowing. The Development of Self, Voice and Mind*, New York: Basic Books.
Brookfield, S. (1994) 'Tales from the dark side: a phenomenology of adult critical reflection', *International Journal of Lifelong Education*, 13, 3: 203–16.
Carr, W. and Kemmis, S. (1986) *Becoming Critical: Education Knowledge and Action Research*, London: Falmer Press.
Chia, R. (1996) *Organizational Analysis as Deconstructive Practice*, Berlin and New York: De Gruyter.
Czarniawska, B. (1998) 'A narrative approach to organization studies', *Qualitative Research Methods Series 43*, London: Sage.
Fineman, S. (1999) 'Emotion and organization', in S.R. Clegg and C. Hardy (eds) *Studying Organization*, London: Sage.
Freire, P. (1972) *Pedagogy of the Oppressed*, Middlesex: Penguin.
Gilbert, G.N. and Mulkay, M. (1984) *Opening Pandora's Box: A Sociological Analysis of Scientists' Discourse*, Cambridge: Cambridge University Press.

Grant, D., Keenoy, T. and Oswick, C. (eds) (1998) *Discourse and Organization*, London: Sage.

Grey, C., Knights, D. and Willmott, H. (1996) 'Is a critical pedagogy of management possible?', in R. French and C. Grey (eds) *Rethinking Management Education*, London: Sage.

Guba, E. and Lincoln, Y. (1994) 'Competing paradigms in qualitative research', in N.K. Denzin and Y.L. Lincoln (eds) *Handbook of Qualitative Research*, Thousand Oaks, CA: Sage.

Hardy, C., Lawrence, T.B. and Phillips, N. (1998) 'Talk and action: conversations and narrative in interorganizational collaboration', in D. Grant, T. Kennoy and C. Oswick (eds) *Discourse and Organization*, London: Sage, 65–83.

Lather, P. (1991) *Getting Smart, Feminist Research and Pedagogy With/in the Postmodern*, New York: Routledge.

Mey, J. (1993) *Pragmatics an Introduction*, Oxford: Blackwell.

Parker, I. (1992) *Discourse Dynamics*, London: Routledge.

Porter, L.W., Muller, H.J. and Rehder, R.R. (1989) 'The making of managers, an American perspective', *Journal of General Management*, 14, 4: 62–76.

Potter, J. and Wetherell, M. (1987) *Discourse and Social Psychology*, London: Sage.

Reynolds, M. (1997) 'Towards a critical pedagogy', in J. Burgoyne and M. Reynolds (eds) *Management Learning, Integrating Perspectives in Theory and Practice*, London: Sage, 312–28.

Sambrook, S. and Stewart, J. (1998) 'No, I don't want to be part of HR', *HRDI*, 1, 2: 171–88.

Sinclair, J.M. and Coulthard, R.M. (1975) *Towards an Analysis of Discourse: The English Used by Pupils and Teachers*, Oxford: Oxford University Press.

Spradley, J.P. (1979) *The Ethnographic Interview*, London: Holt, Rinehart and Winston.

Van Dijk, T.A. (ed.) (1997) *Discourse as Structure and Process*, Vol. 1, London: Sage.

Watson, T. (1994) *In Search of Management*, London: Routledge.

Watson, T. (1999) 'Beyond managism: negotiated narratives and critical management education in practice', *First International Conference on Critical Management Studies*, University of Manchester, 14–16 July.

Watson, T. and Harris, P. (1999) *The Emergent Manager*, London: Sage.

Weick, K. (1995) *Sensemaking in Organizations*, Thousand Oaks, CA: Sage.

Willmott, H. (1997) 'Critical management learning', in J. Burgoyne and M. Reynolds (eds) *Management Learning*, London: Sage, 161–76.

Wolcott, H.F. (1995) 'Making a study more ethnographic', chap. 3 in J. Van Maanen (ed.) *Representation in Ethnography*, London: Sage.

5 Management education

A tool for mismanagement?

Finian Buckley and Kathy Monks

Introduction

The importance of managing employee development has gained increased attention in recent decades particularly following the writings of prominent researchers advocating that future competitiveness advantage can be tracked to the development of the creative human capital of the organization (Pfeffer, 1994; Hamel and Prahalad, 1996). The emphasis on the importance of nurturing and developing intangible and hitherto untapped human creative resources has prompted human resource development (HRD) specialists to rethink traditional training strategies. The perspective has shifted from ensuring that employees had the required skills and competencies to complete the role and tasks assigned to them toward a more holistic view of developing a wide range of employee competencies, particularly those which are unique and which differentiate the organization from competitor organizations.

The Harvard Business School, among others, led a clarion call for founding organizational competitive advantage and advancement on the recognition and development of core competencies. Such advocacy soon created a vogue in 'competency assessment' throughout the business world (Willmott, 1994). This trend developed in parallel with the arrival of the so called paradigmatic shift to viewing organizations as continuously learning entities (see e.g. Senge 1990; Brown and Duguid, 1991; Pedler *et al.*, 1994). The focus on continuous learning and on identifying key competencies accelerated the development of the HRD function and elevated the importance of training within many organizations. Training appeared to move from being primarily functionalist and regulatory in orientation toward being future oriented and an end in itself (Ortenblad, 2002a). This was also supported by the growing awareness that learning (both in the workplace and beyond) did not terminate at the conclusion of formal education but needed to be seen as a lifelong process (Edwards, 1997; Edwards *et al.*, 2002).

Great expectations

Doubtless the challenges facing organizations at the latter end of the twentieth century and at the beginning of the twenty-first century are more complex and chaotic than at any other time in history (Aram and Noble, 1999; Stacey *et al.*, 2000). This has led to the elevation of the HRD function to a core position when organizations either plan for the future or seek to react to unplanned organizational or environmental events which pose challenges. It appears that employee training and development is now firmly identified as the vehicle which will deliver a wide range of organizational benefits (Iles, 1993). These organizational benefits can be characterized and reviewed under three headings: micro-level development, meso-level development and macro-level or organizational development. These headings identify the differential focus of certain developmental approaches. Table 5.1 outlines examples of the different form of learning focus in each category of training/development.

The micro-level approach tends to focus on 'near transfer' (Young, 1993) behavioural and visible skills. Examples of typical outcomes include functional skills such as IT skills, presentation skills, service communication skills, health and safety procedures, machine skills and so forth. This form of training focuses on proximal transfer where the skills or procedures developed are overt and instantly applicable in the function for which they are intended.

The meso-level categorization is typically associated with management level training and development. However, in the era of downsizing, the process of delayering and delegating management responsibilities to a wide range of employees became commonplace (Manz and Sims, 1987). Therefore, management training and development became a more widespread and broader function with more defined and proximal objectives than previously identified (Winterton and Winterton, 1997). Despite this the general objective of the meso-level development process is to bridge the perceived gap between employee competencies and abilities and those required of managers. While many of these competencies are recognized as readily transferable, there is a sense of mystique surrounding aspects of effective management, suggesting a requirement for higher order thought, a significant perspective shift from citizen-employee to citizen-with-organizational responsibility. Inherent in this transfer is the suggestion that more sophisticated training and development techniques are required to bring employees to this 'level' of thinking and performance. Despite the fact that the emphasis in meso-level interventions is manager, rather than role defined

Table 5.1 Expected outcomes of training and development interventions at different organizational levels

Outcome of micro-level training and development	Outcome of meso-level training and development	Outcome of macro-level training and development
Functional role skills	Future oriented management	Organizational-level
IT skills	competencies	learning
Presentation skills	Decision-making	Double loop thinking
Health and safety	Team leadership	Strategic reorientation
procedures	Innovative thinking	Long-term planning
Service	Developmental style	Learning organization
communication	Conflict resolution	Change orientation
Report writing	Employee appraisal	

employee focused, the essential outcome is bounded or normative in that little fundamental organizational change is to accrue. Within this experience, the faces in management positions may change but the philosophy, social and power architecture, and the supporting systems, as well as the organizational objectives, remain relatively static (Alvesson and Deetz, 1999). In essence, the aim of meso-level intervention is containment and control in the short to medium term.

The third category, macro-level or organizational-level change, is by far the most difficult area of management training and development to define, confine and describe. While most top managers recognize this higher order level of management readiness and competence as essential for the future growth and prosperity of their organizations, exactly how this might be achieved is less clear (Höpfl and Dawes, 1995). It is at this level that there is an implicit convergence of the idea that the organization can provide an environment for employee self-actualization and that these liberated employees then lead the organization to the nirvana characterized as the Learning Organization (Ortenblad, 2002b). This category of management training and development requires significant personal development on the part of participants, particularly in what Clarke refers to as 'meta-abilities' as 'they underpin and determine how and when knowledge, skills and competencies are used' (1999: 46). In order to apply these meta-abilities within an organization requires an organizational readiness to adopt new perspectives and cast aside defensiveness. In contrast to Young's (1993) ideation of 'near-transfer' mentioned at micro-level training, transfer at this level might be described as 'far-transfer' in that the manager is not developing actual visible skills but rather perspectives and orientations which may or may not have direct application in the short term or medium term.

Unexpected outcomes

The HRD literature is replete with researchers and practitioners expounding the positive impact of a huge variety of training and development interventions on personal, unit and organizational-level change (Huselid, 1995; Martocchio and Baldwin, 1997; Salas and Canon-Bowers, 2001). There is no doubting that learning is change and that formally designed learning and development opportunities sponsor significant change for many organizations. However, there is a literature, granted minuscule in comparison, which identifies that accepted training and development approaches do not always deliver the predicted change and indeed in some situations can have a deleterious impact on participants and the organizations concerned. This section reviews some of these hidden outcomes including commentary on the widespread absence of valid measurement of the impact that training and development has on actual workplace performance; the frequent misalignment of training with organizational strategy and culture; the impact of non-selection for programme participation on remaining employees; how returning participants can feel isolated in the old workplace and the use of training and development for reasons contrary to the programme objectives. The section concludes with a case study illustrating some of these causes and outcomes which combine in an ill-fated approach to management development.

Transfer to job performance?

Perhaps the most consistent criticism of the effectiveness of training and development interventions is the failure of HRD professionals to measure validly the actual impact of the intervention on organizational performance (Harrison, 1993; Bramley, 1996; Warr *et al.*, 1999). While most professional training providers will seek participant feedback on perceptions of the effectiveness of the training programme (Level 1 in Kirkpatrick's 1959 evaluation of training outcomes framework), this is a separate and distinct concept from the actual behavioural impact of the training on workplace performance (Alliger *et al.*, 1997). Some providers also attempt to measure the impact of the training or development intervention on the knowledge, skills or competencies of the participants (Kirkpatrick's Level 2). Typically, this is attempted by measuring participants' entry level competency and comparing these scores with those measured immediately after programme completion (Warr *et al.*, 1999 refer to these as 'attainment scores'). It might be assumed that significant positive increments in attainment scores confirm the effectiveness of training but the association between these changes and application in the workplace is not necessarily predictive (Alliger *et al.*, 1997). The functional validity of any training programme is if the outcomes have the desired impact on organizational behaviour and performance (Kirkpatrick's Level 3). However, only a tiny minority of training and development providers actually engage in measurement, both prior to and post programme, of the impact of the programme on actual workplace performance (Pfeffer, 1981; Arthur *et al.*, 2003). Even if this approach is utilized, fewer providers or research studies use a control group of non-trainees with which to compare intervention measures. Further controversy surrounds the actual measurement of the application of training and development outcomes in the workplace as this is recognized as an area fraught with difficulties given the array of extraneous factors which may mediate transfer (Doyle, 1995; Winterton and Winterton, 1997; Salas and Canon-Bowers, 2001).

The lack of attention to professional measurement has led to justified criticism of the HRD field and until providers focus on insuring the transfer of training to situated organizational behaviour and the on-going needs of the organization they will legitimately attract such criticism (Berry, 1990; Clarke, 1999; Warr *et al.*, 1999). The effectiveness of training and development interventions (at micro-, meso- or macro-levels) can only be assessed if rigorous appraisal and measurement techniques are employed. However, viewing the organization as a functioning machine and viewing employees as manipulatable human resources whose behaviour needs to be changed or altered to fit the organizational needs is a restrictive reified perspective and may never supply the required validation statistics given the dynamic nature of organizations. Approaching training and development from a more inclusive relational perspective may make traditional point-to-point transfer measurement more difficult but does not preclude more qualitative and longitudinal approaches to the validation of training effectiveness (Clarke, 1999; Kozlowski *et al.*, 2000).

Misalignment of training with organizational motive

The importance of aligning training and development needs with the stated and agreed strategy of the organization is a fundamental given in the area of strategic change (Goldstein, 1993; Huselid, 1995) and in the 'training needs analysis' literature (Taylor and O' Driscoll, 1998). Despite the obvious requirement for the alignment of training and development needs with organizational strategy there is evidence to suggest that this alignment is not always in place (Broad and Newstrom, 1992; Kozowski *et al.*, 2000). It is not unknown for managers and supervisors at a functional level to identify the need for specific forms of employee training and to source this training without any reference to overall organizational strategy. This misalignment may be due to the absence or non-representation of HRD professionals in the strategic planning process of the organization (Ezzamel *et al.*, 1996) or the poor translation of organizational-level strategy to the work practice level. It may also indicate a dislocation of the organizational strategy from the everyday working needs of the units and departments. Kessels and Harrisons' (1998) research and commentary further highlights the importance of not only internal, but also the external consistency of training and development interventions, as the key to success of management development programmes. Hussey (1988) asserts that most training and development exercises engaged in by organizations are neither planned nor assessed in the light of the future orientation and strategic focus of the organization. This is not to say that the training and development exercise is irrelevant to the organization but that the specific alignment of training needs to the organizational strategy is rarer than one might expect (Robinson, 1994).

Workplace climate and support

Evidence exists to suggest that work colleagues who do not participate in on-going training or development interventions (either by personal choice or by not being chosen to participate) can have a negative impact on workplace behaviour (Smith-Jentsch *et al.*, 2001). The non-participants may feel aggrieved at not being chosen to participate and may display their frustration and feelings of inequity in a number of ways (Niehoff and Paul, 2000; Tepper, 2000). A typical reaction facing a participant on return to the workplace might be *'did you learn that on the training course? Well, this is the real world and that won't work here'*.

The attendance at high prestige interventions, particularly restricted entry programmes, may isolate the participants on return to the workplace where they may now be regarded suspiciously as part of an out-group (Linville *et al.*, 1989; Duffy *et al.*, 2002). So, while imbued with new ideas and competencies, the returning participant may be isolated and no longer counted as central to the functioning in-group or seen as part of the core community (Lave and Wenger, 1990). Critical management researchers view these issues as elementary to the understanding of organizational dynamics, where the crucial concept is the power distribution within the organization (Willmott, 1994; Clarke, 1999; Brown and Starkey, 2000).

Research in the area of 'motivation to engage in training' has also indicated that being chosen to engage or participate in a training intervention in itself can have a strong motivating impact, informing those chosen that they are seen as potentially significant contributors to the future of the organization (Ready *et al.*, 1994; Colquitt *et al.*, 2000; Salas and Canon-Bowers, 2001). This motivation is often coupled with a sense that the organization is in a state of readiness for new ideas and new perspectives, especially if the intervention is regarded as representing meso- or macro-level development. If, on return, participants are met with personal rejection by colleagues or resistance from current top management to adopt and accept new ideas and approaches, then, as described by Doyle, participants facing 'organization, cultural and structural barriers left little scope... to transfer their knowledge to the workplace leading to considerable scepticism and cynicism about the cost and motives of development activity' (1995: 9).

Research by Rouiller and Goldstein (1993), followed by Tracey *et al.* (1995) demonstrated that training transfer is highly dependent on the climate of acceptance in the organization or unit to which participants return. If the climate is not supportive or sympathetic then the likelihood of open transfer of ideas skills and abilities reduces significantly. Brown and Starkey (2000) suggest that most training and development interventions are doomed to such a fate as the returnees threaten the current power balance within the organization and are unlikely to have the influence to destabilize the current pervading culture. These findings have led some commentators to suggest that much of the management development engaged in by organizations is a game of 'meaningless outcomes' (Clarke, 1999).

Case study: Roco and Floco[1]

In 2000 two large Irish public sector organizations, Roco and Floco, were faced with significant organizational reviews prompted by external pressures to modernize and to meet new statutory requirements. In particular, both organizations faced considerable pressure to review the levels of participation of women at managerial levels within the organizations.

An equality audit had revealed that while Floco had over 2,500 women employees (52 per cent of total) a review of senior management by gender revealed that less than 20 per cent of top management positions were held by women and this dropped to less than 10 per cent in the top three management grades. One top manager interviewed remarked that there was evidence of a 'huge potential that is not being tapped into, a pool of talent that are not being utilized'.

Roco might be described as a more traditional organization than Floco employing nearly 5,000, of which, less than 700 were women (14 per cent). A diversity audit reported that less than 2 per cent of Roco senior management were women. The nature of Roco's activity (primarily technical and engineering) meant that traditionally it was a male-dominated organization, however, despite changes in gender representation in recent recruitment drives the organization still reflected a very traditional patriarchal culture.

Changes in equality and diversity legislation meant that both organizations could no longer ignore the disparities in gender participation, particularly at management and senior management levels. Internal review reports suggested that both organizations employed a significant number of women who possessed the abilities and experience necessary for management roles. It was suggested that these women required more encouragement and confidence to apply for promotion opportunities as statistics on promotion rates indicated that many more men (and frequently less well qualified) applied for promotional opportunities than did women.

One of the suggested solutions to this problem was to supply these 'high potential women' with an accredited management education experience. Both organizations independently approached a large university business school with a view to securing the delivery of a customized management development programme which would meet the following objectives:

- Fill the competency gap required to facilitate the progression of these 'high potential women' to management positions.
- Encourage participants to become aware and ready to engage in the organizational change and development strategies being adopted by both organizations.

A programme was designed containing the typical portfolio of essential management modules: accounting, marketing, law, organizational behaviour, economics etc. However, the programme designers were sensitive to the experience of other women-only management training providers (e.g. Gray, 1994; Vinnicombe and Singh, 2003) and took care to build the programme on participant self-awareness and with strong self-development foundations. The adoption of a critical and reflective approach avoided the use of traditional examinations and outcome merit listings. Rather, the programme emphasized action-based learning in team and group formats to heighten the supportive nature of the learning process. Particular care was taken to ensure the development and fostering of a positive self-efficacy toward learning within the programme.

The programme was to be run on a day per week release basis at the university over an academic year with about 20 participants enrolling in each class on the programme. Participants applied for entry to the programme in their workplace (to allow for discussion within department for cover etc.). Some participants were approached and were encouraged to apply by their managers.

The programme was evaluated by the providers across the three levels suggested by Kirkpatrick (1959). These measures, post-programme completion, revealed positive participant evaluation of the programme (Level 1) and significant increments in individual competency levels (Level 2); however, it is at the transfer of learning to organizational behaviour (Level 3) where problems arose.

While there was wide agreement that these selected women would be given opportunities to move to more senior positions and become involved in key organizational decision-making, the reality on return was very different. Few promotional opportunities were forthcoming and an example of the resistance to new thinking was illustrated by Floco when they established a new change management team, to review long-term organizational change, but failed to even consider female representation.

It became apparent that the programme was being viewed as 'an equality initiative' and according to one Roco participant 'the training and development function [in Roco] are not involved and therefore do not link the programme to their procedures'.

Both Roco and Floco recognized that the traditional structure of many management positions, and the demands associated with the roles, required revision if they were to become attractive to women and to meet more general quality of working life criteria. Neither Roco nor Floco appeared to make any significant advances on these assurances in the year following programme completion.

This general level of inactivity in both organizations led the participants to become frustrated and feel cheated. Considerable levels of anger were expressed and the elevated levels of enthusiasm and commitment recorded during the programme had deteriorated and were replaced by almost entirely negative sentiments. All participants would have completed as part of their programme action learning reports, professionally outlining how new initiatives might be introduced in their units. These reports sat unopened and inactive in most cases.

The frustration born of this lack of opportunity was compounded by some participants experiencing complaints from fellow workers (particularly male workers who may have felt excluded by the process) about how they were given this positive learning experience while others were not being offered the chance. While this created difficulties for some women in their departments it also created some issues for management in terms of opening promotional opportunities for participants.

Why did management development fail to deliver in Floco and Roco?

An analysis of the case study reveals a complex set of variables and relationships that has led to the frustration of the objectives and effectiveness of the developmental intervention for both the organizations and for the individuals involved. In essence, the laudable strategic objectives expressed by top management were laced with rhetoric and when it came to operationalizing aspects of the diversity programme, little progress was recorded. There are several possible reasons to explain the outcomes in Floco and Roco and these are discussed in the following two sub-sections. The lack of impact of the programme on actual organizational change resides with the inability of the key power holders within the organizations to support the inclusion of the women in key change areas (thus supporting transfer) and to risk re-appraising their collective perception of how the organizations function and should function.

The myth that management development solves all problems

The evidence was stark regarding the lack of participation of women in senior management in both organizations. However, interpretation of these statistics by top management was somewhat self-serving in that they perceived the cause of the non-participation of women to reside within the women themselves. This form of stereotyped attribution is a common and well researched issue in social psychology (Macrae *et al.*, 1996) stemming from causal thinking based on a 'widespread belief that the world is just and that outcomes are usually the just consequences of the actions or attributes' (Mackie *et al.*, 1996: 59). Thus, we typically accept that others get what they deserve and in tandem deserve what they get. Other attribution researchers (e.g. Pettigrew, 1979; Hewstone, 1990) illuminate this issue further by adding that when poor performance of out-group members is recorded (in this case women reaching senior positions), then members of the in-group (male top managers) are likely to ascribe the cause of this to the out-group members themselves. In addition, the cause of the outcome (non-progression) is seen as being caused by internal dispositional factors such as intelligence or ability. The self-serving nature of this defence protects the key stakeholders from the more probable truth that the organization they have moulded is in fact discriminatory and dysfunctional as this would reflect negatively on their self-esteem and leadership competence.

If this is a reason for the non-participation of women at senior management level then it was highly unlikely that the participation of the women on a management development programme would alter the stereotyped attitudes of top management and the structures and practices they employ. It might be suggested that is was the top management who would have benefited from a personal and management development experience! Overall the decision by top management to employ a management development intervention to ready women employees for the prospect of management reflects a static and normative approach to seeing employees as resources that occasionally require adjusting to fit organizational needs. This traditional managerialist viewpoint is blinkered to the complexity of an alternative approach which embraces the relational richness of organizational life (Alvesson and Deetz, 1999). What was required was a more holistic and inclusive review of why women were under represented in senior management and a recognition that issues such as the traditional structures, language, appraisal and promotion systems, and the overall culture of the organizations may have been at fault, and not the women themselves.

The threat of new ideas

When participants returned to their organizations they were in an elevated state of readiness to utilize their new knowledge and competencies. Post-intervention measures administered by the programme providers had indicated significant increases in participant competency levels but also in motivation and readiness to participate fully in the change promised in their organizational strategic plans. The participants as class groups had already delivered a full report proposing a diversity management policy to their senior management team which had received very positive reviews. However, as the weeks passed following programme completion, participants found that they were still engaged in the same roles they were responsible for a year earlier. While they now possessed an expanded social and professional network within their organizations, they found little opportunity to apply their knowledge and skills. This led to high levels of frustration where participants felt that they were now more demotivated than they had been before they entered the programme. They went through a cycle of reactions from excitement to questioning, to frustration, to anger, to disillusionment. Commitment and affective attachment to the organization was seriously impaired as a result.

Brown and Starkey (2000) suggest that such results should not be unexpected given that most organizations (in particular, key stakeholders) exert remarkable energy in maintaining the existing established routines. Accepting the new perspectives that the women returned with would not alone have required a re-evaluation of the stereotypes referred to earlier but would also have required top management to shift their current identity and shared sense of the organization. The presence of these changed employees bursting with new ideas and abilities was ignored and to an extent denied in order to maintain the norm (Walsh and Fahey, 1986). To open up opportunities for these women to express their newly developed ideas would doubtless have put them in a direct conflict with the senior managers in each organization and the power dynamics would become, at the very least, uncomfortable.

Conclusion

Training and developmental interventions are regarded as pivotal to organizational change and development and have been seen as so for decades. Conversely, they can also be viewed as a naïve and simplistic default reaction to organizational problems. The idea that organizations can solve most if not all problems by engaging employees in well designed training or development interventions is to view employees alone as the factor which requires adjustment.

The case study illustrated that the training intervention was founded initially on false premises as the reason for low female participation at senior management level was not with the women themselves but with the patriarchal culture and climate and structures created and supported (admittedly unconsciously) by top management. In advocating a management development model to ready the women for management, top management avoided facing their immediate prejudices and delayed any change strategy for at least a year. However, the management development experience was liberating for the participants and when they returned with new ideas and confidence top management were again facing a threatening scenario. Their reaction was one predicted by the psychodynamic perspective on organizational change: they engaged in defence mechanisms such as denial and rationalization when faced with the women's demands for the organizational changes and opportunities they felt they were promised.

Given that the programme was designed by the providers to prepare the women for future management opportunities, many of the learning sets and exercises were explicitly oriented toward such a changed role. As the programme focussed on self-development first, the participants were grounded in the changes that lay before them if they wished to pursue progression. When the opportunities for participants to engage in the organizational change process were not delivered to the extent they had been led to understand, the participants became frustrated and disaffected.

Participation in the management development programme had been construed by participants as part of a new psychological contract (Turnley and Feldman, 1999; Robinson and Wolfe-Morrison, 2000). In return for their participation and the effort it required, participants expected at least an opportunity to apply their new competencies and perhaps even seek progression within the organization. The breaching of this contract left the participants with a deflated and with a less-trusting perception of senior management.

In conclusion, the case clarifies that if training and management development initiatives are to be employed in an organization then they need to be clearly linked to the organizational need and returning participants require a supportive climate otherwise the intervention may be meaningless. It must also be understood that well designed training and development interventions (particularly meso- and macro-level interventions) may raise the motivation and expectations of the participants. The organization needs to make concrete moves to meet these needs and expectations. In a sense key decision makers need to be ready to shift their perspectives and be ready to abandon comfortable approaches to viewing organizational dynamics. Whether top management are conscious of it or not, a new psychological contract has been established and should be honoured.

Learning is change and, in the first instance, this change occurs at a personal and individual level. Thereafter, it becomes a social phenomenon when new ideas, knowledge or behaviours are shared or exhibited in work settings. Senior management need to reconsider training and development as more than some sort of a band-aid for organizational ills and understand that well-designed and delivered training and development interventions deliver a complex bundle of outcomes such as personal development, self-awareness, expanded cognitive and behavioural heuristics, new workplace competencies, increased motivation, expanded sense of self-efficacy and new expectations regarding work roles and parameters. Only when an understanding of this complexity is integrated into organizational planning and management will we begin to eradicate the token use and misuse of training and development interventions.

Note

1 Due to the sensitivity of the organizations to the outcomes of the process the names have been altered and the authors feel it necessary to keep the description of their areas of activity relatively vague. A series of interviews were conducted with key participants after the programme was completed but the interviewees, while open in interview, did not want much of what they discussed quoted in public fora.

References

Alliger, G.M., Tannenbaum, S.I., Bennett, W., Travers, H. and Shortland, A. (1997) 'A meta-analysis of the relations among training criteria', *Personnel Psychology*, 50: 341–58.

Alvesson, M. and Deetz, S. (1999) 'Critical theory and postmodernism: approaches to organizational studies', in S.R. Clegg and C. Hardy (eds) *Studying Organizations: Theory and Method*, London: Sage Publications, 185–211.

Aram, E. and Noble, D. (1999) 'Educating prospective managers in the complexity of organizational life', *Management Learning*, 30, 3: 321–42.

Arthur, W. Jr, Bennett, W. Jr, Edens, P.S. and Bell, S.T. (2003) 'Effectiveness of training in organizations: a meta-analysis of design and evaluation features', *Journal of Applied Psychology*, 88, 2: 234–44.

Berry, J.K. (1990) 'Linking management development to business strategies', *Training and Development Journal*, 44, 8: 20–2.

Bramley, P. (1996) *Evaluating Training Effectiveness*, 2nd edn, London: McGraw-Hill.

Broad, M.L. and Newstrom, J.W. (1992) *Transfer of Training: Action Packed Strategies to Ensure High Pay-off from Training Investments*, Reading, MA: Addison-Wesley.

Brown, A.D. and Starkey, K. (2000) 'Organizational identity and learning: a psychodynamic perspective', *Academy of Management Review*, 25, 1: 102–20.

Brown, J.S. and Duguid, P. (1991) 'Organizational learning and communities of practice', *Organization Science*, 2: 40–57.

Clarke, M. (1999) 'Management development as a game of meaningless outcomes', *Human Resource Management Journal*, 9, 2: 38–49.

Collquitt, J.A., LePine, J.A. and Noe, R.A. (2000) 'Toward an integrative theory of training motivation: a meta-analytic path analysis of 20 years of research', *Journal of Applied Psychology*, 85, 5: 678–707.

Doyle, M. (1995) 'Organizational transformation and renewal: a case for reframing management development', *Personnel Review*, 24, 6: 6–18.

Duffy, M.K., Ganster, D.C. and Pagon, M. (2002) 'Social undermining in the workplace', *Academy of Management Journal*, 45, 2: 331–51.

Edwards, R. (1997) *Changing Places? Flexibility, Lifelong Learning and Learning Society*, London: Routledge.

Edwards, R., Ranson, S. and Strain, M. (2002) 'Reflexivity: toward a theory of lifelong learning', *International Journal of Lifelong Learning*, 12, 6: 525–36.

Ezzamel, M., Lilley, S., Wilkinson, A. and Willmott, H. (1996) 'Practices and practicalities in human resource management', *Human Resource Management Journal*, 6, 1: 63–80.

Goldstein, I.L. (1993) *Training in Organizations: Needs Assessment Development and Evaluation*, 3rd edn, Monterey, CA: Brookes-Cole.

Gray, B. (1994) 'Women-only management training: a past and present', in M. Tanton (ed.) *Women in Management: A Developing Presence*, London: Routledge.

Hamel, G. and Prahalad, C.K. (1996) *Competing for the Future*, Boston, MA: Harvard Business School Press.

Harrison, R. (1993) 'Developing people: for whose bottom line?', in R. Harrison (ed.) *Human Resource Management Issues and Strategies*, Workingham: Addison-Wesley.

Hewstone, M. (1990) 'The ultimate attribution error? A review of the literature on intergroup causal attribution', *European Journal of Social Psychology*, 20: 311–35.

Höpfl, H. and Dawes, F. (1995) 'A whole can of worms! The contested frontiers of management development and learning', *Personnel Review*, 24, 6: 19–28.

Huselid, M. (1995) 'The impact of human resource management on turnover, productivity and corporate financial performance', *Academy of Management Journal*, 38: 635–72.

Hussey, D.E. (1988) *Management Training and Corporate Strategy: How to Improve Competitive Performance*, Oxford: Pergamon.

Iles, P. (1993) 'Achieving strategic coherence in HRD through competence-based management and organization development', *Personnel Review*, 22, 6: 63–80.

Kessels, J. and Harrison, R. (1998) 'External consistency: the key to success in management development programmes?' *Management Learning*, 29, 1: 39–68.

Kirkpatrick, D.L. (1959) 'Techniques for evaluating training programs', *Journal of ASTD*, 13, 11: 3–9.

Kozlowski, S.W.J., Brown, K., Weissbein, D., Canon-Bowers, J. and Salas, E. (2000) 'A multilevel approach to training effectiveness: enhancing horizontal and vertical transfer', in K. Klein and S.W.J. Kozlowski, (eds) *Multilevel Theory, Research and Methods in Organizations*, San Francisco, CA: Jossey-Bass.

Lave, J. and Wenger, E. (1990) *Situated Learning: Legitimate Peripheral Participation*, Cambridge: Cambridge University Press.

Linville, P.W., Fischer, G.W. and Salovey, P. (1989) 'Perceived distributions of the characteristics of in-group and out-group members: empirical evidence and a computer simulation', *Journal of Personality and Social Psychology*, 57: 165–88.

Mackie, D.M., Hamilton, D.L., Susskind, J. and Rosselli, L. (1996) 'Social psychological foundations of stereotype foundation', in C.N. Macrae, C. Stangor and M. Hewstone (eds) *Stereotypes and Stereotyping*, New York: Guilford Press.

Macrae, C.N., Stangor, C. and Hewstone, M. (eds) (1996) *Stereotypes and Stereotyping*, New York: Guilford Press.

Manz, C.C. and Sims, H.P. (1987) 'Leading workers to lead themselves: the external leadership of self-managing work teams', *Administrative Science Quarterly*, March: 106–29.

Martocchio, J.J. and Baldwin, T.T. (1997) 'The evolution of strategic organizational training', in R.G. Ferris (ed.) *Research in Personnel and Human Resource Management*, Greenwich, CT: JAI.

Niehoff, B.P. and Paul, R.J. (2000) 'Causes of employee theft and strategies that HR Managers can use for prevention', *Human Resource Management*, 39: 51–64.

Ortenblad, A. (2002a) 'Organizational learning: a radical perspective', *International Journal of Management Reviews*, 4, 1: 87–100.

Ortenblad, A. (2002b) 'A typology of the idea of the learning organization', *Management Learning*, 33, 2: 213–30.

Pedler, M., Burgoyne, J. and Boydell, T. (1994) *A Manager's Guide to Self Development*, 3rd edn, London: McGraw-Hill.

Pettigrew, T.W. (1979) 'The ultimate attribution error: extending Allport's cognitive analysis of prejudice', *Personality and Social Psychology Bulletin*, 5: 461–76.

Pfeffer, J. (1981) 'Management as symbolic action: the creation and maintenance of organizational paradigms', *Research in Organizational Behavior*, 3: 1–52.

Pfeffer, J. (1994) *Competitive Advantage through People*, Boston, MA: Harvard Business School Press.

Ready, D.A., Vicere, A.A. and White, A.F. (1994) 'Linking executive education to strategic imperatives', *Management Learning*, 25, 4: 563–78.

Robinson, G. (1994) 'Management development and organizational development', in A. Mumford (ed.) *Gower Handbook of Management Development*, Aldershot: Gower.

Robinson, S.L. and Wolfe-Morrison, E. (2000) 'The development of psychological contract breach and violation: a longitudinal study', *Journal of Organizational Behavior*, 21: 525–46.

Rouillier, J.Z. and Goldstein, I.L. (1993) 'The relationship between organizational transfer climate and positive transfer climate', *Human Resource Development Quarterly*, 4: 377–90.

Salas, E. and Canon-Bowers, J.A. (2001) 'The science of training: a decade of progress', *Annual Review of Psychology*, 52: 471–99.

Senge, P.M. (1990) *The Fifth Discipline: The Art and Practice of the Learning Organization*, New York: Doubleday.

Smith-Jentsch, K.A., Salas, E. and Brannick, M. (2001) 'To transfer or not to transfer? An investigation of the combined effects of trainee characteristics and team transfer environments', *Journal of Applied Psychology*, 86, 2: 279–92.

Stacey, R.D., Griffin, D. and Shaw, P. (2000) *Complexity and Management: Fad or Radical Challenge to Systems Thinking?* London: Routledge.

Taylor, P.J. and O' Driscoll, M.P. (1998) 'A new integrated framework for training needs analysis', *Human Resource Management Journal*, 8, 2: 29–50.

Tepper, B.J. (2000) 'Consequences of abusive supervision', *Academy of Management Journal*, 43: 178–90.

Tracey, J.B., Tannenbaum, S.I. and Kavanagh, M.J. (1995) 'Applying trained skills on the job: the importance of the work environment', *Journal of Applied Psychology*, 80: 239–52.

Turnley, W.H. and Feldman, D.C. (1999) 'A discrepancy model of psychological contract violations', *Human Resource Management Review*, 9, 3: 367–86.

Vinnicombe, S. and Singh, V. (2003) 'Women-only management training: an essential part of women's leadership development', *Journal of Change Management*, 3, 4: 294–306.

Walsh, J.P. and Fahey, L. (1986) 'The role of negotiated belief structures in strategy making', *Journal of Management*, 12: 325–38.

Warr, P., Allan, C. and Birdi, K. (1999) 'Predicting three levels of training outcome', *Journal of Occupational and Organizational Psychology*, 72: 351–75.

Willmott, H. (1994) 'Management education: provocations to a debate', *Management Learning*, 25, 1: 105–36.

Winterton, J. and Winterton, R. (1997) 'Does management development add value?' *British Journal of Management*, 8: 65–76.

Young, M.F. (1993) 'Instructional design for situated learning', *Educational Technology Research and Development*, 41, 1: 43–58.

6 A critical review of researching Human Resource Development

The case of a pan-European project

Sally Sambrook and Jim Stewart

Introduction

In this chapter we draw upon recent research into the connections between organisation practices related to the profession and function labelled Human Resource Development (HRD), and the promotion and achievement of lifelong learning. The research was funded by the European Union and was conducted by partner universities in seven European countries.

We briefly report the findings of the project here but focus more on drawing interpretations from the findings, exploring the problematic status of the concepts of HRD, learning organisations and lifelong learning and reflecting on our experiences of collaborative and comparative research. Thus, the chapter has four related aims

1   To briefly describe the design of the project, then examine the claimed similarities and differences in organisation practices related to HRD across seven European countries.
2   To explore potential factors which might account for these similarities and differences across Europe and extend the comparison to HRD practices evident in USA and Japan.
3   To engage in a critical examination of the concepts of HRD, learning (oriented) organisations and lifelong learning.
4   Finally, based on the experiences of this project, to provide our reflections on the possibilities and limitations of researching HRD, focusing particularly on comparative and collaborative research.

We begin with a straightforward description of our research, but then seek to problematise the project by examining the conceptual and methodological assumptions informing the research design, and the varying extent to which these were accepted by researchers at partner institutions. We use the claimed findings and outcomes to illustrate and explore the problems and dangers of cross-national research and the inherent weaknesses of comparative analyses. We also explore the difficulties and opportunities of collaborative research. Overall, we reflect on the conduct and conclusions of one pan-European research project, albeit from the perspective of just two of the research team, to both provide a useful critique and highlight issues of interest and relevance to others wishing to adopt critical approaches to the study of HRD. However, our ambitions are limited and we do not intend or claim a comprehensive or definitive account of the project and the issues we explore.

Being critical

There is an established, if relatively young, history of thinking 'critically' about organisation and management studies (see e.g. Alvesson and Deetz, 1996; Alvesson and Willmott, 1996), including human resource management (Legge, 1995; Keenoy, 1999). However, it is only recently that such critical thinking has been associated with human resource development (McGoldrick *et al.*, 2001, 2002). For example, the first 'innovative' session specifically established to consider critical perspectives on HRD did not appear at the American Academy for HRD conference until 2002. As the session organisers note, 'What has come to be referred to as the critical manage-ment studies movement in organisational and management theory has seen a growth in activity of the last 10 years, but has hitherto not been acknowledged by the main-stream HRD community' (Elliott and Turnbull, 2002: 971). Elliott and Turnbull proposed this session for several reasons: 'We are concerned that the methodological traditions that guide the majority of HRD research do not allow researchers to engage in studies that challenge the predominantly performative and learning-outcome focus of the HRD field.... We seek to unpick the assumptions behind the performative orientation that dominates much HRD research by exploring with researchers ... whether this tradition is conducive to what we perceive is the greatest tension in HRD, the struggle to reconcile the needs of the individual with the needs of the employing organisation ... We therefore perceived the need to open up HRD theory to a broader range of methodological and theoretical perspectives (2002).' Following the AHRD session in 2002, a second group of UK academics, including one of the present authors, convened a stream on critical HRD at the third international conference on Critical Management Studies held at Lancaster University in July 2003. Some of the papers from that stream will be referenced in this chapter.

The word 'critical' can of course have many meanings (Sambrook, 2003). Some would argue that the word 'critical' does not have to appear for a work to present a critical approach. Others might argue that any good research should be critical – with the word being used in a similar way to the concept of reflexivity, where researchers attempt to 'reveal' their assumptions and 'hand' in crafting the research outcomes. However, when many are engaged in research examining HRD practices, few, until recently, have engaged in the critical (the word is used to suggest 'crucial') debate about that which we label HRD.

For us, being critical (about HRD) involves various philosophical and method-ological factors. We try to move beyond a simplistic and entitive ontology of HRD towards one recognising the complexity, diversity and ambiguity of cognitions and activities associated with facilitating learning and development within organisations. We try not to take for granted assumptions about shared meanings and understandings but seek to expose and explore differences in meanings and potential reasons for these.

This encourages us to analyse discourses of HRD, revealing some of the underlying influences, whether performative or humanistic, for example, which shape HRD action. This also requires a shift from traditional 'scientific' research methods to enable us to access and analyse the multiple, dynamic and contradictory social constructions of what is labelled HRD.

HRD and lifelong learning

Whilst the terms 'HRD' and 'lifelong learning' can be argued to be becoming standard concepts in the lexicon of organisation and management, it is equally arguable that there is little standardisation in definitions, understandings and meanings attached to the concepts. To take HRD as an example, the term is generally acknowledged to have been coined in 1969 by Leonard Nadler and subsequently defined by him in 1970 (Sambrook, 1998), yet two recent books on the subject by Walton (1999) and by Wilson (1999) both refer to HRD as an 'emerging' field of study and reinforce the assertion of Stewart and McGoldrick (1996) that the concept has no universally accepted meaning. (See also Sambrook and Stewart, 1998a,b.) Some seek to clearly define HRD (Swanson, 2001). Some find this task difficult (McLean, 2001). Others flatly refuse (Lee, 2001). Obviously some degree of consensus must be achieved to facilitate researching HRD, whatever 'it' is. Yet, thirty years of debate continue on the meaning of HRD. Different authors and theorists adopt divergent positions on what is and what is not encompassed by the term (see e.g. Weinberger, 1998), and adopt an assortment of methodologies for researching this complex concept. This situation is further complicated by 'national' perspectives (e.g. Tjepkema *et al.*, 2002). Having introduced the topic, and our critical approach, the next section briefly describes the research project.

The research project

The project was funded by the European Commission under its TSER programme, Area 11-Research in Education and Training. Project management was undertaken by a team at the University of Twente in The Netherlands, and a further six partner universities or research institutes were located in Belgium, Finland, France, Germany, Italy and the UK, the last of these being Nottingham Business School. The European Consortium for the Learning Organisation (ECLO) was an additional partner providing access to research sites and commentary on the emerging results. The project was intended and designed to address the following questions.

1   How do HRD departments in learning oriented organisations throughout Europe envision (envisage) their role in stimulating and supporting employees to learn continuously as part of everyday work?
2   What differences in outlook can be found between HRD departments in European organisations and the perspectives on the role of HRD which exist in the USA and in Japan?

3   What strategies do European HRD departments adopt to realise their envisioned role?

4   What inhibiting and facilitating factors do European HRD departments encounter in trying to realise their role, and how do they cope with these factors?

Answers to questions 1, 3 and 4 were sought through empirical research in the seven countries. The second question was addressed by a literature review to identify reported practice in the USA and in Japan. The results were then compared with the European findings. The empirical research consisted of two stages: first, case study research in 28 organisations; and second, a postal or telephone survey of 165 organisations across the seven European countries.

One of the issues we explore later in the chapter focuses on establishing shared meanings of the key research concepts – HRD and lifelong learning – within the project team, particularly given its pan-European composition. However, looking back, it seems that, at the outset, little was done explicitly to develop a working definition or common understanding of these terms. It was as if there was an assumption that we all shared similar definitions and understandings of the concepts. It was only as the project evolved that differences and difficulties emerged in agreeing what constituted HRD and lifelong learning and how these could be researched and reported. We return to critically review these issues later, but first we present the research methods in a more traditional manner to provide the reader with a clear description of what the research involved.

Selection of case organisations

To facilitate subsequent comparative analyses, criteria were determined to select case study organisations. First, they had to be capable of being defined as 'learning oriented'. This term was originally coined by Leys *et al.* (1992) and further elaborated by Tjepkema and Wognum (1996). In essence, the term refers to organisations with the *intention* of becoming learning organisations (Tjepkema and Scheerens, 1998). However, in practical terms, it was necessary to operationalise this concept. This was achieved on the basis of a review of the literature and suggestions from each of the partners, resulting in nine specific criteria (Sambrook and Stewart, 2000), of which case organisations had to meet a minimum of six.

In addition, organisation size and industry sector were also taken into account when selecting the case studies. The size of an organisation was limited to between 500 and 1,000 employees. Industry sector was categorised using a matrix, suggested by the German partners, based on two variables: either the manufacturing or service sector of the economy, and either engaged in 'mass production' or adopted a 'customer orientation'. Each partner agreed to select one organisation from each of the four cells. Thus, in each country the case organisations had to meet six criteria of being 'learning oriented', employ between 500 and 1,000 employees and fill the four cells in the matrix. The first of these criteria was the only one to be consistently applied in the subsequent survey, although analysis of the results allowed comparisons across the variables of size and industry.

Case study methods

In each case study organisation, semi-structured interviews were conducted with a number of senior managers including whoever held board responsibility for HRD and, in some cases, the Chief Executive, with the HRD manager, and with a number of HRD practitioners. These were supplemented by interviews with a number of middle/operational managers drawn from a variety of departments or functions, and with a number of non-managerial and non-HRD staff, again drawn from a variety of functions. In addition, a range of documentary evidence such as mission statements, business plans, policy statements and examples of HRD programmes/materials were gathered and analysed in an attempt to achieve triangulation in the research design.

Interview guidelines were produced for each category of interviewees. These were based on and derived from the research objectives and conceptual framework (Scheerens *et al.*, 1998). These also informed the design of a common format and structure for case study reports produced, as with the interview guidelines, by the project management team following consultation with the project partners. Each partner institution produced a case study report in the agreed format for each of their four case study organisations, who were asked to comment on the accuracy of the reports. The project management team received all 28 reports and produced a comparative report. This was commented on by each partner before it was finalised.

The survey

The survey was conducted in a similar manner. The management team produced a draft questionnaire and partner institutions provided comments and suggestions. Each partner then identified and gained agreement from respondents in organisations that met the agreed criteria. The majority of respondents were senior HRD practitioners. The primary purpose of the survey was to 'test' and extend the findings of the case study research. Thus the design of the survey instrument was primarily structured with scaled responses. A target of 20 respondents in each country was set. This was met precisely only in the UK with other countries surveying between 17 and 39 organisations.

Partner institutions distributed and received completed questionnaires, in some cases translated into their national language. They then returned completed questionnaires, translated if necessary back into English as the project language, to the partner institution in Finland, which undertook statistical analysis and forwarded the results to the project management team who then produced a draft report. The draft was discussed at a final partner meeting held in The Netherlands, following which the report was finalised and submitted by the project managers to the EC.

The literature review

The second question of the project was examined through a literature review. Project partners provided suggestions on appropriate sources detailing HRD practice in the USA and in Japan. The management team then accessed and reviewed the literature and produced a draft paper. This was again commented on and discussed by the partners before it was finalised by the project managers. A working document (see Figure 6.1) was developed, comprising a number of statements relating to the concept of a learning (oriented) organisation, derived from a review of Japanese and American literature. These statements were presented as polarities or dichotomies. This analytical tool was developed to rate Japanese and American models and then compare these with findings from the European project.

1	**Vision on lifelong learning** *'What do we mean by learning organisation?'*	
A consumption		An investment
↑ Japan		America ↑
2	**Vision on learning** *'Why do employees need to learn?'*	
Company-oriented		Job-oriented
↑ Japan		America ↑
3	**Reason(s) for becoming a learning society** *'Why do organisations want to become learning oriented?'*	
Quality of life		Quality of the organisation
↑ Japan		America ↑
4	**Kind of leadership** *'What kind of leadership is used?'*	
Top-down		Bottom-up
	↑ Japan America ↑	
5	**Role of the HRD department** *'How is the HRD function organised?'*	
No HRD department		Centralised HRD department
	↑ Japan ↑ America	
6	**Responsibility for learning** *'Who are responsible for learning and development?'*	
HRD professionals		All employees
	Japan ↑ America ↑	
7	**Role of management** *'What is the role of management in learning?'*	
No responsibility		Responsibility
	America ↑ ↑ Japan	
8	**Role of the HRD professional** *'What tasks should the HRD professional perform?'*	
Co-ordinate learning		Create a learning environment
	↑ Japan America ↑	
9	**Role of the employee** *'Why should I learn?'*	
Commitment to organisation		Commitment to own career
↑ Japan	America ↑	
10	**Skills to develop** *'What do they need to learn?'*	
Spiritual development		New knowledge and skills
↑ Japan	America ↑	
11	**Kinds of learning activities** *'How is learning facilitated?'*	
Integrated in daily work		Separated from work
↑ Japan	America ↑	
12	**Time and money** *'How much do we spend on learning?'*	
Little money, much time		Little time, much money
↑ Japan		America ↑
13	**Recruitment and selection** *'What characteristics are necessary for learning?'*	
Personality		Performance
↑ Japan	America ↑	
14	**Career development** *'How can the employee organise his career path?'*	
Individual paths		Standard career paths
	↑ Japan America ↑	

Figure 6.1 An analytical tool.

Research project findings

As findings have been reported elsewhere (Sambrook and Stewart, 2000; Sambrook *et al.*, 2003; Tjepkema *et al.*, 2002), only a brief overview of the project results are presented here. The overview follows the conceptual framework developed for the project by reporting results under four headings: Organisation context, Role of HRD, HRD Strategies and Influencing factors. There are two limitations that need to be highlighted at this point. First, the findings of the case studies have been through two processes of interpretation; first within the partner institutions and second within the project management team. Second, the findings treat the concepts as unproblematic. This limitation is the focus of a later section of this chapter.

Organisation context

The reasons organisation respondents gave for being 'learning oriented' broadly related to a need to become more innovative in the development and provision of products and services. A strongly related factor is becoming more responsive to and focused on customers. These factors were in turn related to globalisation and associated themes such as increasingly competitive markets and fast(er) changing technologies. The emphasis on employee learning and development is seen as a necessary component of business strategies intended to respond to these changing market conditions.

These findings emerged first from the case studies. They were confirmed by the survey results. The latter failed to identify any significant differences across industries or organisation types. Some minor differences across countries were identified, but these were marginal and not considered significant. Analysis of reported practice through the literature review suggests that this broad European context does not differ significantly from that in the USA and in Japan. This might be explained by the consequences and effects of a globalising economy.

Role of HRD

Both pieces of empirical research suggest a changing role for HRD practitioners. One significant component of this change suggested by the case studies is to provide a much more strategic contribution. This is evidenced, for example, by development interventions and programmes leading attempts to increase the perceived quality of customer service or to increase innovation in the development of products and services. However, this finding is much less clear in the survey results, which suggest that the contribution of HRD remains at a more tactical or operational level. Findings related to what has been termed the 'diffusion' of the function (Horst *et al.*, 1999) are more consistent. Increasing involvement of managers and individual employees in the management of learning and development is a clear direction in the changing role of HRD practitioners.

Some differences across European countries were again suggested by the survey results, but these were again relatively minor. No significant differences were found across industry sectors or organisation types. This suggests that such differences as exist in the role of HRD practitioners are more influenced by national cultures than by industry factors. The literature review indicated stronger similarities between Europe and the USA than with Japan. In the latter, HR practice is much more closely integrated, with less separation between HRM and HRD[1] than in Europe or the USA. In addition, Japan does not have the same tradition of HRD specialists. Management of employee learning and development is part of the role of operational managers rather than the responsibility of HRD practitioners. It might therefore be argued that European organisations are moving towards a 'Japanese model' in respect of the role of HRD. This argument is strengthened by the fact that the survey results showed that respondents expected the 'diffusion' of the function to increase in the future.

HRD strategies and interventions

The case study results suggested a continuing reliance on what can be termed traditional training and development; the provision of standard courses, for example. This finding received overwhelming confirmation in the survey. However, both also suggested some less traditional strategies, and the survey identified strong expectations of significant changes in the future. Some examples of the type of changes identified in the case studies were 'culture change' programmes aimed at increasing the flexibility and adaptability of the work force through changing attitudes and behaviour, and a greater focus on 'informal' learning. Additional examples include facilitating knowledge management and utilising information and communications technology as learning and development tools. The overall findings suggest a gap between the envisioned role and actual HRD practice, but with an expectation that the gap will close over time.

Empirical research findings and our review of the literature suggest that HRD practice in Europe is closer to that in the USA than that in Japan. The latter tends to emphasise learning in the workplace and on-the-job more than the former. However, such learning is more likely to be more formal and planned. There also seems to be more formalised attempts in Japan to facilitate and manage organisational learning through, for example, interdisciplinary teams and quality circles.

Influencing factors

Influencing factors were divided into those that facilitate and those, which inhibit a learning orientation. An interesting conclusion of the case study research is that the same factors can and do have both supportive and inhibiting influences. Such factors include individual motivation to learn; learning culture; clarity on the role of HRD departments/specialists; level of financial resources and time available for or allocated to learning and development. Depending on the 'amounts' or 'quantities' extant in a particular organisation or at a particular time, these factors could either facilitate or inhibit learning and development. The survey results confirmed the significance of these factors. However, they also suggested a clearer picture of their impact. Results of new HRD activities; motivation for learning; positive attitude towards change;

sufficient financial resources and motivation to share knowledge all emerged as facilitating factors. A lack of clarity on the role of HRD; lack of time for managers and lack of time for employees to devote to learning were identified as clearly inhibiting factors. A third set of factors, learning culture; organisation flexibility; time available to HRD practitioners and clarity on HRD goals emerged as neutral and as having no or little influence. It was not possible in the literature review to address the question of influencing factors.

Examining the concepts

So far, we have treated the concepts of HRD, learning organisations and lifelong learning as unproblematic. We have also talked of American, Japanese and European models of HRD as if these too were unproblematic. Here, we seek to problematise the project.

The project sought to produce descriptive accounts of the connections between lifelong learning and HRD practices in learning oriented organisations across Europe. One finding from the UK research is that there is a 'mismatch' between the language of the project and that used in work organisations. For example, the term HRD is not widely used, either in job titles or in talking about specialist practice. The latter was true of specialist practitioners as well as of non-HRD managers and employees. This finding confirms that of other research conducted by one of the present authors (Sambrook, 1998). In addition, outside of formal organisation documents and the conversation of some senior managers, the terms 'learning organisations' and 'lifelong learning' are not part of the vocabulary of organisation members. So, it seems to be the case that the concepts have little or no meaning within organisations, even among those groups, senior managers and specialist practitioners, for example, who are actively promoting their application in attempts to achieve their claimed benefits. There are also problems with the concepts if we confine ourselves to academic discourse(s). Kessels (2002) also identified language as a potential barrier to researching and understanding HRD within Europe.

HRD

The term HRD can, in some ways, be compared with HRM (McGoldrick and Stewart, 1996). One similarity is that both have their origins in the USA (Legge, 1995; Wilson, 1999). A recent review of the American literature identified 18 different definitions of HRD (Weinberger, 1998). While not all mutually exclusive, the author of that review was able to identify five different theoretical domains informing the definitions. Blake (1995; see Walton, 1999) argues that HRD defies definition or boundaries, while an even earlier writer suggests that HRD is 'omnivorous' and compares it to an amoeba which takes nourishment from wherever is expedient (see Wilson, 1999: 9). A complicating factor is the emergence of 'performance improvement' in the USA (Torraco, 1999). Swanson, a leading theorist in America, seems to take his earlier definition of HRD (Swanson, 1995) as a basis for defining performance improvement (Swanson, 1999). A second similarity with HRM is attempts to define HRD in opposition to more established terms such as training, or training and development (Stewart, 1992; Stewart and McGoldrick, 1996; Harrison, 1997; Walton, 1999; Wilson, 1999). The evidence from the project reported here suggests that, as with HRM (Legge, 1995), this may be of more concern to academics than to practitioners (see also Sambrook, 1998).

It might be argued from the previous paragraph that the concept of HRD has emerged to promote and further academic interests and careers (Sambrook and Stewart, 1998a). However, what seems to be beyond argument is that HRD lacks universal acceptance in professional practice, and still lacks a shared meaning or definition. The latter seems to be true even among those communities who regularly use the term to frame and denote a particular approach to that practice (Sambrook and Stewart, 1998b; Stewart, 1999).

There appears to be a growing argument in support of the importance of understanding what we actually mean by 'HRD'. At the 2002 AHRD conference, the Town Forum was the arena for a debate on whether the label HRD was appropriate for the activities it attempted to encompass. Walton (2002) clearly believes that one term – HRD – cannot be used to mean many things to many people, whether it is 'theories' or organisational activities. He cites how Ruona (2000) has previously argued that 'a major barrier for HRD professional is that our work and what we stand for are not yet well understood by others'. However, Walton argues that 'the label we use to designate our domain is a major factor contributing to the creation of such a barrier' (2002: 1). Yet, Ruona (2002) argues for retaining the label whilst we attempt to gain increased clarity of HRD. Re-labelling at this stage would only cause, both within the field and perhaps signal to those outside, further confusion – and what would it be replaced with?

A further consideration is the pursuit of peculiarly national or regional 'models' of HRD. In much American research, there are attempts to build a unifying theory and identify a single model of HRD (see e.g. Swanson, 2002). In our project and in this chapter, we have alluded to an 'American' model. Across the Atlantic, HRD has been emerging in Europe, and here, too, there have been some attempts to 'discover' the 'European' model of HRD, as witnessed by the number of EU funded research projects.

Comparing such models has been the focus of much discussion, and a session was devoted to that occupation at the joint UFHRD/AHRD 2002 European Conference on HRD Research and Practice. However, chairing the session, Stewart (2002) notes, 'This to some extent assumes that there can or might be such a thing as a single European model of HRD, and indeed the same assumption is being applied to the USA. ... Whether we can talk sensibly about a single European model of HRD has provided a topic of research for many of the EC funded project. ... Some of those have and are also addressing directly the comparison with alternative models such as what might [be] termed the American model of HRD. But, we don't know whether it is possible or sensible to talk of a single American model either!'

McLean (2002: 1) states that, 'Certainly in the US the model that predominated early, back in the 60s, was Len Nadler's model ... (which) differentiated training from education and development.' However, 'the predominant model in HRD in the US, and . . . around the world, in spite of all the criticisms about it, is Patricia McLagan's work that started in 1984 through the American Society for Training and Development . . . that resulted in definitions and professional roles for HRD' (2002: 1). McLean notes the debate around what are the supporting theories for, and foundations of, HRD, citing his ongoing public argument with Swanson (McLean, 1998; Swanson, 1999), but suggests that whilst there is discomfort with the models that currently exist, and interest in developing the field, there seems to be 'a move away from trying to create an overriding model and instead trying to create models that are theoretically based' (2002: 2).

A similar argument, but this time in relation to a European model, was presented by Kessels (2002: 1). He noted that HRD practices varied considerably between large and small enterprises and between private and public sector organizations. 'So, searching for an overriding model or theory is becoming increasingly difficult' (2002). He also identified the varied historical contexts of European countries. For example, Germany has a strong tradition of vocational education and close collaboration between schools and companies, where the 'Lernwerkstaff' – the learning organisation – is seen as a prestigious title for an organisation that offers learning opportunities for young people. However, there is also a merger between vocational education and HRD, resulting in a 'fuzzy idea, a blurred structure . . . (which) doesn't fit in the formal HRD discourse' (2002). Kessels also identifies the 'sharp controversy between employers and employees. This very often inhibited the development of joint activities in the domain of HRD', citing the UK as an example, whilst in The Netherlands, 'there is a long history of deliberation and consensus among social partners' (2002: 2). Kessels argues that, 'Europe shows a fragmented map in terms of cultural differences, economic activities, historic backgrounds, regional differences and, not to forget, language barriers. For communication among international practitioners language plays an important role, not only in sharing ideas, experience and knowledge. Language barriers are also a drawback on the academic development of our profession' (2002). The issue of language in pan-European projects is significant in potentially hampering collaborative and comparative research, and a theme we explore later in the chapter based on our own experiences. To summarise, Kessels states that, 'HRD is not regarded as a well-defined generally accepted and recognised domain. In many instances Europeans see HRD as an American invention, imported to Europe, which is helpful as an umbrella to bring together many different activities, but I do not see a real search for a single model or field. We seem to enjoy divergence and difference rather than feeling a need for having a unifying definition or theory' (2002: 3).

It is clear from this discussion that HRD is at best a heterogeneous concept the understanding of which is influenced by national cultures, among other factors. Much recent work confirms this position, and also articulates both the complex roots and complex nature of HRD as a conceptual term and field of practice (Lee, 2003; Vince, 2003). That being the case, it is a small step to identify a number of 'lenses' with which to adopt a 'critical' stance in researching the subject (Sambrook, 2003).

Learning organisation

Kessels' reference to the learning organisation brings us to the second 'contested' concept, recently criticised in both the professional (Sloman, 1999) and academic literature (see Easterby-Smith *et al.*, 2002).

One element in some of these critiques is the necessary connection with the notion of 'organisational learning'. There have of course been significant and influential attempts to theorise this concept and to study its application in work organisations (Moingeon and Edmondson, 1996; Nonaka, 1996). However, such attempts have been subject to recent criticism and claims that satisfactory theories have yet to be developed (Elkjaer, 1999; Prange, 1999; Sun, 2003). To the extent that the notion of 'organisational learning' remains problematic, the idea of 'learning organisations' cannot be said to be capable of operationalisation in any meaningful sense. This has obvious implications for research. In any case, and as with the term HRD, the existence of competing and incommensurable formulations of the concept (see e.g. Swieringa and Wierdsma, 1992; Pedler *et al.*, 1996; Watkins and Marsick, 1993; Senge, 1990; Sun, 2003) suggests significant difficulties in researching the concept.

Perhaps two fundamental and related reasons for difficulties in reaching conceptual understanding of the term is, first, the dominance of established but competing theories of learning, which continue to emphasise the individual as the 'learning unit'; and second, the basic philosophical and psychological assumptions which inform and 'scaffold' those theories (Holmes, 2003). Whatever the case may be, it is clear that the concept 'learning organisation' remains a topic of debate.

A robust defence of the concept has been published by one of the leading theorists which provides a reasoned response to many of these points (Burgoyne, 1999). Even so, our conclusion remains that the concept is problematic. We found in the UK element of the research reported here, varying understanding on the part of practitioners, and little evidence of the various characteristics claimed in the different models actually existing in practice.

Lifelong learning

We now turn our attention to the final concept which was central to our research project. Use of the term 'lifelong learning' can be traced to the 1970s (Scheerens *et al.*, 1998). Its connections with training and development were also recognised at that time. However, as with HRD, the currency of the term is relatively recent. For example, 1996 was the official European Year of Lifelong Learning and the EU Memorandum of Lifelong Learning was published 5 years later (European Union, 2001).

As currently formulated and applied in policy initiatives (Gass, 1996; OECD, 1996; DfEE, 1998), the concept has a significant focus on formal opportunities for education, training and development, and associated structural provision of resources. Such formulations, though, downplay the validity and potential application of theories of learning which suggest that individual learning is both inevitable and continuous (see Burgoyne, 1997; Stewart, 1999). That being the case, application of the concept in the context of work organisations will tend to downplay the role and significance of 'implicit learning' (Chao, 1997), 'incidental learning' (Marsick and Watkins, 1997) and 'informal/accidental learning' (Mumford, 1997). As we have seen, the findings of the research project reported earlier in the chapter suggest that this is the case. Despite the wishes and, in some cases, the efforts of HRD professionals, learning and development practice still relies to a significant extent on traditional and formalised training interventions. This finding was particularly pronounced in the wider survey which investigated practice in 165 organisations across Europe.

An additional problem with the concept as currently applied is that at the same time as downplaying certain theories of individual learning, there is, nevertheless, an emphasis on the individual as the 'learning unit'. This has the consequence of down-playing the social nature of learning and theories such as 'situated learning' which seek to locate learning in social processes (see Fox, 1997; Elkjaer, 1999). Our research project again tends to lend support to this criticism in that HRD practitioners report problems and difficulties in facilitating and promoting what they refer to as 'team learning', 'knowledge sharing' or 'organisation learning'. This is perhaps in part because, as with the concept of 'lifelong learning', professional practice, and indeed conventional wisdom, is primarily informed by theories of individual learning. The concept of lifelong learning as currently understood works to reinforce the primacy of such theories. The empirical findings are a little surprising given the potential relevance of social learning theories to the concept of 'learning organisations'. However, that concept can also be problematic.

Summary

Based on this brief analysis we conclude that researching the relationships and connections between the three concepts discussed would be in any circumstances a difficult project. We do not have to employ critiques from 'critical management' (Alvesson and Willmott, 1996), postmodernism (Alvesson and Deetz, 1996), or indeed to employ the tools of discourse analysis (Oswick *et al.*, 1997; Sambrook and Stewart, 1998a) to critique or problematise the concepts. Our experiences of the project reported here raise additional problems for the conduct of research. These are identified in the next section.

Implications for comparative and collaborative research

The research issues that have been raised for the authors by the research project can be considered under the two headings of 'comparative' and 'collaborative'.

Comparative research

The previous section has established the problematic status of the three main concepts used in the research. Of particular importance is the question of the 'mismatch' of language used by academics and those studied in work organisations, and the extent to which this allows valid comparisons to be made. This is, though, just one facet of language use. There can be, and are, potential and actual differences in meanings attached to conceptual terms among academics, and among individuals within and across work organisations (Sambrook, 1998). A particular example of the former in the current project is the matrix of industry sectors devised and proposed by the German partners. The dichotomy of 'mass production' versus 'customer orientation' uses concepts with potentially multiple connotations and meanings. The choice between the two was in fact rejected by the UK case organisations. As the UK project partners, we applied definitions negotiated as acceptable to representatives of the case organisations in order to 'allocate' each to one of the four cells. This might be considered an example of the social and negotiated nature of reality (see Sambrook, 1998). We then communicated our definitions to the project management team and the other partners. It remains probable, however, that across the 28 cases organisations have been allocated to cells against varying understandings of the dimensions and associated criteria. As well as having implications for comparative research, the example also illustrates issues for collaborative research (see the following paragraphs).

Conceptual meanings and understanding is an issue that is likely to have greater significance in international research. The obvious problem of national languages and the need for translation is probably only the tip of a large iceberg of varying understandings and interpretations associated with cross-national research. A simple example from this project is the search for examples of 'good practice'. What might be considered 'good practice' in varying cultural and national contexts is itself problematic. As an attempt to overcome this, the project elaborated the meaning of the term through the use of concepts such as 'interesting', 'novel' and 'innovative'. However, given different traditions and their influences on approaches to professional practice, what is considered 'novel' or 'innovative' in one cultural context may be considered established or normal practice in another. So, valid comparisons again become questionable.

Collaborative research

The issues discussed so far have implications for collaborative research across national boundaries. There are though two other issues that arise irrespective of the comparative focus.

The first issue is that of communication within the team of researchers. Advances in information and communications technology may be thought or argued to have overcome many difficulties associated with this issue. However, our experience suggests that face-to-face discussion and debate remains the most satisfying, productive and effective communication process when conducting collaborative research. The project reported here enjoyed only a small number of partner meetings. There was, therefore, a heavy reliance on fax and email. In addition, much of the communication by those methods was, of necessity, channelled through the project managers, with less direct communication among the project partners. One consequence of this is that the management team become arbiters of the various and varying views expressed. This can be considered a legitimate role, and we would endorse that view (but see final section). We also believe though that, at times and in relation to some of the more significant and important issues that inevitably occur in research projects, being placed in the role of arbiter is an unfair burden. There are times when full participation in decisions of all partners is the best or ideal process. It is at such times that problems of communication become more sharply focused.

The second issue is that of methodological orientation. This is an added complication to that of conceptual understanding, though the two can be directly connected. In the present case, the overall research design was produced by the project managers, and partner institutions were invited to participate. That being the case, significant differences in methodological position would, presumably, have led to the invitation being declined, and therefore few or no problems in relation to methodological decisions. However, the often-claimed broad methodological distinctions and disputes (Gill and Johnson, 1997; Easterby-Smith *et al.*, 2002) deflect attention from less obvious though significant epistemological nuances. For example, at one meeting to discuss the results of the survey, there was a variety of views on the appropriateness and validity of the statistical analysis of the data. There remains, therefore, the potential for disagreement around particular methods and the means of their application and, perhaps more importantly, the status of research data and the claims that they might support. There is, of course, a direct connection here with the issue of communication since open debate can and may resolve any disagreements that arise. With limited opportunities for such debate though, the issue can gain greater significance.

Summary and conclusion

This chapter has described the results of a pan-European research project. These seem to suggest a changing role for HRD practitioners across Europe which, in turn, appears to be associated with closer links with business strategies; an emphasis on innovation and customer responsiveness in those strategies; a 'diffusion' of HRD responsibility and practice, and application of innovative HRD strategies and methods. Contributing factors influencing both business strategies and HRD roles included globalisation, technological development and interest in and application of the ideas of 'lifelong learning' and 'the learning organisation'. Each of the concepts forming the focus of the research can though be considered problematic.

Adopting a critical and reflexive stance, our experience of working on the project has led to the identification of some issues of relevance to the design and operation of similar projects. These issues relate to variability in understandings and definitions of conceptual terms, and to engaging in comparative and collaborative research. While these issues have been discussed separately here, the experienced reality has been that they are closely interrelated and woven into the research process.

Note

1 What constitutes HRM, HRD and the relationship between them is much debated. Here, we define HRM as those activities associated with attracting, selecting, evaluating, rewarding and relating to employees, and HRD as those activities associated with facilitating the learning and development of employees and their employing organisation. However, we note that there is much potential overlap between and contested territory within these concepts. Both authors have explored this relationship in more detail elsewhere (see McGoldrick and Stewart, 1996; Sambrook, 1998; McGoldrick *et al.*, 2002; Stewart and Harris, 2003). Exploring issues of integration and separation contribute to developing a more critical understanding of these concepts.

References

Alvesson, M. and Deetz, S. (1996) 'Critical theory and postmodernism approaches to organization studies', in S.R. Clegg, C. Hardy and W. Nord (eds) *Handbook of Organization Studies*, London: Sage Publications.

Alvesson, M. and Willmott, H. (1996) *Making Sense of Management: A Critical Introduction*, London: Sage Publications.

Blake, R. (1995) 'Memories of HRD', *Training and Development*, March, 49, 3: 22–28.

Burgoyne, J. (1997) 'Learning: conceptual, practical and theoretical issues', *BPS Annual Conference*, Herriott Watt University, Edinburgh.

Burgoyne, J. (1999) 'Design of the times', *People Management*, 5, 11: 38–44.

Chao, G.T. (1997) 'Organization socialisation in multinational corporations: the role of implicit learning', in C.L. Cooper and S.E. Jackson (eds) *Creating Tomorrow's Organizations*, Chichester: John Wiley.

DfEE (1998) *The Learning Age: A Renaissance for Britain*, London: HMSO.

Dixon, N. (1994) *The Organizational Learning Cycle*, Maidenhead: McGraw-Hill.

Easterby-Smith, M., Burgoyne, J. and Araujo, L. (eds) (1999) *Organizational Learning and the Learning Organization*, London: Sage Publications.

Easterby-Smith, M., Thorpe, R. and Lowe, A. (2002) *Management Research: An Introduction*, 2nd edn, London: Sage Publications.

Elkjaer, B. (1999) 'In search of a social learning theory', in M. Easterby-Smith, J. Burgoyne and L. Araujo (eds) *Organizational Learning and the Learning Organization*, London: Sage Publications.

Elliott, C. and Turnbull, S. (2002) 'Innovative Session', *Proceedings of the Annual AHRD Conference*, Hawaii, February–March.

European Union (2001) Memorandum of Lifelong Learning, lifelonglearning@cec.eu.int.

Fox, S. (1997) 'From management, education and development to the study of management learning', in J. Burgoyne and M. Reynolds (eds) *Management Learning: Integrating Perspectives in Theory and Practice*, London: Sage Publications.

Gass, R. (1996) *The Goals, Architecture and Means of Lifelong Learning*, Luxembourg: Office for Official Publications of the European Communities.

Gill, J. and Johnson, P. (1997) *Research Methods for Managers*, 2nd edn, London: Paul Chapman Publishing.

Harrison, R. (1997) *Employee Development*, London: Chartered Institute for Personnel and Development.

Holmes, L. (2003) 'The learning turn in education and training: liberatory paradigm or oppressive ideology?', *Critical Management Studies 3 International Conference*, Lancaster University, July.

Horst, H., Sambrook, S. and Stewart, J. (1999) 'The role of HRD within learning (orientated) organizations in creating opportunities for lifelong learning', *ECLO International Conference*, Glasgow.

Keenoy, T. (1999) 'HRM as holograms: a polemic', *Journal of Management Studies*, 36, 1: 1–23.

Kessels, J. (2002) 'HRD practice: a comparison of European and US models. Perspectives of HRD in Europe', *Proceedings of European Conference on HRD Research and Practice*, Edinburgh, January. Published on the EHRD website http://www.b.shuttle.de/wifo/ehrd-per/ste02a.htm (accessed 15 April 2002).

Lee, M. (2001) 'A refusal to define HRD', *Human Resource Development International*, 4, 3: 327–41.

Lee, M.M. (2003) 'The complex roots of HRD', in M.M. Lee (ed.) *HRD in a Complex World*, London: Routledge.

Legge, K. (1995) *Human Resource Management: Rhetorics and Realities*, Basingstoke: Macmillan.

Leys, M., Wijgaerts, D. and Hancké, C. (1992) *From Learning in the Workplace to Learning Organizations: Seven European Companies Move Beyond Training Policies*, Brussels: SERV-Stichting Technologie Vlaanderen.

McGoldrick, J. and Stewart, J. (1996) 'The HRM-HRD Nexus', in J. Stewart and J. McGoldrick (eds) *HRD: Perspectives, Strategies and Practice*, London: Pitman Publishing, 9–27.

McGoldrick, J., Stewart, J. and Watson, S. (2001) 'Theorizing human resource development', *Human Resource Development International*, 4, 3: 343–56.

McGoldrick, J., Stewart, J. and Watson, S. (2002) 'Researching human resource development', in J. McGoldrick, J. Stewart and S. Watson (eds) *Understanding Human Resource Development: A Research-Based Approach*, London: Routledge, 1–17.

McLean, G. (1998) 'HRD: a three-legged stool, an octopus, or a centipede', *Human Resource Development International*, 1, 4: 375–7.

McLean, G. (2001) 'If we can't define HRD in one country, how can we define it in an international context?', *Human Resource Development International*, 4, 3: 312–26.

McLean, G. (2002) 'HRD practice: a comparison of European and US models. HRD models in the United States', *Proceedings of European Conference on HRD Research and Practice*, Edinburgh, January. Published on the EHRD website http://www.b.shuttle.de/wifo/ehrd-per/ste02a.htm (accessed 15 April 2002).

Marsick, V.J. and Watkins, K.E. (1997) 'Lessons from informal and incidental learning', in J. Burgoyne and M. Reynolds (eds) *Management Learning: Integrating Perspectives in Theory and Practice*, London: Sage Publications.

Moingeon, B. and Edmondson, A. (eds) (1996) *Organizational Learning and Competitive Advantage*, London: Sage Publications.

Mumford, A. (1997) *Management Development: Strategies for Action*, 3rd edn, London: IPD.

Nonaka, I. (1996) 'The knowledge-creating company', in K. Starkey (ed.) *How Organizations Learn*, London: International Thomson Business Press.

OECD (1996) *Lifelong Learning For All*, Paris: OECD.

Oswick, C., Keenoy, T. and Grant, D. (1997) 'Managerial discourses: Words speak louder than actions?', *Journal of Applied Management Studies*, 6, 1: 5–12.

Pedler, M., Boydell, T. and Burgoyne, J. (1996) *The Learning Company*, 2nd edn, Maidenhead: McGraw-Hill.

Prange, C. (1999) 'Organizational learning: desperately seeking theory?', in M. Easterby-Smith, J. Burgoyne and L. Araujo (eds) *Organizational Learning and the Learning Organization*, London: Sage Publications.

Ruona, W. (2000) 'Should we define the profession of HRD? Views of leading scholars', *Proceedings of the AHRD Conference*, Raleigh-Durham, NC, 8–12 March.

Ruona, W. (2002) 'Town Forum', *Proceedings of the Annual AHRD Conference*, Hawaii, February–March.

Sambrook, S. (1998) *Models and Concepts of Human Resource Development: Academic and Practitioner Perspectives*, PhD Thesis, Nottingham: Nottingham Business School.

Sambrook, S. (2003) 'A critical time for HRD?', *Critical Management Studies 3 International Conference*, Lancaster University, July.

Sambrook, S. and Stewart, J. (1998a) 'HRD as a discursive construction', *Leeds–Lancaster Conference on Emergent Fields in Management*, University of Leeds, Leeds.

Sambrook, S. and Stewart, J. (1998b) 'HRD as a discursive construction', *Professors Forum, IFTDO World Conference*, Trinity College, Dublin.

Sambrook, S. and Stewart, J. (2000) 'Factors influencing learning in European learning oriented organization: issues for management', *Journal of European Industrial Training*, 24, 2/3/4: 209–219.

Sambrook, S. and Stewart, J. (2002) 'Reflections and discussion', in S. Tjepkema, J. Stewart, S. Sambrook, H. Horst ter, M. Mulder and J. Scheerens (eds) *HRD and Learning Organizations in Europe*, London: Routledge, 178–87.

Sambrook, S., Stewart, J. and Tjepkema, S. (2003) 'The changing role of HRD practitioners in learning-oriented organizations', in B. Nyhan, M. Kelleher, P. Cressey and R. Poell (eds) *Facing Up to the Learning Organization Challenge*, CEDEFOP Reference Series 41-Vol II, Luxembourg: Office for Official Publications of the European Communities, 221–46.

Scheerens, J., Tjepkema, S., Horst ter, H. and Mulder, M. (1998) 'Conceptual framework', *Role of HRD in Learning Organizations: European Concepts and Practices*, The Netherlands: University of Twente.

Senge, P.M. (1990) *The Fifth Discipline: The Art and Practice of the Learning Organization*, London: Doubleday.

Sloman, M. (1999) 'Seize the day', *Learning Centre, People Management*, 5, 10: 31.

Stewart, J. (1992) 'Towards a model of HRD', *Training and Development*, 10, 10.

Stewart, J. (1999) *Employee Development Practice*, London: FT Pitman Publishing.

Stewart, J. (2002) 'HRD practice: a comparison of European and US models. Introduction', *Proceedings of European Conference on HRD Research and Practice*, Edinburgh, January. Published on the EHRD website http://www.b.shuttle.de/wifo/ehrd-per/ste02a.htm (accessed 15 April 2002).

Stewart, J. and Harris, L. (2003) 'HRM and HRD: an uneasy relationship', *People Management*, 9, 19: 58.

Stewart, J. and McGoldrick, J. (eds) (1996) *HRD: Perspectives, Strategies and Practice*, London: Pitman Publishing.

Sun, H.-C. (2003) 'Conceptual clarification for "organizational learning," "learning organization," and "a learning organization"', *Human Resource Development International*, 6, 2: 153–66.

Swanson, R.A. (1995) 'HRD: performance is the key', *Human Resource Development Quarterly*, 6: 207–13.

Swanson, R.A. (1999) 'HRD theory, real or imagined?', *Human Resource Development International*, 2, 1: 2–5.

Swanson, R.A. (2001) 'Human resource development and its underlying theory', *Human Resource Development International*, 4, 3: 299–312.

Swanson, R.A. (2002) 'Theoretical assumptions underlying the performance paradigm of human resource development', *Human Resource Development International*, 5, 2: 199–215.

Swieringa, J. and Wierdsma, A. (1992) *Becoming a Learning Organization: Beyond the Learning Centre*, New York: Addison-Wesley.

Tjepkema, S. and Scheerens, J. (1998) 'Working documents', *Role of HRD in Learning Organizations: European Concepts and Practices*, The Netherlands: University of Twente.

Tjepkema, S. and Wognum, A.A.M. (1996) 'From trainer to consultant? Roles and tasks of HRD professionals in learning orientated organizations', *ECLO International Conference*, Copenhagen.

Tjepkema, S., Stewart, J., Sambrook, S., Horst ter, H., Mulder, M. and Scheerens, J. (2002) (eds) *HRD and Learning Organizations in Europe*, London: Routledge.

Torraco, R.J. (ed.) (1999) 'Performance improvement: theory and practice', *Advances in Developing Human Resources*, No. 1, Academy of Human Resource Development, San Francisco, CA: Berrett-Koehler.

Vince, R. (2003) 'Towards a critical practice of HRD', *Critical Management Studies 3 International Conference*, Lancaster University, July.

Walton, J. (1999) *Strategic Human Resource Development*, Harlow: Financial Times Prentice Hall.

Walton, J. (2002) 'Town Forum', *Proceedings of the Annual AHRD Conference*, Hawaii, February–March.

Watkins, K.E. and Marsick, V.J. (1993) *Sculpting the Learning Organisation: Lessons in the Art and Science of Systemic Change*, San Francisco, CA: Jossey-Bass.

Weinberger, L. (1998) 'Commonly held theories of human resource development', *Human Resource Development International*, 1, 1: 75–93.

Wilson, J. (1999) *Human Resource Development*, London: Kogan Page.

7 HRD beyond what HRD practitioners do

A framework for furthering multiple learning processes in work organisations

Rob F. Poell

Among all the misconceptions about human resource development, one of the most persistent and obfuscating ones is the idea that HRD practitioners are the core actors on the learning and performance stage (Van der Krogt, 2002). Although it is common nowadays to assert that employees are self-responsible for their own learning and careers, with their managers in a coaching role, in practice HRD professionals still spend most of their time co-ordinating, designing and delivering training to employees (Hytönen *et al.*, 2002; Tjepkema *et al.*, 2002; Nijhof, 2004). There is little evidence to suggest that managers are enthusiastically taking on new roles supporting employee learning or that employees are engaging in completely new ways of self-directed learning. It is often forgotten that employees and managers have always been involved in learning at the workplace, much more so than HRD practitioners ever have. Only in the past ten years has attention in HRD literature been targeted (anew) to implicit and self-directed learning processes occurring within work environments. Before that, until the mid-1990s, HRD was really about training, about trainers, and about what trainers could do to improve the transfer of training (Broad and Newstrom, 1992). At first, the workplace was regarded as the site where employees applied what they had learned in a training setting (Robinson and Robinson, 1989). Later, the focus shifted and the workplace came to be seen as an important learning environment in its own right (Simons and Streumer, 2004).

This chapter proposes a model of learning in the workplace in relation to the activities of HRD practitioners. The model makes clear that there is a lot of HRD beyond what these HRD practitioners do. First, the basic components of the model will be outlined. Next, the model will be built up gradually. Finally, the strengths and weaknesses of the model in terms of advancing our understanding of HRD will be discussed and a research agenda presented.

Three types of learning activity combined

If HRD is defined as outside intervention in employee learning and development processes, how are these learning processes influenced and in which directions exactly? Eraut *et al.* (1998) asserted that besides formal training and education arrangements, the most important sources of learning are the challenges in the work itself and interactions with other people in the workplace (Van Woerkom, 2003).

Therefore, it is important for HRD to investigate such implicit and self-directed learning practices, in order to realise its full potential for competence development. Several HRD actors are relevant in their possible impact on such learning processes, including supervisors, managers, work preparation staff, trainers, consultants, trade unions, works councils, professional associations and so forth. Important independent variables in this connection are characteristics of the work setting, the existing organisational structure and culture, various learner characteristics, various characteristics of the intervention and the dynamic interplay between individual learning and outside intervention (Poell, 1998; Van der Krogt, 1998; Van der Sanden, 2001).

Learning in the context of work and organisation is strongly contingent upon individual employees' daily experiences in the workplace. Much of this learning remains implicit (Van Woerkom, 2003). For instance, becoming a better salesperson or learning to communicate with multiple constituencies are competencies often acquired through unconscious experience. In some cases, however, employees deal with their experiences more consciously, for example, when they conclude they have been unsuccessful, think about how they might improve, and try out a better way the next time. In still other cases, dedicated experts or HRD practitioners design a learning situation or an activity for employees to learn from; for instance, a training course, an educational cd-rom, or a performance evaluation meeting. Employees may ask for guided learning themselves or be exposed to it by their manager or an HRD practitioner.

The three types of employee learning activity can be modelled as shown in Figure 7.1 (Poell, 2001): implicit, self-directed and guided learning. All three types of employee learning can occur in both an individual and a collective setting. Taking into account the fact that self-directed learners can also ask for support from experts, coaches, counsellors and so forth, Figure 7.1 represents the way in which six employees (1–6) learn, both on their own terms and as a result of outside intervention.

In Figure 7.1, the six horizontal arrows represent implicit learning, the small ovals represent individual self-directed learning, the large ovals represent collective self-directed learning, the small rectangles represent individual guided learning, the large rectangles represent collective guided learning, the top-to-bottom arrows represent outside intervention, and the bottom-to-top arrows represent asking for support. These elements will be introduced and explicated in more detail in the following paragraphs.

Implicit learning activities

Figure 7.2 shows the basic learning process in any organisation: implicit learning (Tomlinson, 1999). The six arrows indicate that these six workers learn on a continuous basis over time. The notion that employees learn a lot from doing their everyday job, without being aware of it necessarily, has been around for a long time. Some examples of implicit learning activities include solving everyday work problems, finding out by coincidence what approach works out best, unintentionally copying what an experienced colleague tends to do, and bringing someone else's job to a good finish in an emergency. This type of learning has been referred to as learning-by-doing and as

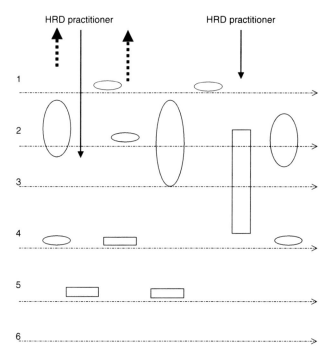

Figure 7.1 Six employees engaging in different combinations of implicit, self-directed and guided learning activities.

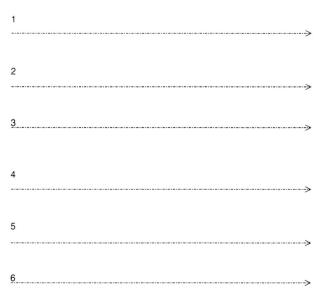

Figure 7.2 Implicit learning at work in six employees.

experiential learning (Kolb, 1984). Marsick and Watkins (1990) called it incidental learning, whereas the term everyday learning was coined by Van Biesen (1989). The main similarity among these concepts is that they do not require any pedagogical structuring or intention to learn, or even an awareness of learning on the part of the learning employee.

Self-directed learning activities: individual and collective

The second type of learning activity does require an awareness and an intention to learn as well as some form of pedagogical structuring on the part of the learners themselves. Managing one's own learning process is a good way to describe this type, which is often referred to as self-directed learning (Candy, 1991) or informal learning (Marsick and Watkins, 1990). Donald Schön's book *The Reflective Practitioner* (Schön, 1983) describes professionals who engage in self-study and who learn consciously and explicitly through reflection within and upon their work experiences, a prime example of self-directed learning. In relationship to implicit learning, self-directed learning refers to shorter periods of time when employees learn more consciously, explicitly, and intentionally than is normally the case. During these periods, however, the implicit learning processes still go on, often independent of the self-directed learning that takes place, although the two activities can also mutually reinforce one another.

A distinction can be made between individual and collective self-directed learning. Some examples of individual self-directed learning (the small ovals in Figure 7.3) include paying more attention to a recurring problem, looking up something one wants to know more about, asking an experienced colleague for advice, and actively seeking new learning experiences. A few examples of collective self-directed learning (the large ovals in Figure 7.3) are tackling a mutually experienced work problem together, asking (and giving) structured feedback from (and to) direct colleagues, collectively inviting an expert for concrete advice, and collaborating on a proposal for work improvement. The notion of learning from and with one another in the workplace was made popular by Nancy Dixon (1994), building on insights around cooperative and collaborative learning (Johnson and Johnson, 1999). Another related concept is inter-colleague consultation (Driehuis, 1997), also popular among professionals.

Guided learning activities: collective and individual

The third type of learning activity, presented in Figure 7.4, is structured by an outside agent for the learning employee, therefore it is referred to as guided learning (Billett, 2000). These activities are commonly known as training courses or educational programmes (Romiszowski, 1982), for which transfer enhancing measures have to be designed to make the learning effective in the workplace (Robinson and Robinson, 1989). Other related terms are instruction learning, formal learning and structured learning (Jacobs and Jones, 1995). Two common characteristics

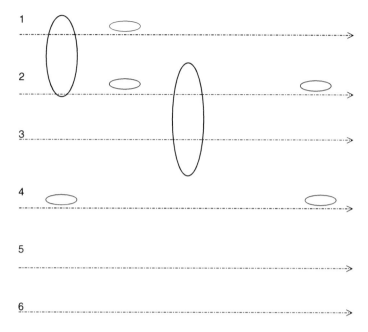

Figure 7.3 Self-directed learning, both individually and collectively, in six employees.

among these concepts are the large degree of preparation and design by an expert and the considerable amount of organisation and intervention by an educator, trainer or adviser.

Again, a distinction can be made between individual and collective guided learning activities. Quite often, such efforts are collective (the large rectangles in Figure 7.4), as in the examples of attending refreshment training, receiving workplace instruction, participating in course activities and being sent to a seminar by one's supervisor with a view to informing the whole team of latest developments. However, individual guided learning activities (the small rectangles in Figure 7.4) are also quite prominent where there is a one-on-one relation of the learning employee with the educator, trainer or adviser. One may think of individual instruction or forms of supervision. Two well-known concepts in this connection are coaching (Locke and Latham, 1990) and mentoring (Galbraith and Cohen, 1995). Examples of individual guided learning activities include having a job review with one's supervisor, receiving individual instruction at the workplace, carrying out a difficult assignment under the supervision of an expert and being inducted into a job by a mentor or coach.

It has to be mentioned here that employees can also ask for support in self-directed learning themselves (the vertical arrows in Figure 7.4), for instance through taking the initiative to call in advice for complex problem-solving, through having a counsellor's input to draw up a personal development plan, through mobilising the

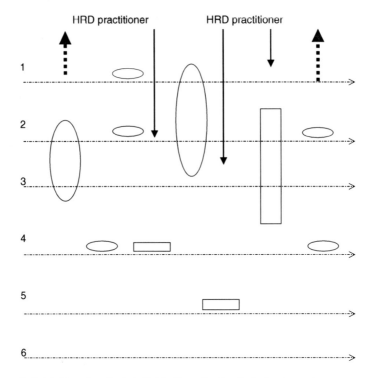

Figure 7.4 Guided learning, both individually and collectively, in six employees.

resources and expertise one has available in the social environment and through consciously putting part of one's learning process in the hands of an expert. This is guided learning at the initiative of the learner.

Multiple learning processes

It is worthwhile to note, going back to Figure 7.1, that workers can have very different patterns in combining learning activities. Worker no. 6 is learning mainly by doing, by experience, with little or no conscious reflection or explicit planning (but even no. 6 does learn!). Worker no. 1 conducts individual self-directed learning activities as well (an 'active learner'). Worker no. 5 is learning mainly in settings pre-organised by others (besides everyday implicit learning). Worker no. 3 is looking mainly for collective learning activities, with an emphasis on self-directed group situations. Workers nos. 2 and 4 have quite multi-faceted learning patterns: they are learning in all kinds of situations and settings.

However, in all six cases the everyday implicit learning always continues. This can be problematic in the case of self-directed learning, as mentioned above, but is usually far more troublesome in the case of guided learning. It is relatively easy for self-directed learners to take into account their own implicit learning activities, but it is far more difficult for outside experts to do so when designing training programmes, especially collective ones. This is where the problem of training transfer surfaces, in that the distance between the training programme and the implicit learning activities of a participant is often hard to bridge, especially for the learners themselves. Reasoning from the model presented here, transfer is really the challenge of combining multiple (implicit, self-directed and guided) learning activities into a coherent learning pattern by the learning employee. This is the very thing that HRD practitioners (and managers) cannot do for employees and, therefore, the reason why employees are much more powerful than HRD practitioners when it comes to organising learning processes. While managers usually have some opportunities to change the work of employees (and therefore, their everyday learning opportunities), the influence of HRD practitioners is restricted largely to guided learning (i.e. training) situations (Van der Krogt, 2002). The bottom line here is that no one can force employees to learn anything or, as Kessels (1999) put it, to 'be smart against their will'.

Strengths and weaknesses of the model

What can this model offer that HRD literature has not produced yet? In the first place, it draws on various well-established traditions within the HRD field to interlink the activities of employees, managers and HRD practitioners in various constellations distinctively within a single framework.

Second, it places employees at the forefront of HRD theorising. By doing so it can explain why in HRD practice employees are often accused of being resistant to change, of showing a lack of motivation or of failing to take on self-responsibility for their work, learning and careers. Self-directed learning means that employees actually self direct what they need to learn and how they like to go about doing that. As long as their notions in this respect fit with the ideas of the people trying to intervene from the outside (i.e. managers and HRD practitioners offering guided learning), all is well. When, however, actual conflicts of interest or opposing viewpoints have to be played out, which is often the case, the idea that individual and organisation needs can always be aligned turns out to be an illusion and terms like resistant, unmotivated and irresponsible enter the discussion.

A third strength of the model is that it brings the issue of power into the field of HRD, which has been conspicuously absent to date, except for the work of Ron Cervero and Arthur Wilson (1996; see also Wilson and Cervero, 1997). Underlying the three different types of learning are different conceptions of who decides about what is learned, why and how. The model also provides insight into which actors are powerful in which domains of learning, thereby accounting for many of the problems experienced by HRD practitioners concerning their less than strategic position, their low status and recognition within organisations and their lack of support from management – even if they adhere to management's problem definitions (Hytönen *et al.*, 2002; Poell and Chivers, 2003; Poell *et al.*, 2003).

Finally, the model can also be used as a pragmatic tool to think through various ways in which coherent sets consisting of various learning activities can be organised.

In all its simplicity, the model is emancipatory in the sense that not only HRD practitioners can easily use it but employees and managers as well. It can even act as a (language and planning) tool for discussion among these parties in clarifying priorities and preferences.

A potential weakness of the model, on the other hand, is that it may be used as a technical tool *only*, by HRD practitioners *only*, thereby not realising its emancipatory potential. On a more conceptual level, dividing all possible learning activities into only three main categories is of course oversimplifying organisational reality. More work should be done to elaborate upon each of the three categories and refine them into meaningful sets of conceptually valid subcategories of learning activity. A final weakness of the model proposed here that should be mentioned is its relative inability to shed light on the content of learning, especially when it comes to implicit learning. The model rather focuses on the way in which learning takes place in a work context. It should (and can) be elaborated for various types of work context (i.e. work content and work relations) tied to different learning contents. Such an effort, however, is beyond the scope of the current chapter.

Implications for HRD research and practice

Key questions informing a research agenda that arise from the perspective described earlier are the following:

1   How do various types of learning activity take place and what are their outcomes?
2   Which constellations of various types of learning activity can be distinguished and what are their outcomes?
3   What is the impact of outside intervention on employee learning activities and outcomes?
4   What is the impact of employee learning activities and outcomes on outside intervention?
5   Which mechanisms have the largest impact on the interaction between HRD practices and learning activities/outcomes?
6   To what extent do learning activities and outcomes, as moderated by HRD practices, depend on the work setting, on the existing organisational structure and culture, on various learner characteristics, on various characteristics of the intervention and on the dynamic interplay between individual learning and outside intervention?

Especially the fifth question, about the mechanisms that moderate the effect of HRD on learning, seems relevant for a *critical* HRD research agenda. In part because this is the least elaborated question conceptually, let alone empirically, and in (larger) part because providing a better insight into these mechanisms enables employees, managers and HRD practitioners to play the organisational game called organising learning with a fuller understanding of the determinants and consequences of possible actions that they have at their disposal. Interesting mechanisms to include in further studies along these lines encompass the negotiation of (shared) meaning

(Billett, 1996), power distribution (Wilson and Cervero, 1997), organisational conflict (Rahim, 2002), identity formation (Winch, 2003) and participation (Lave and Wenger, 1991; Van Woerkom, 2003).

The proposed model can contribute to the debate on critical HRD by providing a means to discuss learning in organisational contexts as a contested domain heavy with oft-ignored power issues and conflicts of interest. Besides this, as Fenwick (2003) asserts, critical HRD operates from the principle that the inherent logic of human development prevails over an economic rationale for learning. In putting employees and both their implicit and self-directed learning first, the model presented in this chapter reflects this very principle. In other words, performance follows learning (Bierema, 1996).

HRD practice can benefit, as illustrated earlier, from applying the model to better understand the interplay of implicit and self-directed employee learning with outside intervention by HRD practitioners and managers. If not necessarily to bridge the gap between employee interests and corporate concern with learning and development, the model can at least provide an insight into the social–organisational dynamics and problems associated with such contested processes.

References

Bierema, L.L. (1996) 'Development of the individual leads to more productive workplaces', in R.W. Rowden (ed.) *Workplace Learning: Debating Five Critical Questions of Theory and Practice*, San Francisco, CA: Jossey-Bass.

Billett, S. (1996) 'Situated learning: bridging sociocultural and cognitive theorising', *Learning and Instruction*, 6, 3: 263–80.

Billett, S. (2000) 'Guided learning at work', *Journal of Workplace Learning*, 12, 7–8: 272–85.

Broad, M.L. and Newstrom, J.W. (1992) *Transfer of Training: Action-Packed Strategies to Ensure High Pay-Off from Training Investments*, San Francisco, CA: Addison-Wesley.

Candy, P.C. (1991) *Self-Direction for Lifelong Learning: A Comprehensive Guide to Theory and Practice*, San Francisco, CA: Jossey-Bass.

Cervero, R.M. and Wilson, A.L. (1996) *What Really Matters in Adult Education Program Planning: Lessons in Negotiating Power and Interests*, San Francisco, CA: Jossey-Bass.

Dixon, N.M. (1994) *The Organizational Learning Cycle: How We Can Learn Collectively*, London: McGraw-Hill.

Driehuis, M. (1997) *De lerende adviseur: Een onderzoek naar intercollegiaal consult in organisatie-advisering* [*The Consultant as a Learner: A Study of Peer Consultation in Organisational Consultancy*]. PhD thesis, Technical University of Eindhoven, The Netherlands.

Eraut, M., Alderton, J., Cole, G. and Senker, P. (1998) *Development of Knowledge and Skills in Employment*, Brighton: University of Sussex.

Fenwick, T.J. (2003) *Dancing With the Devil: Towards a Critical HRD*, from www.ualberta.ca/~tfenwick/ext/pubs/aerc03.htm (Retrieved 27 December 2003).

Galbraith, M.W. and Cohen, N.H. (eds) (1995) *Mentoring: New Strategies and Challenges*, San Francisco, CA: Jossey-Bass.

Hytönen, T., Poell, R.F. and Chivers, G. (2002) 'HRD as a professional career? Perspectives from Finland, The Netherlands, and the United Kingdom', in W.J. Nijhof, A. Heikkinen and L.F.M. Nieuwenhuis (eds) *Shaping Flexibility in Vocational Education and Training*, Dordrecht: Kluwer Academic Publishers, 227–42.

Jacobs, R.L. and Jones, M.J. (1995) *Structured On-the-Job Training: Unleashing Employee Expertise in the Workplace*, San Francisco, CA: Berrett-Koehler.

Johnson, D.W. and Johnson, F.P. (1999) *Joining Together: Group Theory and Group Skills*, 7th edn, Boston, MA: Allyn and Bacon.

Kessels, J.W.M. (1999) *Verleiden tot kennisproductiviteit [Tempting Into Knowledge Productivity]*, Inaugural lecture, Twente University, The Netherlands.

Kolb, D. (1984) *Experiential Learning*, Englewood Cliffs, NJ: Prentice-Hall.

Lave, J. and Wenger, E. (1991) *Situated Learning: Legitimate Peripheral Participation*, New York: Cambridge University Press.

Locke, E.A. and Latham, G.P. (1990) *A Theory of Goal Setting and Task Performance*, Englewood Cliffs, NJ: Prentice-Hall.

Marsick, V.J. and Watkins, K.E. (1990) *Informal and Incidental Learning in the Workplace*, London: Routledge.

Nijhof, W. (2004) 'Is the HRD profession in the Netherlands changing?', *Human Resource Development International*, 7, 1: 57–72.

Poell, R.F. (1998) *Organizing Work-Related Learning Projects: A Network Approach*, PhD thesis, University of Nijmegen, The Netherlands.

Poell, R.F. (2001) *Learning Projects Viewed From a Network Perspective*, Paper presented at the Centre for Research in Education, Equity and Work (CREEW), University of South Australia, Adelaide, 27 November.

Poell, R.F. and Chivers, G.E. (2003) 'Experiences of HRD consultants in supporting organisational learning', in B. Nyhan, P. Cressey, M. Kelleher and R.F. Poell (eds) *Facing Up To the Learning Organisation Challenge: Selected European Writings*, Luxembourg: Office for Official Publications of the European Communities, 247–64.

Poell, R.F., Pluijmen, R. and Van der Krogt, F.J. (2003) 'Strategies of HRD professionals in organising learning programmes: a qualitative study among 20 Dutch HRD professionals', *Journal of European Industrial Training*, 27, 2/3/4: 125–36.

Rahim, M.A. (2002) 'Toward a theory of managing organizational conflict', *International Journal of Conflict Management*, 13, 3: 206–35.

Robinson, D.G. and Robinson, J.C. (1989) *Training For Impact*, San Francisco, CA: Jossey-Bass.

Romiszowski, A.J. (1982) *Designing Instructional Systems: Decision Making in Course Planning and Curriculum Design*, London: Kogan Page.

Schön, D.A. (1983) *The Reflective Practitioner: How Professionals Think in Action*, London: Temple Smith.

Simons, P.R.J. and Streumer, J. (2004) *Work Related Learning*, Dordrecht: Kluwer Academic Publishers.

Tjepkema, S., Stewart, J., Sambrook, S., Mulder, M., Horst ter, H. and Scheerens, J. (2002) *HRD and Learning Organisations in Europe*, London: Routledge.

Tomlinson, P. (1999) 'Conscious reflection and implicit learning in teacher preparation: recent light on an old issue', *Oxford Review of Education*, 25, 3: 405–24.

Van Biesen, F. (1989) 'Alledaags leren in arbeidsorganisaties' [Every-day learning in organisations], *Ontwerp*, Tjidschrift voor Volwassenen educatie, 1: 4–11.

Van der Krogt, F.J. (1998) 'Learning network theory: the tension between learning systems and work systems in organizations', *Human Resource Development Quarterly*, 9, 2: 157–77.

Van der Krogt, F.J. (2002) 'Managers en werknemers creëren leersystemen? De lastige positie van HRD'ers' [Managers and workers create learning systems? The difficult position of HRD practitioners], in P. Bührs, H. Dekker, R.F. Poell, S. Tjepkema and S. Wagenaar (eds) *Organiseren van de HRD-functie*, Alphen aan den Rijn: Kluwer.

Van der Sanden, J. (2001) 'Opleiden vanuit een constructivistisch perspectief' [Training from a constructivist perspective], in J.W.M. Kessels and R.F. Poell (eds) *Human Resource development: Organiseren van het leren*, Alphen aan den Rijn: Samsom, 53–66.

Van Woerkom, M. (2003) *Critical Reflection at Work: Bridging Individual and Organisational Learning*, PhD thesis, Twente University, The Netherlands.

Wilson, A.L. and Cervero, R.M. (1997) 'The song remains the same: the selective tradition of technical rationality in adult education program planning theory', *International Journal of Lifelong Education*, 16, 2: 84–108.

Winch, C. (2003) 'Occupational identity and vocational education', *Educational Philosophy and Theory*, 35, 1: 117–22.

8 Place

A (re)source for learning

Ginny Hardy and Colin Newsham

> The world is the house where mortals dwell.
> (Heidegger)

Introduction

We work in places; we live in places; we learn in places. Everything that we do happens in a physical place of some kind. We may meet and interact virtually but we are still bound, bodily and physically, to places. And yet place, that physical context within which HRD, and everything else, happens is taken for granted and rarely discussed. In this chapter, we introduce the idea of 'place' and how it might inform, and add a different critical perspective to HRD practice.

We want to show the way in which a greater awareness of the places in which we live and work and learn, of our immediate contexts, can be used to support individual and organisational learning and the design of learning events. It is also an excellent starting point for thinking about issues of social and environmental responsibility, an aspect of a critical approach that is increasingly important both to individuals and to organisations. Businesses and organisations can often seem to be context-free – free of any connections to the social or natural world around them, to 'place'. They exist in a vacuum, not in real physical spaces that need water, heat and light, and have surroundings, neighbours and a history. Training and development in this area can too easily focus on teaching *about* social and environmental 'issues'. There is a danger that the content of such courses are about 'out there', distant places and global problems, 'somewhere else' to where we are and somewhere separate from ourselves. For us the emphasis is on 'knowing' our own place, our own context and our immediate connection to the wider environment and using that to support HRD processes of any kind.

We begin by looking at the concept of place and at our own, as authors, very different relationships to place. Then we explore how we use these ideas and experiences of place to support learning and change. We look at the use of the physical environment in our learning events and the ways in which we can raise awareness of the relationship between individuals, organisations and places. We also focus on the use of 'place' as a metaphor. We end by looking at the implications for the design of work and learning spaces. For this chapter, our emphasis is on our *practice* rather than on a theoretical discussion of place.

Experiencing place

One of the attractions of the concept of place is its looseness, its openness, its reluctance to be pinned down. From the physical identifying features of landscape or simple location dots on maps, through to our experiences of places and the meanings that we put upon them. Place-name, fireplace, out-of-place, displace, in place, replace, workplace, place in the sun, common place, dwelling place – what do we mean by place? It might be a physical space – a wood, a city square, stepping stones across a stream. It could be a wider area, a region like the Lake District or The Cairngorms. It is unique. It is the relationship between a physical reality and our experience of that physical reality. Place is more than location, it is also about meanings. A place could be a building; an office, a college, a lecture theatre, a house, a room. It could also be an imaginary place from a book or a dream. Everything that we do happens in a place of some kind. Roaming cyberspace is still done from that particular internet cafe in Paris or that desk by the window in Notting Hill.

When it comes to our own experiences of place, there is something of a difference. Colin has lived and worked all his life in one place, a pattern that once applied to most people when travel was slow and difficult. Today, few people live and work in the same place; few people remain in the same place throughout their lives. We can travel much further in any day and we are likely to move much more with our work (Massey and Jess, 1990). This is now the dominant pattern and fits with Ginny's experience. Traditionally, place and identity were closely linked. Now our sense of place has been problematised. Tuan (1977) describes 'place as security', a sense of belonging, which he contrasts with 'space' which is freedom; 'we are attached to the one and long for the other'.

Colin's Story

I have lived in the same place all my life, the family farm, 70 hectares of undulating grassland with a river running through it and close to Lancaster University, the city, and the M6 motorway. Banton House was the name of the farm my parents purchased in 1960, for the production of milk, lamb, and beef. Following a diversification process over the last 10 years, the farm is now called Forrest Hills and has a fly-fishing lake, a 9-hole golf course and two wooden lodges used as meeting rooms or classrooms by Lancaster University and other businesses and organisations. (For details of the process of the development see Newsham, 2002.)

The family farm was not only a business but a way of life, passed down from generation to generation with an overriding sense of pride in looking after the countryside for the future. This responsibility is firmly rooted in my sense of place. My life and work still revolves around the 'place', the 'farm' but there are no animals, no food is produced, just working with people, mowing golf greens, advising fishermen to which flies are catching best that day, organising corporate activity events for companies, providing outdoor training facilities and meeting space for departmental away days from the local university, attending and presenting at local, national and international conferences, talking to the 'neighbouring' farmer, whether it is over the hedge or in Sweden, and designing workshops for students and organisations. While mixing and communicating with all these people I still keep one foot in my traditional farming past by visiting farming relatives and going to the local cattle markets – perhaps as a sense of security, something I trust, a familiar feeling, fond memories.

Living and working in the same place, knowing it through the seasons and having to make a livelihood from that place has given me a deep connection to it. Producing the food that your animals need to thrive, which fields will grow better grass, where the wet areas are, the drains, where birds nest and wild hares lie during the day, these have all been an essential part of my learning background and are very much a local and specific knowledge. As a farmer you have to be connected 'in place'. Long term thinking, forward planning, seasons, cycles of life's reproduction, stock replacement, relationships to who you are, where you are, what you do, combine with the immediate, the unexpected, weather changes, crop failure, illness. Potentially others can learn from this experience, this connection to place.

Recently I went to a conference where a speaker from the National Farmers' Union said 'A farmer is someone who produces food'. Yet despite having no animals and producing no food, I still think of myself as a farmer. For me it is more about what you do and your relationship to a place than it is about what you produce. Farming is about managing the unpredictable and uncontrollable and about having an intimacy with the land and none of that has changed! The skills are the same too – you have to be flexible, creative and self-reliant. All of the very different things that I do are linked together by the place. Everything I do is connected to that.

Ginny's Story

I've lived in many places and felt connected to many more. Many rural but some urban. Place has always been significant, impossible to separate the 'where I am' from 'what I am doing' and 'how I feel'. In some places I feel caged, closed down. In others more alive, expansive, able to move and breath. I have no one place but seek out those aspects of place that seem to support life and learning.

I first came to Lancaster University as a student. My overwhelming impression was of uniformity and a lack of 'normal' life – no children, no dogs, no real sense of any wider community. Later I became a lecturer in management learning. The community had become a little more diverse by then – more and more students from other countries; 'town' people using facilities and conference delegates from all walks of life. Even the pre-school centre my daughter had attended moved site and became part of the main hill top buildings. I walked a lot – around the parkland of campus; beyond the perimeters to footpaths and lanes leading past farms and down to the stepping-stones across the River Conder. I had no real awareness of the bordering farm, of what was produced and by whom.

My own sense of intimately knowing a place comes from childhood. As a child, our relationship to place tends to be very physical. Mike Pearson writes about a particular Welsh concept *y filltir sqwar* or 'the square mile' – 'to the age of eight, we know a patch of ground in a detail we will never know anywhere again' (Pearson, 2000). He quotes D.J. Williams, 'When the many things I remember actually happened [ ] I haven't much of an idea. But I can *locate* most of them with a degree of certainty – *where* such and such a thing happened and *where* I was standing when I heard what I heard'.

Going back there, and despite many changes, I have a sense of knowing the place, the light, the landscape, individual trees and streams.

In the Management School I was very conscious of the spaces in the building – long, often-blank corridors with closed doors to individual academic's rooms. Teaching rooms with plastic furniture of uniform sizes and proportions. No worse than many other management schools. No better either. My interest grew in how place both immediate and distant, past and present, affects our learning.

Two very different places. One modern, standing out on the hillside, mainly white buildings and visible for miles around. The other rooted in history, stone and wooden buildings, remains of a settlement, a bronze age axe, an indicator of earlier life, set into a hollow and blending into their surroundings. Both places of work and learning. The land of one bordering the land of the other. Two very different stories and two very different relationships to place.

Practising place

Our interest in place, and our different experiences of it, have led us to work together in developing learning events and activities both for management students and for organisations. As well as being a way to raise discussion of environmental issues we have also designed activities for a wide range of purposes including helping groups work with diversity and as part of organisational change processes.

We encourage people to think about their own stories of place, how they came to be where they are. It could be a simple list of places they have lived or worked in. It might also include other places that are significant. Massey and Jess (1990) suggests reviewing your own personal migration history – moves made yourself but also in previous generations – where did parents, grandparents move to and from and why. (As well as being a way of exploring our relationship to place, it is also a gentle way in which to introduce discussion about diversity.) Thinking of childhood places and drawing a map of it can also be a useful starting point. With all of these activities the idea is on highlighting things normally taken for granted and reminding ourselves of the significance of place. We also work with the idea of place in two different yet complimentary ways: place as we experience it physically, and place as metaphor.

On the workshops that we run, we try to make the most of the natural environment. Forrest Hills, Colin's 'place', is situated close to an urban area, a university campus and a motorway yet feels distant and wild. Most people we work with, live and work in a built and mediated environment. Working outdoors in woodland, alongside lakes or the river, in fields – or indoors in the wooden lodge overlooking one of the lakes, highlights the contrast with their normal environment. By engaging with place and being 'in place', we put an emphasis on the physical and the immediate, allowing learning to happen rather than trying to make things happen. This contrasts with much of management and HRD theory and practice where there is often an emphasis on 'controlling' and 'predicting' as a way of dealing with the complexities of our social, economic and physical world.

One event we ran involved HRD students, from many different countries, on a year long Masters course. The day began with the simple act of walking the quarter mile from campus to Forrest Hills. People chatted in small groups or pairs. Questions came up about the meaning of place-names, such as Barrow Greaves and Conder, and landscape features. Straight away the context was shifted; awareness raised about the beauty of the surrounding landscape. Travelling at walking pace, instead of driving, forces you to slow down in other ways too and see things you would not normally notice. There was awareness of the contrast between the two places, the contrast between indoors and outdoors. They were relaxed. They were able to be informal and so relate to each other and to staff in different ways. Different strengths came to the fore and different ways of encouraging and supporting each other.

We had organised a mixed format of activities with a high degree of choice – introduction and initial warm-up activities (literally as it was late autumn and very cold); tree planting, outdoor art activity, an exploration of place exercise, informal discussion and walks. A library of books relevant to both the setting and the topic of the module were provided, allowing informal learning and discussion in the warm and comfortable lodge. Many students took advantage of this informality of both place and design to get to know each other better, walking and talking in small groups, working together on the activities and sharing lunch.

Eating together, something not normally done, was again important. Food is an excellent place-related vehicle for discussion. It embodies cultural differences and allows these to be discussed yet in a non-threatening way. We now also try to source food for our events locally and have information about it available. One student commented on the fact that the staff made tea for everyone – Susan Scott (2000) writes about how we can use such 'ritualised domestic acts' to 'ground us in place' and make us question some of our ideas about distinctions between domestic and wild.

Rather than follow the design of a traditional outdoor management development session we focussed on actual tasks, such as tree planting, that needed doing and that foster a different awareness of and connection to place. Planting trees was very significant to the students. The contact with the earth. The physicality of the task. The contrast with the emphasis on the abstract and the mental in much of their course.

Art, too, is another way of slowing down and being aware of place in different ways. The British artist Andy Goldsworthy works directly, usually outdoors, with materials from nature. He talks of his art as a 'way of learning and understanding'.

It was very important to me when I discovered that I could actually learn from making art. [ ] it acted as a kind of vehicle for getting information. Learning how ice freezes.

(Friedman and Goldsworthy, 1990)

Students spent some time producing their own sculpture out of a group of young willow trees, something none of them had ever tried before and were convinced they couldn't do. Weaving the willow branches and experiencing the intense cold on the shaded hillside, they were also suprised and delighted to have made an attractive structure.

Thinking critically about place

Barclay and York (2001) have outlined some of the ways in which physical, working environments impact on areas like social status and power, group and individual behaviour and organisational culture. They introduce an exercise in which students seek out artifacts that illustrate cultural use of space. We use an exploration of place and apply it to particular learning or workplaces as a way of developing an awareness of immediate context. What does place mean to us? What do we know about the place where we are right now? Its history? Its physical landscape features? Where is the nearest running water? Where does the water from that tap actually come from? What buildings or settlements were here before? Who are the immediate neighbours? How can we develop our own specific and local knowledge? We can develop these questions further as part of a process of critical reflection (Reynolds, 1999). Who or what benefits from this particular space or building? What impact do particular places have on our work or learning?

Michael Hill, in talking about cross-organisational working, emphasised the need to

> have a *sense of place and passion for place* and incorporate it into every facet of what you do. To be directed by *place* when you choose how to structure your organisation. To know the *place* that you inhabit, its needs and wants, when you are choosing what activities to undertake. To be respectful of and rooted in *place* when you decide what to teach and what to research. To understand the *place* of others when you choose your partners and when you form new, broader networks beyond your own place.
>
> (Hill, 2000)

We encourage people to think about their own places of work or learning. What does the design and layout of buildings and rooms say about the values and culture of the organisation? About expectations for what happens in a particular space? Who or what is included or excluded within any place? Out of place? What form do borders, boundaries and edges take? We can think about questions such as these literally but also metaphorically.

An airport is an archetypal boundary place, a transition zone. It lacks any real sense of place but offers movement, travel, possibility and excitement. In myths and fairy tales the crossroad plays a similar role – anything can happen there. We can talk of liminal places such as the crossroad but also in time. Midnight and midday are times of mythical power and significance. What are the borders and boundaries, the liminal places in our own lives? In our places of work or learning? Who crosses borders or is in exile? (Giroux, 1992; Said, 1993) Someone crossing a border can be in a powerful position; they can see things that others may take for granted, they can ask naive questions, they can introduce new ideas and experiences. Such a role is an important one for an HRD professional or external consultant. We have to encourage some border crossings. We have to experience that shift that allows us to see things differently.

We have written earlier about using walking as a way of bringing about different connections to place, seeing different things. Walking can be a simple way of connecting with the our environment (Thoreau, 1937) but it can also be a type of border crossing (Solnit, 2000).

> A solitary walker, however short his or her route, is unsettled, between places, drawn forth into action by desire and lack, having the detachment of the traveller rather than the ties of the worker, the dweller, the member of a group.
>
> (Solnit, 2000)

Earlier we outlined our two different stories of place. These include crossing borders and boundaries of our own respective social and working communities – farming and academic. We use this position to look at how we are able to interact respectively with these professions, being able to challenge and ask 'naive' questions.

One activitiy in which we explicitly use the natural environment as metaphor, is our 'river walk'. We invite people to walk along the river Conder as it flows through Forrest Hills. We ask them to apply the metaphor of the river to their own situation. For example, we have done this with students beginning a new process of learning; with managers involved in an organisational change process and with participants at conferences. In each case individuals were able to understand and if appropriate express, their own complex ideas, cultural differences and feelings in ways they had not done before. The river provides a wealth of imagery – from rocky rapids and large boulders to deep water and sandy banks including much that we had not noticed! Even with groups who have never met before and where we have used photographs rather than the actual river, the effect has been dramatic – easy and animated discussion and an appreciation of others' perspectives.

The combination of physical, bodily involvement in natural settings with physical features such as a wood, river, fields offers a powerful way of making sense of a wide range of individual, group and organisational processes. We can draw on the 'systems' processes of ecology – succession, cycles of change, growth and decay – and apply these metaphors of place at the level of individual, group or organisational learning. We can use them to make sense of our own experience, to make sense of the way in which we work with others or in which groups of people work together. We can also apply them to organisations as metaphors for change, decision making etc.

Our own working practices also mirror our professional practice. A crucial part of this process is that we intermingle writing papers or designing learning events with walking, clearing brambles and mowing grass. We use a variety of methods of working with groups – practical, physical tasks, structured exercises, individual and paired walking, all designed to encourage flow and learning. We actively encourage sense-making and learning through the use of journal writing, reflection (individual and group) feedback, storytelling, art work, theory and ideas.

We are currently involved in a process of designing new working and learning spaces and adapting existing buildings and outdoor areas drawing on these ideas of place. We want to create spaces that people want to be in, that encourage them to be creative and that encourage a closer sense of connection to the environment around them. There is a blurring of boundaries between inside and outside with partially covered entrances and mixing areas – places to encourage informal interaction. There is strong use of natural materials and indoors high levels of natural light. This work draws on ideas from 'natural architechture' (Pearson, 2001; Day, 2002). We also incorporate art work that fully represents place – not just famous local landmarks but images put together by people related to a place and incorporating their meanings; something that celebrates 'local distinctiveness' (www.commonground.org.uk, last consulted November 2004) and acknowledges the wider community of an organisation. Again the idea is to stimulate discussion and encourage engagement with the local and immediate context.

In order to support a critical HRD we believe that we need this level of support and security that comes from being 'rooted in place'. With a sense of belonging comes a sense of obligation, both to that place and the people in it. By developing close connections to our particular places we are more likely to try to respond to them sensitively.

Conclusion

We have argued that the concept 'place', which we have usefully applied to our own work and learning, can be applied to HRD and organisational learning much more generally. The environment around us, whether building or landscape, region or room, is something everyone has an attachment to, feeling for, and experience of throughout their lives although with the pressures of modern organisational life this awareness can often be dormant. Metaphors of place such as borders and boundaries are exciting and useful. By working with our physical environment, the local, the immediate, and activities like walking, artwork and critical reflection, we can more consciously develop this connection to place as a resource for wider learning and organisational change.

These ideas can be used to raise awareness of the natural environment and our contribution to social and environmental responsibility; as a way of working with diversity and difference and as a way of relating theory and practice more closely. We can also look again at our own places of work and learning and question their design and suitability and find ways of adapting spaces to more fully support and compliment our purposes.

In essence, what would we see if we put 'sense of place' at the heart of everything we do?

References

Barclay, Lizabeth and York, Kenneth (2001) 'Space at work: exercises in the art of understanding physical indicators of culture', *Journal of Management Education*, 25, 1: 54–69.

Buttimer, Anne and Seaman, David (eds) (1980) *The Human Experience of Space and Place*, London: Croom Helm.

Canter, David (1977) *The Psychology of Place*, London: Architectural Press.

Casey, Edward S. (1993) *Getting Back into Place: Towards A Renewed Understanding of the Place World*, Bloomington, IN: Indiana University Press.

Day, C. (2002) *Spirit and Place*, London: Architectural Press.

Friedman, Terry and Goldsworthy, Andy (1990) *Hand to Earth: Andy Goldsworthy Sculpture 1976–1990*, Leeds: The Henry Moore Centre for the Study of Sculpture.

Giroux, Henry (1992) *Border Crossings: Cultural Workers and the Politics of Education*, New York: Routledge.

Gladwin, Thomas N., Kennelly, James J. and Krause, Tara-Shelomith (1995) 'Shifting paradigms for sustainable development: implications for management theory and research', *Academy of Management Review*, 20, 4: 874–907.

Heidegger, Martin (1962) (trans.) *Being and Time*, London: Blackwell.

Hill, Michael (2000) 'Managing knowledge for regional development', *Symposium*, Sundsvall, Sweden.

Kaplan, R., Kaplan, S. and Ryan, R.L. (1998) *With People in Mind: Design and Management of Everyday Nature*, Washington, DC: Island Press.

Lave, J. and Wenger, E. (1991) *Situated Learning: Legitimate Peripheral Participation*, Cambridge: Cambridge University Press.

Macauley, David (1997) 'Be-wildering order: on finding a home for domestication and the domesticated other', in Roger S. Gottlieb (ed.) *The Ecological Community*, New York: Routledge.

Massey, Doreen and Jess, Pat (eds) (1990) *A Place in the World: Places, Cultures and Globalization*, Milton Keynes: Open University Geography.

Newsham, Colin (2002) 'Implementing multifunctionality on the farm', *Journal of Education and Extension*, 8, 2, Wagnegen University, The Netherlands.

Pearson, D. (2001) *New Organic Architechture*, London: Gaia Press.

Pearson, Mike (2000) 'The Square Mile', *Abstracts From the Conference Between Nature*, Lancaster University, July.

Pearson, Mike and Shanks, Michael (1997) 'Performing a visit: archaeology of the contemporary past', *Performance Research*, 2, 2: 41–53.

Reynolds, Michael (1999) 'Critical reflection and management education: rehabilitating less hierarchical approaches', *Journal of Management Education*, 23, 5: 537–53.

Said, Edward (quoted in McLaren, Peter and Leonard, Peter (eds) (1993) *Paulo Freire – A Critical Encounter*, New York: Routledge).

Scott, Susan L. (2000) 'At home and Wild: women in wilderness', *Abstracts From The Conference Between Nature*, Lancaster University, July.

Solnit, Rebecca (2000) *Wanderlust: A History of Walking*, London: Verso.

Thoreau, Henry (1937) 'Walking', in Brooks Atkinson (ed.) *Walden and Other Writings by Henry David Thoreau*, New York: The Modern Library.

Tuan, Yi-Fu (1977) *Space and Place – The Perspective of Experience*, Minneapolis, MI: University of Minnesota Press.

9 Critiquing codes of ethics

Monica Lee

Introduction

One of my favourite modes of writing is to reflect upon some aspect of my life or my experience – to use that to draw out the points I wish to make. For some, this is disconcerting and indulgent – for others it is too revealing of me – the 'author' who should be shrouded by the power of the invisible 'authority'. I am, however, going to indulge myself again, as the role of the 'author' in ethical situations is part of the point I wish to make here. In doing this I am adopting the perspective that each of us interprets 'reality' and our own position in that from our own perspective, and thus we 'author' our world (Lee, 2002). The personal examples that I describe here each illustrate one particular area that I wish to cover: reification, time dependence, individual understanding of the nature of ethical codes and the challenge of emotion, but have implications for the others. Before exploring them, however, I shall set the scene by looking at what is meant by codes of ethics and the nature of 'author'ity.

Codes of ethics

As Hatcher and Lee (2003) have argued, HRD is a profession that is clearly linked to and propounds democratic values within organisations that are themselves often not run on democratic principles or structures. HRD, therefore, finds itself in the forefront of the battleground between people-centred and for-profit motifs, and thus operating in an environment fraught with ethical quandaries. Dalla Costa (1998: 59) says 'When the government is focused on competitiveness, and society is fixated on budgets, growth assumes greater importance than quality of life'. Many HR related professional bodies have addressed the need for guidance expressed by their members by adopting codes of ethics. Figure 9.1 gives an example of those adopted by the American Society for Training and Development, chosen because of their compactness rather than as an endorsement or criticism. Many different examples can be produced, most of which run to several pages and some of which are longer and more detailed – see, for example, those of the Academy of HRD on www.ahrd.org.

American Society for Training and Development (ASTD)

Code of Ethics

The ASTD Code of Ethics provides guidance to members to be self-managed human resource development professionals – Clients and employers should expect from ASTD members the highest possible standards of personal integrity, professional competence, sound judgment, and discretion. Developed by the profession for the profession, the ASTD Code of Ethics is the Society's public declaration of its members' obligations to themselves, their profession, and society.
I strive to...

- recognize the rights and dignities of each individual.
- develop human potential.
- provide my employer, clients, and learners with the highest level quality education, training, and development.
- comply with all copyright laws and the laws and regulations governing my position.
- keep informed of pertinent knowledge and competence in the human resource field.
- maintain confidentiality and integrity in the practice of my profession.
- support my peers and to avoid conduct which impedes their practicing their profession.
- conduct myself in an ethical and honest manner.
- improve the public understanding of human resource development and management.
- fairly and accurately represent my human resource development/human resource management credentials, qualifications, experience, and ability.
- contribute to the continuing growth of the Society and its members.

Figure 9.1 ASTD Code of Ethics.

Codes of ethics are not limited to professional bodies. Many organisations already have codes of ethics or are in the process of establishing them. This is done in the belief that once we develop a value it becomes a criterion of significance for us (Rokeach, 1973; Hultman and Gellerman, 2002). Core values (such as peace, equality, freedom, respect and sustainability) do not change dramatically over time since they represent an end state or outcome (Hatcher, 1993; Gilley *et al.*, 2001).

The core value, enshrined within a code of ethics, acts with mediating power and as a goal post. This is particularly true of human rights issues. As Hatcher (2002: 133) argues 'Human rights violations occur through daily HR activities such as employment, recruiting, training, promotion, and laying off of employees. Therefore, by ensuring the security of employees and facilities, identifying and managing environmental issues, and attempting to make a positive contribution to the societies and cultures within which the companies operate, HRD is intimately involved in human rights in many organisations. The capacity of individual HRD professionals to mitigate these and other human rights abuses is in most cases limited. However, collectively, as a profession and as a field of study, we can and should make a significant contribution to upholding human rights.'

Despite (or because of?) the battleground within which HR functions, economic success is also linked to codes of ethics. Korten (1995: 7) argues for the 'creation of life-centred societies in which the economy is but one of the instruments of good living – not the purpose of human existence'. Similarly, 'As a core value, sustainability can provide the understanding that economic success and ecosystem survival are both worthy and necessary goals for individuals, organisations, societies and Nature' (Stead and Stead, 1996: 130; Hatcher, 2002: 125–31). Indeed, it can be argued that organisations that exhibit core values such as stakeholder service, social responsibility, ethics and sustainability are able to transcend the conflicts that arise between human fulfilment, environmental protection and economic success; that the adoption of codes of ethics has a clear impact upon the social, economic and performance environment of the organisation. Hatcher takes this further by arguing persuasively for the need to include ethics and social responsibility within organisations and HRD, not just because this is a 'good' thing, but also because those companies that have codes of ethics outperform those that do not, and because of the cost of misbehaviour. 'Less than stellar behaviour associated with organisations and their leaders accounts for losses of almost $3 trillion a year in the United States alone (Estes, 1996), and, worldwide, the figure may be triple' (Hatcher, 2002: 4).

A code of ethics has tremendous power – it helps establish some norms for a profession and for newcomers to become socialised into a profession. It delineates and clarifies acceptable and unacceptable behaviours. All professions have codes of ethics of some sort, though not all have then written down or thought through. It could be argued that recent financial scandals, such as Enron, are a good example of an unwritten code of ethics that allowed greed to take precedence over probity. In considering and writing down codes of ethics, thereby exposing them to public scrutiny, professions take a large step towards acting ethically.

Therefore, when we establish core value as an ethical code we are marking what is important for us, both now and what we would like to see in the future. Establishing a code of ethics is therefore a way of making a clear signal about how we would like the future to develop, as well as saying something about our current society. They are a collective statement of responsible behaviour. They form the rules by which organisations can govern themselves in the same way that principles *can* guide the actions of individuals.

Authority

The operative word in the previous sentence is 'can'. The establishment of a code of ethics does not mean that those to whom it applies will necessarily act in an ethical manner. Höpfl (1999) makes a distinction between Auctoritas, or moral authority, and Potestas, or the rights of office. '*auctoritas* is a capacity to initiate and inspire respect. It can be an attribute of either persons or of institutions, customs and practices, but with the conspicuous difference that as an attribute of institutions and practises authority is a stabiliser and consolidator, something exempting them from the flux, but as an attribute of persons it may well be *de*stabilising' (Höpfl, 1999: 222). Obviously to have a safe pair of hands, and to be calm and unflustered, keeping your head when all about are losing theirs, are authoritative attributes which may preserve and stabilise institutions. But equally, *auctoritas* is initiative, the capacity to set things in motion, and that may be indispensably valuable, but it is not as such stabilising. Either way, '*auctoritas* is precisely *moral* authority, and this is both its strength and its limitation. It is an imputed right to be listened to, a capacity to elicit respect, to be consulted or a consultant, to guide, to steer; it is *not* a right to command, or to decide, determine, rule, order, legislate, arbitrate, still less a power to compel'. In contrast, he argues that *potestas* 'is the property of an office, not a person. It means the right to act derived from an office ... And, unlike *auctoritas*, it *can* be assigned, distributed, redistributed, shared around and/or withdrawn, for all of this may, in principle, be done to or with offices' (Höpfl, 1999: 223). The role of the whistle-blower is a good example of this. When someone feels sufficiently compromised, ethically, to risk their job and colleagues in order to step out of line and call attention to what they see as malpractice they are asserting their moral authority over that of the power of office. They are saying that their code of ethics is being contradicted by the one that they see in practice around them.

At the start of this chapter I made a point of raising the issue of authorship and authority. I am the author of my world, as I am of this chapter, and in my world it is 'I' who interprets whether the situations I find myself in have ethical connotations and what these might be, and whose individual code of ethics comes to bear. Professional codes might dictate what my ethical behaviours ought to be, but even so, I have the responsibility of deciding if I will comply or suffer the consequences of not complying. Therefore, if we wish to establish a code of ethics that is relevant to a group of people, each the author of their own worlds, then those who are implicated in the process must be able to see it as legitimate.

> Legitimation must establish some plausible connection between what people value already and what is to be legitimated. The strength of the link established between these constitutes the force of the legitimation. Plausibility demands at a minimum that what is being legitimated should not be out of proportion to the goods in terms of which it is legitimated: an association that can promise its associates immortality can demand more of them than an association that can merely offer them an attractive package of benefits.
>
> (Höpfl, 1999: 231)

In other words, I am not going to follow a particular code of ethics unless I believe in its benefits. Let us assume that key people in a profession have deliberated for hours on end, have consulted with their membership, and have designed a code of ethics that (should have) a high level of legitimacy. The question is 'will I follow it?', and the answer is 'I don't know'! Like many professionals in HRD I have a strong desire to work towards a better way of doing things. I dislike hypocrisy intensely and have several times risked a great deal in support of my principles. In other words – like many others – I do reflect upon my actions and thoughts quite regularly with the intention of 'doing my best' for the human condition (which I hasten to add, includes – at least in my view – doing my best for the environment and non-humans also).

I would like to consider myself a principled person – but I am not sure I could tell you what my principles are, and as soon as I find I 'have a principle' and start to consider it, I can find a case in which the application of that principle would be counter productive – or, in my view, unethical. Where do I stand on war? I don't know. How about abortion? I don't know. What of riches? I don't know – and so on. Even hypocrisy can sometimes have its benefits – can it not? This is not because I don't know what ethics are, but because it seems wrong to make an unwavering stand on such emotionally charged and situated issues. When there are many sides to the debate how do we know which is the right one, and under what circumstances, and what are the dangers in raising that chosen side above all others?

Reification

An example of this might be seen as we all sit at the start of a participative training session, and as part of good practice negotiate out 'learning contract' and in doing so all agree to be open and honest with each other, to maintain confidentiality and to trust each other. However, do we ever actually do so, and what would be the effects on the session if we really did? In my experience each of these contractual promises is taken with a pinch of salt. We are open to a certain level, but even in sessions designed to bring feelings to the surface, true openness seems hard to achieve, and if it does arise it is often destructive to the people involved and the objectives of the session – do we not really mean 'open, but only in a nice way'. Similarly, we agree to confidentiality, but what do we mean? Nothing goes outside the room? Can we tell others what happened for us, but not talk of others – and if so, how do we talk about interactions that might have had a lasting effect upon us? When we agree to confidentiality do we not really mean that we won't talk about things that are not important to us? Trust is an even harder one – do we really mean it when we say that we will trust people that we hardly know – people who (if they are work colleagues) might have a major effect upon our careers in a few years time? Do we not promise to trust and at the same time reserve the right to only reveal certain aspects of our selves? We successfully manage to survive the training session (as in life) by the application of a certain level of hypocrisy.

In doing so, we fall into the danger of reifying each of these concepts we have agreed upon, such that they take on a life of their own – we know we are honest with each other because we have agreed this, and thus we do not need to revisit it – honesty (or whatever) sits like another piece of furniture in the room with us – one that we can ignore now that it is there. We might occasionally refer to it, and take turns to sit on it, but to what extent do we internalise it? We follow the rules (*potestas*) and promise 'honesty' but self preservation means that we introduce small print that modifies how honest we are in any particular situation – indeed, it might even be more ethical to keep silent on some points (*auctoritas*). There can be good reasons, at times, to reify the aspects of a code of ethics, but do we really want a code that allows (or even encourages) people to pay lip service to it? Does this reduce its legitimacy?

Applicability and time-dependence

Of course, codes of ethics cannot be set in stone. They need to be able to develop and change as society and the needs of a profession changes. Let me give another example. The medical profession is one that is renowned for its strong code of ethics and its focus upon ethical behaviour – to the extent that malpractice is considered to be extremely serious, and is punished. In the 1970s I was diagnosed as having a hormone imbalance, which at the time was believed to be a direct indication of a brain tumour on the pituitary gland. The particular hormone had only recently been isolated in humans and I was one of the first cases to be identified. I was interested in the field and able to talk to the consultants as a colleague and in a knowledgeable way, and so was not overtly emotional about notions of brain tumours, best methods of operating and so on. My hormone levels became extremely high and in discussing this one of the consultants told me, as a colleague, that my case was being used as a cautionary tale, as a small amount of my blood had contaminated another sample. The man, like me, was told that he had a brain tumour, though he was, unknowingly, completely clear. He was so upset that he committed suicide shortly after being wrongly diagnosed. My condition was not, in fact, due to a brain tumour and is manageable, although it will remain with me for life as does its treatment. What also remains with me is the knowledge that someone committed suicide because of me.

It seems to me that no ethical principles were broken here. It is easy to say that there should have been no possibility of contamination and the man shouldn't have been misdiagnosed – but at the time medical science was not as advanced as it is now. The consultant was doing the best he could, ethically, in telling as many people as possible of the need to be absolutely scrupulous in avoiding contamination and this has probably helped the much cleaner approach that exists nowadays. It is also easy to say that I should never have been told. I am sure he would not have told me of this if our relationship had been of a normal submissive patient/doctor variety, rather than one of colleagues, but that wasn't the sort of relationship I had or would wish to have. I like to know as much as I possibly can about my condition and to be able to make informed decisions, not act as a passive recipient. That approach carries with it the risk of unwanted knowledge and the responsibility for dealing with it. It is easy to say that it was the doctors who were responsible for the situation, not me – yet I still feel responsible, in some way, for another person's death.

Despite working under a strong code of ethics and with the best of intentions, a situation developed under which each of the parties, including the man who committed suicide and myself, could from some perspective be seen as ethically tainted. The code of medical ethics at the time did not cover this situation, and I can't see how it could be changed to do so, under the circumstances prevailing at the time, without compromising other codes – such as that of my right to information. Codes of ethics can be seen as a reflection of society's values, and thus could and should be changed to address changing societal values. Nowadays, we might view the scenario I describe above through a different lens.

Different lenses

The lens through which we view codes of ethics differs, not just with time, but also with the form of society and the nature of the individual. For example, we differ in whether we believe in the need for differentiated ethical codes. Tufts Richardson (1996) suggests that the strength of the perceived need for ethical guidelines is, itself, associated with personality type, and with form of culture – thus for some, and in some less complex societies, ethics were an unnamed part of life, and do not need to be visited or considered as a separate issue or practice. For example,

> in the Vedic period in India, harmony and integration were realized through ritual experience. The ritual act brought into being the ethical balance through one's essential participation in the order of the world. Ethics was undifferentiated from affirmation. …Native American culture likewise does not differentiate ethics from the upbringing of a traditional culture. The puberty rites include a vision quest, where the young person experiences being apart from the traditional routines long enough to find a personal, separate, vocation or orienting symbol for their life. …In societies that are pluralistic, on the other hand, puberty rites need to initiate the young person into commitments into social rules and values that in traditional societies are already internalized and secure. The need for ethics per se therefore tends to evolve in diverse and pluralistic societies, where the individual knows there is more than one truth and multiple ways to live rightly.
>
> (Tufts Richardson, 1996: 33–4)

Thus Tufts Richardson argues that the need for explicated ethics tends to evolve in diverse and pluralistic societies, where there are multiple ways to live rightly. Thus, from the standpoint of those who do not see society as pluralistic, the collective establishment of codes of ethics, independent from the society's normal mores, is irrelevant or unnecessary. The development of a code of ethics, therefore, is more relevant to those who are faced with issues of diversity and plurality, as in current complex western society. Within western society, different people follow different spiritual paths, and seek different end-points to their spiritual journey, and these paths are associated with different ethical foci. It follows from this that the code of ethics that I might develop will be different in focus to one developed by another person – though of course, the closer we are in our world view and in our agreement of what is good and evil, and what should be created for the future, the closer our codes might be. Having said that, the HR professional remains poised on the interface between a care for people and profit. A profession, being a fairly homogenous grouping that does not have to make the day to day decisions of its members can suffer from groupthink when developing a code of ethics, and thus risks not addressing individual differences in ethical aspiration and values. The notion of individual difference in the focus of ethicality raises another concern.

Role of the individual and emotion

I have already mentioned problems of reification, through which the very existence of the code can mean that lip service is paid to it such that the import of the code is ignored – in other words, the code can become a 'law' which is followed to the letter, but not in spirit. This is particularly the case in those codes which are punitive, and can thus force people to comply, such as that of the Medical Profession, and might be seen to occur less in others that are more aspirational, such as that of ASTD. My concern, however, has a slightly different focus. Much of the time, as we go about our daily business, we encounter situations which feel as if they require some ethical deliberation, yet which require an immediate response or for which there are no codes to guide us.

An example of this can be seen in some team development/conflict resolution work I was doing with a senior manager (SM) and his close team from a multinational organisation. The team had been having a lot of problems working together, which is why I became involved. The cats-cradle of issues gradually started to untangle and a level of openness started to emerge. As it did so, the atmosphere became tenser and a high level of emotion was clearly just below the surface. In facilitating this, I was making sure everyone had their say and was truly 'listened to' rather than just 'heard'; I was trying to maintain a calm and trustable persona whilst privately being worried about the potentially destructive nature of where we were going. Everyone was on the edge of their seats and fully and deeply engaged, when one member of the team finally made some very personal comments about the SM's leadership style.

The room went silent and I knew that I had to intervene within the next second or so, and that the nature of my intervention would be critical. It seemed to me that I could work with the emotional charge to bring the issue to a head, or take a safer route and encourage him to rationalise the feedback by asking him what he *thought* about it. I quietly said 'How do you feel about that?'. He was silent for a second and then started crying. Years of tension of caring deeply for his team, and not being able to balance that with the harsh judgements demanded of senior management, and of not wanting to delegate for fear of overloading them tumbled out. His team were incredibly supportive, both about the problems he faced and of his emotion, pointing out that they much preferred him as a vulnerable 'real person', than the remote 'senior manager' persona he had adopted as a safety-blanket. The whole process took several days, and on the night of the turning point I did a lot of soul searching, wondering what the next day would bring. As it was, people came together the following day in a much more positive mood and with a real impetus to build upon what had happened. Obviously this was not the only issue, but many of the more minor issues resolved themselves as the whole team started to work together in a different way. Feedback I got, both at the time and several years later, suggested that my risk in focusing on feelings in that way had been well worth it for all involved – but what a risk!

My soul searching revolved around questioning why I had acted as I did, and what the consequences of that, and acting differently, might be. In encouraging (forcing?) a senior manager in a 'hard' industry to reveal his weaknesses to his team had I in effect destroyed him and his career? What sort of trauma had I put him through?

What about his team? Had it completely shattered any chance of them working together? What would be the effects on each of them? What if I had played it safe and asked him what he thought of the comment rather than what he felt – would the same result have been achieved without the emotional breakthrough? I suspect not, in which case we would have ended up with yet more 'talking round the houses', and short-term satisfaction of the team having talked, but no long-term development. Would it have been ethical for me to have 'chickened-out', and accepted payment for a half-job knowing that I had not done the best I could? What of the power involved? Was it right that one person should be placed in, or accept, such a position of trust that others could be severely emotionally shaken by their actions? Was I really being trusted to keep people safe whilst being employed and therefore trusted to resolve the conflict? And so on.

More generally, the question that remains with me is 'Where does the responsibility lie for managing people's emotions in a situation like this?' with the correlate 'Is there any way that a code of ethics that covered responsibility for emotion could have helped?'. Given the power that is wielded by the trainer/developer in such situations, it certainly feels as if there is a need for some sort of code of ethics to cover it, but is it possible? Emotions arise quickly and can be focused by a word or a gesture – both the emotion and the trigger are often subconscious, unknown to the actors, until they burst upon the scene. They can't easily be designed or regulated. They require immediate response that doesn't allow for deliberation about the ethics involved. The outcome is unknown, such that we can only guess whether the response might help or harm – and, of course, notions of help and harm are relative to the people and situations involved. We can't develop guidelines from one situation about what might be helpful in another.

Similar examples can be found in online conversations, where it is harder to gauge the other person's reaction to our words without body language to help us. In theory, when online we have more time to contemplate our reply, but in practice, particularly if the topic is emotional, we often reply immediately with whatever words we have available – yet those words when read by another or by ourselves at a later date, become amplified and strengthened, just because they are written down and can be mulled over, such that they have greater power than was intended at the time.

On a daily basis we come across complex situated events such as this in which we have to act – in that doing nothing can have as powerful effect as doing something, so even a non-response counts as an act. We might like to think that we are guided by codes of ethics and our own principles, but, in reality, our actions or inactions are down to ourselves as individuals. We might seek to justify them in retrospect by reference to wider generally agreed or upheld ethical considerations, but at the time of decision-making and acting we have to rely on our own patterns of behaviour and interpretation of the situation. Given time, we might turn to an ethics decision-making scheme or process that helps us to make the 'right' decision, but that time does not always exist. Furthermore, in many instances, we cannot make an objective choice, as the consequences of our 'choice' only become apparent once the choice is made, and we have no way of knowing what would have really happened (as opposed to our replayed possible scenarios) if we had acted differently.

In other words, I am suggesting that it is the moral authority or *auctoritas* that is brought to bear in any given situation. This might or might not be in accordance with or supported by *potestas* (in this case, the overarching and agreed code of ethics). To break this down further, we can make a distinction between the spirit and the letter of the law. In acting with moral authority it might be that we come across situations which are, at the least, ambiguous, or even in which we find that we have to break the letter of the law if we wish to preserve its spirit. We cannot assume a close knit and comfy fit between a code of ethics and the process of acting in an ethical manner. At times we have to assert our personal codes of ethics, and hope that by doing so we contribute to a strengthening, or re-examination of the collective code of the profession or organisation we are engaged in.

In conclusion

We need codes of ethics – individually as part of our spiritual journeys, and collectively, in order to guide our development and help an ethical future emerge – but we also need to be aware of the difficulties and pitfalls to avoid the False God of reification, and to be aware that the current drive towards the establishment of such codes is, itself, culturally bound and ethically problematic. Furthermore, we need to be aware that the role of *auctoritas* is, at times, to challenge *potestas* and a code of ethics is only as good as the moral authority that underlies it. In establishing professional or organisational codes of ethics we need to incorporate elements of individual difference and flexibility – such that the codes can develop as ethical practice develops, thereby establishing inclusivity and so minimising the need for whistle-blowers, and (as Hatcher, 2002 points out) thereby enhancing performance and productivity.

Acknowledgement

This chapter is based upon a paper (Lee 2003) and I would like to thank Tim Hatcher for his helpful comments on that paper.

References

Dalla Costa, J. (1998) *The Ethical Imperative: Why Moral Leadership is Good Business*, Reading, MA: Perseus Books.

Estes, R. (1996) *The Tyranny of the Bottom Line: Why Corporations Make Good People Do Bad Things*, San Francisco, CA: Berrett-Koehler.

Gilley, J.W., Quatro, S.A., Hoekstra, E., Whittle, D.D. and Maycunich, A. (2001) *The Manager as Change Agent*, Cambridge, MA: Perseus Publishing.

Hatcher, T. (1993) 'Improving ethical performance: the personal ethics process', *Performance and Instruction*, 32: 21–8.

Hatcher, T. (2002) *Ethics and HRD: A New Approach to Leading Responsible Organisations*, Cambridge, MA: Perseus Publishing.

Hatcher, T. and Lee, M. (2003) 'HRD and the democratic ideal: the conflict of democratic values in undemocratic work systems', in J.Winterton (ed.) *Proceedings of 3rd European HRD Conference*, Toulouse.

Höpfl, H. (1999) 'Power, authority and legitimacy', *Human Resource Development International*, 2, 3: 217–35.

Hultman, K. and Gellerman, B. (2002) *Balancing Individual and Organisational Values*, San Francisco, CA: Jossey-Bass.

Korten, D.C. (1995) *When Corporations Rule the World*, San Francisco, CA: Berrett-Koehler.

Lee, M.M. (2002) 'Who am I?: self development in organisations', in Michael Pearn (ed.) *Individual Differences and Development in Organisations*, Chichester: J Wiley & Sons Ltd, 17–34.

Lee, M. (2003) 'On codes of ethics, the individual and performance', *Performance Improvement Quarterly*, 16, 2: 72–89.

Rokeach, M. (1973) *The Nature of Human Values*, New York: Free Press.

Stead, R. and Stead, J.G. (1996) *Management for a Small Planet*, 2nd edn, Thousand Oaks, CA: Sage.

Tufts Richardson, P. (1996) *Four Spiritualities: Expressions of Self, Expressions of Spirit*, Palo Alto, CA: Davies-Black Publishing.

Part II

Theoretical debates

10 Good order

On the administration of goodness

Heather Höpfl

Eastern Academy of Management, San Jose, Costa Rica 2001

There were several practitioner speakers but the most impressive was the young man from a large well-known multinational. He was very good. He looked good. His talk was persuasive and his overhead transparencies colour co-ordinated with his tie. He was well groomed with a Kurt Russell haircut and an all-American smile. He demonstrated by reference to slide after slide that his company was doing well in Costa Rica. He showed us targets and how the company had exceeded them. He told us his corporation was good for Costa Rica and then showed us slide after slide to demonstrate how and why. His company was making things better for the local people. He was an emissary for good. He brought a commitment to corporate values.

He was very good at all this and he exuded charm, enthusiasm and professionalism. He was a real star. He wasn't only good, he was exemplary and outshone his fellow speakers. It was all so good, so wholesome, so well co-ordinated. It made you wonder where they produced such superb corporate models or perhaps I should say where they *reproduced* such accomplished missionaries.

A good set of results

In organisational terms, the strategic direction of the organisation involves the construction of the organisation as a purposive entity with a trajectory towards a desired future. Consequently, organisational strategy as an indicator of movement towards this future is about the way in which such a desired state can be reached, targets set and achievements measured. In such movement towards better and better performance, it is inevitable that the purposive nature of the action takes precedence over the individual in the service of (Latin, ad-ministrare, to serve) desired results. The organisation constructs itself in textual and representational terms in relation to such desires. These representations range from the explicit use of rhetoric in marketing its products and images to the more subtle construction of the organisation as a fictive entity in the construction of statements, strategies and structures, and function to regulate the organisation through definition (Latin, de-finire, to finish, to finalise). The fundamental characteristic of the organisation as a purposive entity is its directedness and, clearly, there is a relationship between the direction as orientation, direction as command of the organisation and the rhetorical trajectory. In a specific sense, the organisation as a rhetorical entity *wants something* of the employee, of the customer, the competitor, the supplier and the general public and, therefore, what is not the organisation is always defined as deficient in relation to it – not as good. Therefore, representations of the organisation – images and texts – need to be received as convincing by its various audiences. For example, recent years have seen the elaboration of the rhetoric directed towards employees in the pursuit of greater commitment, improved performance, invocations to quality and in the construction of ornate narratives of organisational performances, in exhortations towards greater goodness. However, in such representations, the organisation is an abstract entity removed from the activities of the physical bodies of which it is made up. Without a body, the pain of labour itself becomes an abstraction so that embodied pain is exiled from the organisation as a site of production. Such an elaborate vision of goodness, truth and beauty cannot admit the possibility of what counter definition must construe as ugliness and dissent. Consequently, it is the abstract 'good' which is venerated and administered and not the labouring bodies which are in need of ministry.

Administration and ministration

The notion of a discourse of maternity subverts the dominant social discourse to challenge order, rationality and patriarchal regulation. What this contributes to organisational theory is the capacity to make transparent the effects of the production of meaning, to render explicit the patriarchal quest of the organisation, to make problematic the notion of trajectory, strategy and purpose and to question 'ordinary' notions of the good. Therefore, by presenting the organisation as maternal, this chapter seeks to offend conventional definitions of the goods of organisation in order to allow the mother/motherhood/maternal body to enter. Thus, whereas the text of the organisation is about regulation and representation, of rational argument, perfect and perfectible relationships and rhetorical trajectory, the embodied subject speaks of division, separation, rupture, tearing, blood and the pain of labour. So good becomes defined in terms of a recursive seduction to the notion of order and what is not good, the physical, becomes the province of hysteria. Consequently, despite management desires to demonstrate success and achievement by recourse to metrics, comparatives, benchmarks and results, organisations are more of metaphysics than of matter.

One might provocatively characterise this relationship in terms of the ways in which organisations as purposive and rhetorical entities define themselves in counter-distinction to notions of the feminine and madness. Lacoue-Labarthe (1989: 129) speaks of the major threats to representation as being women and madness and, in part, this is because in the hystera (Gk. *womb*) and the psycho*logical* condition of hysteria (as a disturbance of the nervous system thought to be brought about by uterine dysfunction) there is a common concern with the function of reproduction – a contest between representation and definitions of reproduction, between reason and body. In the organisational world, disorder cannot be badness or madness because the logic of organisation assumes that these conditions can be corrected by reason. In this sense, redemption and cure requires submission to *psychology* (regulation of the psyche by the logos). If that which is defined as deficient, the employee, the organisational member, will only submit to superior logic s/he will *realise* the extent of his/her disorder. S/he can be turned around (*converted*) and induced to 'make a clean break between fantasies and reality' (Irigaray, 1985: 273). S/he can be converted by and conformed to psychology: 'the wisdom of the master. And of mastery' (Irigaray, 1985: 274). When organisations exhort their employees to specific standards of performance, behaviour, conformity and so on, they hold up a mirror to the deficient condition of their members and confronts them with 'reality'. However, this is a reality which kills. The physical is destroyed by the reflection and as mere reflection, is rendered inanimate. All that is now permitted to be reflected back is the organisation's own construction, a sublime illusion, and so what the organisation member can reflect back to him/herself is mortification of the body. If the organisation can convert its members to the power of the logos, it is able to demonstrate control over hysteria and disorder and, by implication, over the physical and embodied reproduction. So defined, organisational members are infinitely reproducible and, reproduced, assured that goodness and an absence of madness are synonymous with order and sanity. However, *in order* to sustain this logic, the focus must remain on the organisational speculum so that a consistent reflection is maintained. The organisational member must be conformed to the rule of the logos and possessed by it, must become the property of that logos in the sense that as *property*, the member maintains what is *proper* to that construction. So organisations seek to *cure* their members of their disordered otherness and to offer alternative and convincing definitions of reality. All this in the service of good order.

The psychology of goodness

In other words, the (hysterical) disordered state must be subjected to regulation by psycho-*logy* – regulation by (logical) discourse. Organisations, thus, construct themselves as means of salvation, as bulwarks against destruction and danger. So strong is the conviction that the right path of the organisation leads to good that the organisation believes it can serve to restore a *proper* way of *seeing* things. However, if this cannot be achieved there is no option, the organisational member must conform to propriety or be exiled from it. Mortified in the flesh and now annihilated even as mere reflection, a lack of propriety cannot be admitted. If the organisational member cannot be cured or refuses to be conformed, this is a considerable challenge to the trajectory of the organisation and so the masculine identity of the organisation *hangs in the balance*. The improper must be eradicated to sustain the illusion of purpose, to preserve good order and *for the good of the organisation*.

So it seems, organisations have a purposive commitment to the pursuit of some notion of good, circumscribed and defined, logical and metrical. Jung has argued that the pursuit of 'sterile perfection' (Dourley, 1990: 51) is one of the defining characteristics of patriarchal consciousness. Order and rationality function to exclude the physical. Whitmont puts forward the view that the *control* of passions and physical needs traditionally have been valorised because they idealise maleness (Whitmont, 1991: 243) and gives emphasis to the '*merely* rational' (Whitmont, 1991: 243).

Organisations then, as expressions of collective expectations, render physicality 'dirty' corrupting and, by implication, not good. Indeed, the corollary of this emphasis on rationality is a distrust of natural affections and the loss of compassion (Whitmont, 1991: 245). Without compassion, the organisation cannot *admit* the suffering that is caused by the pursuit of rationality. Goodness, it seems, is self-referential and abstract.

Compassion

Without compassion, the paternal discourse of organisation, dominated by the rationality and the rejection of dependency, reduces the notion of the maternal to nurturing, domestic and servicing functions. For an organisation the loss of the maternal leaves the questing behaviour of organisations as unrelieved rationality and power motivation. Whitmont puts forward the view that historically it has been fear of the feminine, [as disorder or hysteria], which has led to the degradation of women but he also goes on to say that there is a contemporary problem of masculinisation. This he argues has resulted in abstract dogmatic mental attitudes and a sterile and over-rationalistic social world (Whitmont, 1991: 200). It is precisely in this excessive rationality and the preoccupation with measurement that embraces goodness in order to exclude it. Consequently, organisations are given to producing totalising discourses which *seek to capture* all aspects of organisational life. These are totalising if only to provide comfort from the physicality which they lack. What this means is that, reduced to discourse, organisation construct themselves without re-membering the body. Therefore, the discourse of the organisation can never offer the prospect of completion, of embodied subjectivity. Such constructions seek to exclude and, more particularly, they seek to exclude the possibility of the maternal. This is because the maternal threatens to disrupt the discipline and sterility of the paternal logos. The maternal poses a threat to the logic of the self-serving and totalising narratives of the organisation.

At a simplistic level, this is one reason why organisations, as collective expressions of one-dimensional patriarchy, have been keen to turn women into homologues of men – a task greatly assisted by the equity feminists. However, they have also sought to turn men into ciphers of masculinity through the relentless pursuit of perfectionism and ratio-nality. By containing the feminine within the purposive logic of futurity, organisations as directive entities have sought to defend themselves against the threat posed by their very presence, ambivalence and physicality. Yet, the result of all this purposive striving and collective questing is, nonetheless, an inevitable sterility. This is because the patri-archal logos substitutes words, exhortations and their reproduction as text for bodies, physicality and embodied reproduction. In privileging constructions over physicality, the organisation comes to reproduce itself as text and understand itself in metaphysical terms as the product of its own reproduction. Within this logic, the organisation seeks to reassure itself of its own beneficence: the good is whatever the organisation says it is.

Reproducing good

As part of the obsession with definition, organisations have been fanatical about metrics and monitoring. Elsewhere, I have examined the etymology and significance of the matrix as an organ and instrument of reproduction (Höpfl, 2000a,b, 2002) and argued that embodied reproduction is replaced by the reproduction of text. The matrix is regulated so that its cells show location and defining characteristics on the basis of power relations. This power derives from the ability to define, to authorise and regulate the site of production. Understood in this way, the matrix defines what the organisation regards as good and what is worthy of reproduction. In the substitution of words for the natural products of the embodied matrix, reproduction of homologues is guaranteed. Men and women in the service of the organisation, reproduce themselves in relation to what is defined as good and, therefore, produce only sons.

The appropriated matrix deals on the level of the abstract alone. Despite the totalising rhetoric which it produces, it is not sustainable and therefore seeks to construct for itself icons of what it lacks. For the paternal matrix, perfection comes from striving. Consequently, the matrix gives birth into a world of obsessive reproduction and insatiable desire. Paternal reproduction arises from the sense of lack that only the acknowledgement of the maternal matrix could satisfy. However, so configured, the paternal matrix can only construct for itself representations of the things it lacks. Consequently, care, creativity, quality, ethics, emotions and so on become the abstract products of the sterile matrix – acknowledged to be good but divorced from goodness.

No good at all

In this context, it is not surprising that organisations function at variance to the bodies who work in and for them. Consequently, people in organisations are always struggling with issues that arise from the substitution of textual matrices for physical ones. They are rendered abstract by loss of contact with their physicality as organisations reduce them to categories and metrics. But, from the point of view of the maternal, the position is more serious. In the relentless pursuit of future states, organisations as purposive entities seek to construct for themselves the empty emblems of the object of the quest: high quality standards, improved performance, an ethical position, dignity at work, care for staff and so on. In part, this is because the purposiveness of organisations is without end – indeed, *can* never end – and, therefore, the notion of any real completion is antithetical to the idea of trajectory. Strategy gives birth to more strategy, rhetoric to more rhetoric and text to more text and so on. The good is never attained. The construction of goodness as abstract organisational categories is intended to console in the absence of the hope of restoration. Moreover, the vicarious and representational has more seductive power than the physical and disordered other. These emblems function as an anamnesis to register the loss as representation. For this reason alone, the emblem of loss is melancholic and pervades the organisation with melancholy. It cannot offer consolation because ironically it can only recall that there is a loss. So, the emblem of the lost object provides a false reassurance that completion itself can arise from a construction. So, when an organisation lays claim to goodness, it constructs a notion of goodness which serves its strategic ends.

The argument presented here makes the case for a greater understanding of the way in which there is an organisational angst about the feminine as dissident, disorderly and disjunctive. That the feminine is not so easily seduced into the illusions of future satisfactions and abstract relations causes a number of tensions and oscillations. These occur between the purposive nature of organisational trajectory and progress into the future and the ambivalence of compassionate members of organisations as dissident. The paradox at the root of this argument is one of power. Those who are not easily seduced by corporate promises, by subjugation to futurity and by notions of perfectibility are dangerous and disordered. Such positions are equated with the feminine as hysterical and needing to be cured by submission to logic and good order. Where organisational members do not accept these definitions or merely pay lip-service to them, the extent of their participation is controlled and regulated. These positions cannot easily be reconciled because they pose the physical against the metaphysical and in doing so implicitly challenge the organisation's construction of good. Yet ambivalence and dissidence have important political significance for changing the nature of work.

In seeking to construct themselves both as sublime manifestations of male desire and as unattainable ideals, organisations lay themselves open to inevitable failure. The therapeutic project of *saving* the organisation via the rule of logic, via insistent authority, and via psychology, is a process of mortification. Moreover, it is founded on a masculine sublime fabricated to reflect the male ego – narcissistic and inevitably melancholic. The feminine has no place, no reflection, no role in this construction other than to the extent that, in an entirely selective way, it serves as an object within the construction. In this construction, the feminine is hysterical and has to be kept out because, by posing a threat to its mere representational form [to mimesis], it threatens good order. Only if the feminine is prepared to submit itself to the symbol of the masculine construction (the erection) can it even enter into reflection. However, even then it must show a *proper* reflection *appropriate* to its status as a *property* of that construction. Where the feminine lacks *propriety* it is reduced to nothing. The goodness of the organisation is textual and representational. It has nothing to do with compassion and virtue. These are the defences which protect psychology as regulation by the logos from failure and subversion. It is a phallocentric psychology which credits itself with initiative, achievement and purpose and which defends its position by either relegation or cancellation. Clearly, part of this defence rests on power over the control of reflection, theorisation and discourse, and on the control of categories and their meanings.

The heroic good

Organisations want to create a heroic notion of the good, a confident and bold representation of the future – and this is inevitably a masculine construction. The feminine is required to remain silent or to present itself according to its representation as viewed through the male gaze – to produce itself in a way which ensures its own annihilation. What then does the idea of the maternal contribute to an understanding of goodness and organisations? In part, it is to do with borders and their demarcation, exile and homelessness, strangeness, estrangement, the boundary of the body, sociality and love; it concerns ethics and motherhood. These are complex issues which deserve further elaboration. Certainly, the writings of Julia Kristeva are a good place to start (Höpfl, 2000a). Maternity, motherhood and the maternal body play a significant part in the dynamics of her psychoanalytical writing.

Kristeva sees the client–patient relationship as rooted in love and characterised by, what she terms, 'herethics of love' (Kristeva, 1987: 263) – an implicit ethical practice. These are writings from exile and according to Docherty (1996) there is considerable potential in this position. He argues that 'the postmodern narrative of characterisation…eradicates the distinction between the ethical and the political' (Docherty, 1996: 66) because it draws the reader into 'disposition' [*sic*], in other words, it puts the reader into a suitable place, it inclines the reader, or to use the Greek word for this disposition, *ethos*, it establishes the place of the ethical by involving the reader in the search for '*the good*' so, Docherty argues, re-establishing the place of the political. Thus, for Docherty, 'to read postmodern characterisation is to reintroduce the possibility of politics, and importantly of a genuinely historical political change, into the act of reading' (Docherty, 1996: 66, 67).

Writing from exile

Postmodern characterisation then involves 'first, the confusion of the ontological status of the character with that of the reader; second, the decentring of the reader's consciousness, such that she or he is, like the character, endlessly displaced and "differing"; and, third, the political and ethical implications of this "seeming otherwise," shifting from appearance to different appearance in the disappearance of a totalized selfhood' (Docherty, 1996: 67). This has political consequence, that is, that there is 'a marginalization of the reader from a centralized or totalized narrative of selfhood' which renders 'the reading subject-in-process as the figure of the dissident' (Docherty, 1996: 67). To support this view Docherty refers to Kristeva's identification of the experimental writer and, as Docherty says, '*crucially*, women' as types of dissident. So, the argument runs, what these two 'share is the impetus towards marginalization and indefinition; they are in a condition of "exile" from a centred identity of meaning and its claims to a totalized Law or Truth' and, further, he adds that exile itself is a form of dissidence 'since it involves the marginalization or decentring of the self from all positions of totalized or systematic Law (such as imperialist nation, patriarchal family, monotheistic language)'. Hence, Docherty puts forward the proposition that postmodern characterisation, 'construed as writing in and from exile, serves to construct the possibility, for perhaps the first time, of elaborating the paradigmatic reader of these new novels as feminized' (Docherty, 1996: 68) 'always dispositioned towards otherness, alterity'. Hence, postmodern characterisation permits the ethics of alterity and the opportunity to explore what it means 'to speak from the political disposition of the Other'. Docherty's view of postmodern writing raises some important issues not least the problem of authorship and authority (Höpfl, 2003) but it does make an important contribution to an appreciation of the role of exile and estrangement. Here is the possibility of the political and a challenge to grand notions of goodness. Here is the possibility of the ethics of the interpersonal, the encounter with otherness, the reconciliation of logos and physis. The idea of men accepting and valuing their feminine qualities would not be considered strange within a community of nurturing, which had a genuine concern for the other, which adopted an embodied notion of the good. However, there are broader issues here which require careful analysis.

Eagleton argues that against the 'ideal of compassionate community, of altruism and natural affection...(there is) a threat to rationalism' and says that 'the political consequences of this are ambivalent' (Eagleton, 1990: 60). On the other hand, for the feminine, this site of ambivalence might be the very starting point of a political praxis within the discourse of maternity. And whereas Eagleton warns against 'a fantasy of mother and father in one, of love and law commingled' (Eagleton, 1990: 263) it is perhaps this very conciliation which might bring the pursuit of ends and goodness together (see also Whitmont, 1983). In other words, to redefine the good. However, a serious caution must remain and that is one put forward by Baudrillard in his critique of rationality in which he argues that the reduction of male and female to categories has produced an artificial distinction which objectifies the feminine. By this line of argument, the feminine is now constructed as a category of the masculine and, by implication, the power of the feminine to manifest itself in ambivalence is lost. In other words, Baudrillard sees femin-*ism*, per se, as ensnared within the construction of a phallic order (Baudrillard, 1990). This is a position with which Kristeva is familiar (Kristeva, 1984). As her biographer Toril Moi puts it, 'The problem is that as soon as the insurgent "substance" speaks, it is necessarily caught up in the kind of discourse *allowed by* and *submitted to* by the Law' (Moi, 1986: 10). The desire to confront this problem of inevitable capture is fundamental to Kristeva's work and yet she acknowledges that to attempt to use language against itself is to create an untenable position – a position which is all too familiar to women writers when they attempt to deviate from the notion of mastery and this piece of writing is itself not excluded from this judgement. Writing is inevitably about coming up with the goods and in academic life this is about producing good textual sons.

So after all, this chapter is about *good* practice, about behaviour, gesture, ways of interacting, about the micro-politics of organising. It is not about abstract goodness and unattainable futures. These belong to the province of insatiable organisation. Here is simply the hope of a compassionate community and an invocation to the practice of goodness.

References

Baudrillard, J. (1990) *Seduction*, London: Macmillan.

Docherty, T. (1996) *Alterities*, Oxford: Clarendon Press.

Dourley, J.P. (1990) *The Goddess, Mother of the Trinity*, Lewiston: The Edwin Mellen Press.

Eagleton, T. (1990) The *Ideology of the Aesthetic*, Oxford: Blackwell.

Höpfl, H. (2000a) 'The suffering mother and the miserable son, organising women and organising women's writing', *Gender, Work and Organization*, 7, 2: 98–106.

Höpfl, H. (2000b) 'On being moved', *Studies in Cultures, Organisations and Societies*, 6, 1: 15–25.

Höpfl, H. (2002) 'Corporate strategy and the quest for the primal mother', *Human Resource Development International*, January, 11–22.

Höpfl, H. (2003) 'The body of the text and the ordinary narratives of organisation', in B. Czarniawska and P. Gagliardi (eds) *Narratives We Organise By*, Amsterdam: John Benjamins.

Irigaray, L. (1985) *Speculum of the Other Woman*, (trans.) G. Gill, Ithaca, NY: Cornell University Press.

Kristeva, J. (1984) *Desire in Language: A Semiotic Approach to Literature and Art*, (trans.) T.S. Gora, A. Jardine and L. Roudiez, Oxford: Basil Blackwell.

Kristeva, J. (1987) *Tales of Love*, (trans.) L. Roudiez, New York: Columbia University Press.

Lacoue-Labarthe (1989) *Typography*, Stanford, CA: Stanford University Press.

Moi, T. (ed.) (1986) *The Kristeva Reader*, Oxford: Blackwell.

Whitmont, E.C. (1983) *Return of the Goddess*, London: Routledge and Kegan Paul.

Whitmont, E.C. (1991) *The Symbolic Quest, Basic Concepts of Analytical Psychology*, Princeton, NJ: Princeton University Press.

11 Deconstructing the human in Human Resource Development

Christina Hughes

Introduction

As an undergraduate in the early 1980s I was asked to imagine that God was female. This might now appear a rather passé idea given contemporary feminist knowledge of the linguistic primacy of the masculine. Once nouns such as chairman and policeman were presented as the grammatically acceptable forms of gender neutrality. Today concerns over political correctness have taught us to hear the male in those 'man' suffixes. However, for a working class woman, who a few short months previously had been working as a secretary and who had managed to obtain a place at university through part-time study, the idea of God as female was tantalising. It was, as you might understand, a moment that Mezirow (1978) describes as perspective transformation. Knowledge that God might be female was not simply added to my already growing stock of feminist knowledge. It contributed to transforming the way I experienced the world.

This aspect of my biography, and my continuing interest in exploring new ways of thinking and seeing, brings me to the concerns of this chapter. It could be thought that, as a feminist, I would be pleased to see that the name given to the field of study that is concerned with individual and organisational learning and development is configured in the gender neutrality of the term 'human resource development'. This might even be viewed as a feminist victory. The term 'human' has become the gender neutral arbiter of female/male interests and has replaced what we now know is the sexist terminology of he/man language. It can certainly be argued that naming a field of knowledge 'human resource development' is preferable to previous terminology such as manpower planning. It is also the case that, in contrast to terms such as 'mankind', the use of 'human', as in phrases such as 'human kind' or 'human race', take us further, linguistically, towards an egalitarian world. However, rather than argue that the 'human' in human resource development (HRD) stands in for both female and male interests, I shall suggest that it continues to privilege the masculine subject. Indeed, my purpose in this chapter is to illustrate how the male[1] continues to lurk within the seeming gender neutrality of terms such as 'human'.

To achieve my purpose, I shall draw on contemporary feminist theorising that is concerned with the linkages of language to identity and power. Since my student days in the 1980s, feminist interest in language has gone beyond drawing attention to the dominant masculine in common nouns. It has demonstrated the far reaching associations between masculine terminology and the most status rich or privileged ideas in our society. It has also reversed the common assumption that language simply describes an already formed world by illustrating how language actually shapes our view of that world and, importantly, our view of our self. For example, feminist post-structuralist analysis indicates how language is organised in terms of hierarchically organised pairs with the male in the ascendant position. Simple examples of this would be male/female, culture/nature, reason/emotion, mind/body and public/private. Nevertheless, as Plumwood (1993) indicates, this hierarchisation is not confined to these simple binaries. Using the concept of dualism, Plumwood demonstrates how language contains networks of strongly linked, contiguous webs of meaning. This means that we need to trace how meanings extend beyond binary pairs and consider how terms are connected in rhyzomatic ways to one another. One way of doing this is to trace the linkages between the first named object in a binary pair with the first named object in other pairs. Men, for example, are noted for their powers of reason whereas, stereotypically, women are mostly associated with being emotional. The public world appears to be the natural (*sic*) world of men whereas the private realm of the family is seen as the natural (*sic*) domain for women. Given the hierarchical nature of these ideas, it comes as no surprise that, generally, we believe that it is better to act out of reason than to be subject to the whims of emotion. We also receive far more material rewards, and greater status, for the work we do in the public spheres of life than the unpaid work of family. In so doing, we are encouraged to revere, and we also internalise as the normative standard, masculine ways of being in the world.

This point is very important when we turn to what it means to be 'human'. What are the webs of meaning that are associated with humanity? Plumwood's (1993: 46) analysis of dualism highlights how 'the concepts of humanity, rationality and masculinity form strongly linked and contiguous parts of this web'. As Hekman (1999: 85) notes, the consequence of this is that rationality, humanity and masculinity constitute 'the ideal type that forms the central core of modern social and political theory'. As I shall now explore in more detail, the field of HRD is no exception. Here, the major theories and practices of HRD are based on a humanist personhood that privileges the masculine, self-directed, autonomous, choosing subject. I begin by outlining this concept of the person in humanist discourses and then proceed to detail the Enlightenment and Cartesian heritage of such ideas. This is compared to a post-structuralist analysis. Post-structuralism illustrates how some subject positions, such as the autonomous 'I' of the self-directed, choosing subject of humanism, are only fully open to some members of society. The problem for women, who actually form the majority of employees and students in the human resource field, is that the constructions of these masculine subject positions are not so available to us. We might strive to act in ways prescribed in classic HRD texts but this can leave us either with a sense of discomfort or the feeling that there are equally valuable ways of acting and organising that are not being recognised. What are the practical and political options we have available to us to enable us to challenge the resultant sense of inferiorisation that is central to how these aspects of dualism work? This is my concern in the final part of this chapter.

The masculinity of HRD: the Cartesian heritage

I have commented that there is a contiguous web of meaning that associates the term humanity with masculinity and rationality. One of my purposes here is to outline the research that seeks to explain how this situation has arisen. However, before I do so, I want to draw attention to how particular ideas about rationality are central to the field of HRD. Garrick (1998: 152) comments that HRD discourses are 'unashamedly linked to market economics'. This is perhaps best summed up in the phrase 'Your Employees Are Your Best Economic Advantage'. The main imperative for the human resource developer, therefore, is to ensure that the productive capabilities of employees are enhanced and developed. This is achieved, of course, through encouraging employee learning and training, through organisational development and learning and by linking organisational strategies to HRD policies and practices. This means that being a developer of the human capital that is necessary for this is a major role for a HRD specialist (Watkins, 1991).

Human capital theory is commonly related to the extent to which education and training constitute investments in individuals that give rise to increased productivity or an increased economic yield. This relationship is measured through national economic returns to education in terms of Gross Domestic Product or the impact of training on company profits. Importantly, for the discussion here, there is a very particular conception of the individual at the heart of human capital theories. Specifically, the individual is perceived to be 'utility maximising' and, as the terminology implies, to act rationally in their choices is to act in one's own self-interest. This rational choice theory is defined as 'the idea that all action is fundamentally "rational" in character and that people calculate the likely costs and benefits of any action before deciding what to do' (Scott, 2000: 126). Within rational choice theory, therefore, the individual is conceptualised as primarily motivated by the rewards and costs of their actions and the likely profit they can make (Scott, 2000). Such explanations put forward the idea (predominant in our society) that to be a rational person one acts in a dispassionate and objective way. Here, there is no room for emotions and feelings but for a cool analysis of the 'facts'. When there is a choice to make, one simply makes a list of options and their associated advantages and disadvantages and, coolly and calmly, makes the 'right' choice.

In terms of HRD, we can see that such a theory encourages us to believe that rational individuals will invest in their own education and training and will take opportunities for development offered to them by their organisations when they arise. When employees refuse or are unable to take such opportunities we might find other 'rational' explanations for their behaviour. For example, human capital theories also use choice explanations to account for the levels of investment women make in education and training. Here it is suggested that because young women know that as adults they will be primary carers of their families they make rational choices not to invest in initial education and training. More recently, women's increasing participation in paid labour and their higher investments in education have produced alternative 'choice' explanations. In relation to the high proportion of women in part-time paid employment, for example, human capital theorists argue that women choose employment that requires less energy and time because this compensates for the greater time they will have to spend on domestic work. Such a view confirms the idea that, generally, women are not committed to their careers or are not interested in furthering their job prospects through education and learning opportunities. Such a theory, therefore, upholds ideas that women put family and domestic life before employment. This in turn maintains, as inalienable, the belief that family care is, really, women's work.

Within humanist theorising, therefore, strong connections are made between the ways that individuals make choices and our assumptions about them as people. Making choices in the prescribed rationality of weighing up the options and making an informed choice is seen to confirm that the individual is a coherent, orderly, rational and, indeed, sane person. Thus, in today's flexible and competitive employment markets, it is patently rational, in this economic sense of rationality, to enhance one's employability by assessing where skills and knowledges will be needed, exploring the available options, and making suitable choices to invest in these areas through further education and training. Not to make choices in this way is to be regarded as faulty or lacking in this respect. Those employees who do not take these opportunities, mainly working class women and men, older people and part-time workers, appear foolish or foolhardy because their lack of action is not in their self-interest. They are certainly not the 'utility maximising' individuals of rational choice theory.

We can see, therefore, that central to one of the major theoretical strands of HRD[2] is the idea of the person as a freely acting agent who, consciously and deliberately, is able to make choices. But why do we perceive this as a particular masculine conception of the individual? Through an exploration of conceptualisations of rationality from Aristotle to the present day, Lloyd (1996) offers a historical account of why this economically based conceptualisation of rationality is equated with masculinity. Lloyd begins by exploring responses to the question 'What separates humanity from the rest of the animal kingdom?'. She notes how rationality was seen as *the* mark of distinctiveness. Given that the possession of rationality was a unique human trait, it logically followed that, initially at least, women as fellow (*sic*) human beings could not be excluded from having reason. Nonetheless, up to the seventeenth century woman's reason was regarded as inferior to that of men as she was perceived to be more emotional and more impulsive. It was with the development of Cartesian conceptualisations of rationality in the seventeenth century that woman was fully cast out so to speak. Descartes developed a conception of rationality that was based on a systematised and orderly method. In so doing, he separated mind from body and reason from emotion. This formulation of rationality as an act of the mind, and distinctive from emotion, reified the possibilities for polarisation between these two sphere. In consequence it reinforced assumptions that detachment and autonomy are associated with the masculine and emotion and feeling are associated with the feminine. In this respect, Lloyd comments:

> The search for the 'clear and distinct', the separating out of the emotional, the sensuous, the imaginative, now makes possible polarisations of previously existing contrasts – intellect versus the emotions; reason versus imagination; mind versus matter. . . . the claim that women are somehow lacking in respect of rationality, that they are more impulsive, more emotional, than men is by no means a seventeenth century innovation. But these contrasts were previously contrasts **within** the rational. What ought to be dominated by reason had not previously been so sharply delineated from the intellectual. The conjunction of Cartesian down-grading of the sensuous with the use of the mind-matter distinction to establish the discrete character of Cartesian ideas introduces possibilities of polarisation that were not there before.
>
> (1996: 154, emphasis in original)

It is important to note that many feminist responses do not reject the notion of a rational consciousness that forms the essence of the humanist subject (Weedon, 1997). Indeed, Walkerdine (1990) and Lloyd (1996) illustrate how we can understand the development of feminist activism as a response to the polarisation that set up women and men as the essentially different persons popularised through texts such as 'Women are from Venus, Men are from Mars'. One of the consequences of the extreme opposition set up by Cartesian thinking was that women were excluded from the forms of education enjoyed by their brothers. Women were trained in the domestic arts whilst their brothers enjoyed subjects such as science, mathematics and Latin. This division in educational rationale was based on the idea that women were frivolous and flighty by nature. They were thought not only to have weaker bodies but also weaker minds. Education was seen as too taxing for women and would lead to madness or worse. Feminist responses rejected such naturalistic explanations and argued from a social constructionist position that, if women were frivolous and weak, it was because they were excluded from forms of education that enabled them to be trained in reason. Feminists, therefore, lobbied for equality of access to education and training. In this way, feminist activism sought to bring women within the sphere of the rationality to which their brothers had access. Clearly, therefore, this does not undo the idea that Cartesian thought privileges a masculine concept of rationality. Indeed, it can be said to further legitimise it as the normative and the desired.

The desire to be 'human': post-structural perspectives

I have argued that a major way in which we think about an employee's engagement in education and training at work is premised on a particular idea of being human. This individual acts independently because s/he is free of any constraints imposed by social structural influences such as gender, ethnicity, class, age or ability. The primary motivation of this person is their self-interest and, when presented with choices, such individuals are able to detach themselves from their feelings to explore potential options in order to make the 'right' choice. Because this is such a normative perspective, failure to act in this way implies that one is faulty in some regard. What I want to offer here is an alternative way of thinking about personhood. In particular, I shall draw on post-structural perspectives where choice is explored as an aspect of subjectivity. Here the consciousness and deliberateness of 'rationality' might be subverted by both conscious and unconscious desire.

From a post-structuralist perspective, desire is constituted through discourses through which one is subject of and subject to. As I have indicated, one of the major discourses of HRD is that of a particular type of rational subject. One might desire, therefore, to be this kind of person. However, from a post-structuralist view, not all subject positions are equally available. Individuals have differential access to particular discursive positions. Discourses, therefore, have different gendered, raced, class, age and ability implications and we can only 'pick up the tools that are lying there'. For example, the subject position of the humanist subject, that is as experiencing oneself as 'continuous, unified, rational and coherent' (Davies, 1991: 43) is mainly available to White middle class males. This means that middle class masculine subjects will find that it is far more achievable to become, for example, a 'proper' corporate employee in terms of exercising instrumental rationality, objectivity and control. For women, the achievement of such a subject position is both tenuous and ambivalent.

One example of this arose during a research interview I conducted recently (Hughes, 2004). Sian, my research respondent, told me of the difficulties she had sometimes remaining calm during meetings. She described one occasion when she said she 'totally lost it'. Sian also described the consequent shame she experienced at her behaviour. She said:

> You've sabotaged yourself because you've let it out the bag. It's the bit of being found out. I call it the Fraudian complex. Not the Freudian complex. So you're the fraud. Because you always feel like the fraud. I shouldn't really be here.

Sian's sense that she did not belong in this organisational space, and the feelings of fraudulence it gave rise to, can be understood in terms of a failure to achieve the objective rationality required of organisational members. She had been found out as an emotional person subject to bursts of anger. However, before we assume that this is simply a woman's problem, we should be mindful of Kerfoot's (1999) comments in respect of the achievement of appropriate masculinity. She notes how 'Ever concerned with their own and others' judgements of themselves as to their competence at being "on top of" situations, masculine subjects must at all times labour at being masculine and to conceal or downplay personal fears and weaknesses that stimulate a questioning of this competence' (pp. 187–8). Male managers, therefore, also have to ensure that they are operating fully within the parameters of appropriate masculinity. However, women who occupy management positions are in a particular situation. They straddle an uncomfortable line between being seen as either too masculine or too feminine. For example, the expression of anger is seen as unfeminine as, indeed, is not expressing emotion at all. Crying, on the other hand, locates women leaders as exhibiting wimpish femininity. I doubt, therefore, that Sian is alone in experiencing a sense of fraudulence in organisational spaces that privilege the middle class White masculine subject or that she is the only person who consistently fails to live up to its normative expectations.

When faced with situations such as this, a reasonable response from an employee of any sex is to strive to fit into dominant ways of behaving. Sian resolved to take a little card with her to meetings to remind her how to act properly. The words on this card were 'Keep Your Cool'. Sian portrayed her decision in terms of a straightforward choice between continuing to show passion and feeling in meetings or acting within the regulatory parameters of hegemonic organisational discourses. On the basis of utility maximisation we can applaud Sian for making the 'right' choice. However, one of the issues that post-structuralist theorising has explored in relation to choice is its illusory nature. One may feel autonomous and free to choose. But the power of regulatory discourses means that such choice is both 'forced' and of false appearance. This can be contrasted with humanism where an opposition is set up between autonomy and submission. Within humanism, one is either autonomous or submissive. Thus, one is either acting freely or one is forced to do something one would choose not to do. However, post-structuralism reminds us of the significance of desire. Thus:

> the subject's positioning within particular discourses make the 'chosen' line of action the only possible action, not because there are no other lines of action but because one has been subjectively constituted through one's placement within that discourse to **want** that line of action.
>
> (Davies, 1991: 46, emphasis in text)

Walkerdine (1990) discusses the illusion of choice in relation to psychological perspectives of 'good' child rearing. She reflects on how middle class discourses of child rearing urge parents to avoid humiliating a 'naughty' child through overt threats and sanctions as this will damage the child's growing sense of being an autonomous being. Rather, parents are encouraged to offer a child a 'choice' of different behavioural options whilst conveying to the child that there are, of course, 'right' and 'wrong' choices that can be made. In this respect, strong connections are made between 'choice' and 'consequences' and the agency of the individual (Laws and Davies, 2000). Over time, such a child, who desires to be 'good', wants to make the 'right' choices. A parallel case can be made for the 'good' employee. Sian's desire to fit into the organisational order, and to be seen as a 'good' colleague, means that she has to take up, as her own, the discourse of rational objectivity. In this way, agency is perceived to be the simultaneous act of free will and submission to the regulatory order. Thus, in the act of 'choosing', and experiencing this choice as an individual act of will, we are submitting to the requirements of particular regulatory discourses. Sian desired to become the dispassionate employee who can remain suitably objective and detached during meanings and, in this sense, experienced her choice as an act of free will. However, the consequences of not making that choice are manifold and reflect not only on her future career prospects but also on her psychological sense of well-being.

Post-structuralism demonstrates the achievement of this seeming paradox, that issues of agency and structure inhabit the same act, through the attention that has been given to the twinning of mastery and submission. Butler (1995: 45–6) notes in this regard that:

> The more a practice is mastered, the more fully subjection is achieved. Submission and mastery take place simultaneously, and it is this paradoxical simultaneity that constitutes the ambivalence of subjection. Where one might expect submission to consist in a yielding to an externally imposed dominant order, and to be marked by a loss of control and mastery, it is paradoxically marked by mastery itself… the simultaneity of submission as mastery, and mastery as submission, is the condition of possibility for the subject itself.

These processes of regulation, to which one submits, become internalised in terms of self-regulation. For example, the desire to be good means that one must master (*sic*) the subject position of the 'good' employee. One way this is achieved is through repetition. The more we repeat a practice or an action the greater our mastery of it. Mastery, itself experienced as the achievement of the humanist self, is the ultimate self-regulation of our actions and behaviours. Thus, we make a little note to remind ourselves to 'Keep Your Cool'. We practice this regularly and when we achieve this state of being, we have in these moments accomplished key aspects of humanist discourses – individuality, choice, a recognition of the consequences of one's actions, autonomy and responsibility (Davies *et al.*, 2001).

Critical tasks for human resource developers: a deconstructive approach

My aim in this chapter has been to unmask the masculinity that inhabits the term 'human' in HRD discourses. My methodological approach has been one of deconstruction. Deconstruction has been a significant tool in the politics of feminism and has facilitated an understanding of how truths are produced (Spivak, 2001). Politically, its purpose is to lead to 'an appreciation of hierarchy as illusion sustained by power. It may be a necessary illusion, at our stage in history. We do not know. But there is no rational warrant for assuming that other imaginary structures would not be possible' (Boyne, 1990: 124). In order to expose the illusory nature of hierarchy, deconstruction begins by exploring, and exposing, the existence of hierarchy in the organisation of language. For example, this chapter has demonstrated the linkages between masculinity and rationality that comprise an ascendant view of being human. Second, deconstructive approaches are not concerned to reverse this hierarchy, as this would simply maintain hierarchical organisation. Rather, they seek to dis/replace this hierarchy for more egalitarian textual forms through, for example, the creation of new terms and languages. It is notoriously difficult to achieve this second purpose of deconstruction. This is because we have to use the terms of any dominant discourse to challenge that discourse. It is necessary, however, because deconstruction illustrates how so much of what is said is bound up with what cannot be, and is not, said.

Critical theorists have turned to the concept of critical literacy as one practice that aims to contribute towards the development of non-hierarchical ways of knowing and being. Critical literacy is a pedagogic act that can be developed within HRD discourses and practices. Davies (1997) has illustrated how critical literacy is a set of practices that draws on post-structural theories of selfhood and language. It encourages the development of skills and habits but does not seek to separate theory from practice. One of the imperatives of critical literacy is that we must learn to look beyond the content of the text and to see, and critique, how this content works upon us to shape meaning and desire. In consequence, critical literacy aims to develop a reflexive awareness of how speaking-as-usual constructs our understandings of ourselves and of others (Davies, 1997) and so maintains, rather than overturns, traditional gendered hierarchies. It is, in this regard, concerned with the relationship between the construction of selves and regimes of truth. To do critical literacy we need to develop the capacities through which we can read against the grain of dominant discourses and the privileged positions that are constructed within them. In this respect, Davies (1997, see also Hughes, 2002) has set out five tasks that are required.

Know well dominant forms of thought

We have seen that central to HRD is a conception of the human that has its roots in the masculinity of Cartesian rationality. We might now explore other aspects of HRD in order to recognise the gendered nature of its language, theories, questions and concerns. For example, Townley (1994) notes the gendered history evident in debates over the name and image of the UK based Institute of Personnel Management.[3] Townley comments:

> The association changed its name six times from its initial inscription as the Welfare Workers' Association in 1913, until finally deciding on its present [IPM] title in 1946. Debates centre on the image projected – welfare was thought to reflect the feminine – with elements amongst the membership, conscious of employment prospects, wishing to insert more strenuous terms into the title. In 1924, the name changed to Industrial Welfare Workers, in 1931 to the Institute of Labour Management, only finally deciding on the Institute of Personnel Management, in 1946, when, for the first time, male membership of the Institute exceeded female membership.
>
> (1994: 15–16)

One might also consider the assumptions inherent in key strands of adult development theory where research has primarily been based on research on the lives of North American middle class males. Or we might turn to adult learning theory that replicates much that I have discussed above in terms that the ideal adult learner is a self-directed, autonomous agent.

In coming to know the masculine basis of these conceptualisations we then need to come to understand how we have been encouraged to master its discourses. Even whilst we might reject such ways of knowing, we cannot assume that, even if we desire to do so, we can free ourselves so easily, and never totally, from such powerfully dominant discourses. Brah's (1999: 8) use of the Althusserian idea of interpellation is useful here as it denotes how we are 'being situated' and 'hailed' socially, culturally, symbolically and psychically, all at once [and thus] it takes seriously the relationship between 'the social and the psychic'. How have we been hailed or situated by this, and other, discourses? To answer this question it is not necessary to reject these discourses, although we might, but it is necessary to know how dominant discourses work on us, and on others, and why we are so powerfully committed to, or rejecting of, such discourses. This will help us come to understand why we might take up, or we might be persuaded by, particular forms of argumentation.

Move beyond dominant forms of thought to embrace multiple ways of knowing

The second task is to move beyond linear and rational thought and to embrace and celebrate multiple and contradictory ways of knowing. This is because this will help us to undermine the power of dominant discourses. It will also encourage movement through openness and openings and raise questions for us about the truth of different ways of knowing. What alternative, and multiple, ways might we know the rationality of the employee who refuses to engage in education and training? Can we understand their humanity in terms of a cyborg (Haraway, 1991), an exile (Benhabib, 1992) or a nomad (Braidotti, 1994)?

Read, speak and write oneself into the possibilities of different discourses

The third task is to read, speak and write ourselves into the possibilities of different discourses and contexts. What alternative languages or textual forms might we use to express our experiences? For example, how might we use poetry, song, myth and literature to understand, and reconfigure, HRD? When we do so, how does our conceptualisation of the world change?

Engage in moral and philosophical critique

Fourth, we need to engage in moral and philosophical critique of discourse. This is not to assert our moral superiority or ascendancy over others but it is to more fully understand how truth is constructed at different points in time and in different discourses. In this Gee (1996) offers two principles that he argues should form the basis of ethical human discourse. These are that we should ensure that any conceptualisation that we choose should not harm someone else and that we have an ethical obligation to make explicit any tacit theory if we have reason to believe that this theory will give us an advantage over another. One example of this comes from the field of equal opportunities. Many feminists have had an enormous commitment to equality and have worked with a variety of policy makers and organisational leaders to realise their visions. Here, a considerable focus has been to find policies that will remove the 'glass ceiling'. This is work that is mainly beneficial to middle class women working within professional and management fields. As Shaw (1995: 215) remarks:

> much equal opportunities work is irrelevant to the bulk of women who are nowhere near managerial grades. The individualistic strategies advocated for potential high-fliers may be effective, but they do not touch the working conditions of the majority. Indeed, if they did, there is a good chance that they would be abandoned, for equality of opportunity, in and of itself, implies no commitment to equality.

What version of equality are we talking about when we engage in talk with business leaders? What version of equality are business leaders speaking of when they talk to us? Who benefits from this view? Is this made clear to all concerned?

Recognise the limits of critique and potential transformation

The fifth task that Davies (op. cit.) notes is that we have to recognise the limits of any critique or potential transformation. Central to this is developing a reflexive awareness of ourselves as sentient beings and the place of language and meaning in the production of feeling. In this respect Lankshear *et al.* (1997: 83) describe how fast capitalist texts, with their talk of empowerment and self-directed employees, promote visions of ' "enchanted workplaces" where hierarchy is dead and "partners" engage in meaningful work amidst a collaborative environment of mutual commitment and trust'. Such discourses work on the subject to produce similarly enchanted employees. Whilst critical literacy is concerned to develop skills and knowledges that enable us to at least recognise enchantment when it occurs, freeing ourselves totally from such mirages is never totally possible. Nevertheless, unless we constantly strive to move beyond the intellectual pictures that hold us captive (Moi, 1999) we will fail to understand the power of linguistic forms nor develop the capacity to use them well (Davies, 1997).

Conclusion

My work in this chapter has been to challenge the idea that the concept of the human at the centre of HRD is egalitarian and gender neutral. I have argued that the facts of the matter are quite the contrary. The dominant version of the human in HRD privileges a masculine subject who acts within the terms of utility maximisation and rational choice. I have offered an alternative understanding of the subject who is constructed through discourse and, as a consequence, is multiply located and subjectively always in process. In posing these two alternatives, I have suggested that, for those who seek more egalitarian workplaces and practices of HRD, it is necessary to engage in the tasks of critical literacy. This is important work for human resource developers many of whom view their heritage arising from Freirean conscientisation theories and egalitarian politics. It is a radical agenda and involves the development of learning, and unlearning workshops, through which individuals can come to know how dominant discourses are shaping their desires, judgements and ambivalences and through which we can seek out new languages and new ways of being. It is, nonetheless, necessary work.

Notes

1 My use of 'male' in this chapter is used to refer to subject positions rather than sexed bodies. There are many forms of masculinity some of which it is perfectly possible for women to take up.
2 As I indicate under Critical Literacy Task 1, this analysis can be made to many other dominant theories within the field of HRD.
3 The UK based Institute of Personnel Management has now, of course, merged with the Institute for Training and Development and, with chartered status, is now named the Chartered Institute of Personnel and Development.

References

Benhabib, S. (1992) *Situating the Self: Gender, Community and Postmodernism in Contemporary Ethics*, Cambridge: Polity.

Boyne, R. (1990) *Foucault and Derrida: The Other Side of Reason*, London: Unwin Hyman.

Brah, A. (1999) 'The scent of memory: strangers, our own, and others', *Feminist Review*, 61: 4–26.

Braidotti, R. (1994) *Nomadic Subjects*, New York: Columbia University Press.

Butler, J. (1995) 'Contingent foundations: feminism and the question of "postmodernism"', in S. Benhabib, J. Butler, D. Cornell and N. Fraser (eds) *Feminist Contentions: A Philosophical Exchange*, New York: Routledge, 35–57.

Davies, B. (1991) 'The concept of agency: a feminist poststructuralist analysis', *Social Analysis*, 300: 42–53.

Davies, B. (1997) 'Constructing and deconstructing masculinities through critical literacy', *Gender and Education*, 9, 1: 9–30.

Davies, B., Dormer, S., Gannon, S., Laws, C., Taguchi, H., McCann, H. and Rocco, S. (2001) 'Becoming schoolgirls: the ambivalent project of subjectification', *Gender and Education*, 13, 2: 167–82.

Garrick, J. (1998) *Informal Learning in the Workplace: Unmasking Human Resource Development*, London: Routledge.

Gee, J. (1996) *Social Linguistics and Literacies: Ideology in Discourses*, 2nd edn, London: Taylor & Francis.

Haraway, D. (1991) *Simians, Cyborgs and Women: The Reinvention of Nature*, London: Free Association Books.

Hekman, S. (1999) *The Future of Differences: Truth and Method in Feminist Theory*, Cambridge: Polity.

Hughes, C. (2002) *Key Concepts in Feminist Theory and Research*, London: Sage.

Hughes, C. (2004) 'Class and other identifications in managerial careers: the case of the lemon dress', *Gender, Work and Organization*, 11, 5: 526–43.

Kerfoot, D. (1999) 'The organization of intimacy: managerialism, masculinity and the masculine subject', in S. Whitehead and R. Moodley (eds) *Transforming Managers: Gendering Change in the Public Sector*, London: UCL Press, 184–99.

Lankshear, C., Gee, J., Knobel M. and Searle C. (1997) *Changing Literacies*, Buckingham: Open University Press.

Laws, C. and Davies, B. (2000) 'Poststructuralist theory in practice: working with "behaviourally disturbed" children', *Qualitative Studies in Education*, 13, 3: 205–21.

Lloyd, G. (1996) 'The man of reason', in A. Garry and M. Pearsall (eds) *Women, Knowledge and Reality: Explorations in Feminist Philosophy*, New York: Routledge, 151–65.

Mezirow, J. (1978) 'Toward a theory of practice', *Adult Education*, 28, 2: 100–10.

Moi, T. (1999) *What is a Woman?*, Oxford: Oxford University Press.

Plumwood, V. (1993) *Feminism and the Mastery of Nature*, London: Routledge.

Scott, J. (2000) 'Rational choice theory', in G. Browning, A. Halcli and F. Webster (eds) *Understanding Contemporary Society: Theories of the Present*, London: Sage, 126–38.

Shaw, J. (1995) 'Conclusion – feminization and new forms of exploitations: the changing language of equal opportunities', in J. Shaw and D. Perrons (eds) *Making Gender Work: Managing Equal Opportunities*, Buckingham: Open University Press.

Spivak, G. (2001) *Political Discourse: Theories of Colonialism and Postcolonialism* (http://landow. stg.brown.edu/post/poldiscourse/spivak/spivak1.html (accessed 03 March 2001).

Townley, B. (1994) *Reframing Human Resource Management: Power, Ethics and the Subject at Work*, London: Sage.

Walkerdine, V. (1990) *School Girl Fictions*, London: Verso.

Watkins, K. (1991) 'Many voices: defining human resource development from many disciplines', *Adult Education Quarterly*, 41, 4: 241–55.

Weedon, C. (1997) *Feminist Practice and Poststructuralist Theory*, 2nd edn, Oxford: Blackwell.

12 The self at work

Theories of persons, meaning of work and their implications for HRD

K. Peter Kuchinke

> They had called for workmen and saw that, instead, human beings had arrived.
>
> (Max Frisch)

Frisch's poignant observation of the situation of immigrant workers (*Gastarbeiter*) in West Germany in the 1960s who came to a country that was in need of labour but not prepared to integrate others into society, is taken here as the point of departure to investigate alternative constructions of the self in relation to work. The assertion at the outset is that the majority of HRD research and theorizing is based on an instrumental and commodified view of persons, a stance that is not only limiting in a practical sense but equally questionable from ethical and intellectual points of view. That HRD as a field of research and of practice focused on people in organizations should have adopted so intently a functionalist paradigm (Burrell and Morgan, 1979) might be explained by its proximity to the behavioural sciences, the need for legitimacy in academia and organizations, and the dominance of a managerialist discourse (Deetz, 1992). The foreclosure of alternative perspectives should, however, also be seen as a loss of opportunity to bring to the fore ignored areas of organizational life and to expand understanding, theorizing, and practical application. When, as Barley and Kunda (1992) have suggested, managerial emphasis has shifted over the past 25 years from rational to normative modes of coordination (e.g. "productivity through people" rather than through systems, policies and procedures), renewed and vigorous investigation and theorizing about people in organizations is likely, indeed, to yield fresh insight, and broader understanding. Organizations might find lessons from the experience of German *Gastarbeiter* policies: where persons are reduced to factors in the production process. Ethical, social, personal, and work-related problems result.

The focus of this chapter, then, is on the self at work, with self being used to denote the inner nature and qualities of persons, the awareness of their identity and being, as well as their interests (The American Heritage Dictionary, 1982). The focus on the self, then, implies a broader and deeper investigation, a look behind the mask (the meaning of the Latin *persona*) and includes aspects of being such as consciousness, ego, soul, and heart (Flew, 1979). Theorizing the self moves beyond facet characteristics investigated by contemporary organizational psychology, and seeks understanding of the deeper aspects of persons.

The chapter will proceed along the following major themes: the neglect of the self and the prevalence of the compartmentalized functional view of persons in psychology, HRD, and related management sciences; the need for a more complete view of the self for intellectual, ethical, and practical reasons; epistemological issues related to investigating the subject; a brief historical treatise of thinking about the self; a tri-part classification of theories about the self; a critique and extension of the classification scheme; and implications for theorizing and practicing HRD.

The disappearance of the self in management studies

Observations of the dearth and paucity of theories about the self in the social sciences have been made repeatedly. McGoldrick *et al.* (2002: 397), for example, suggested an increased attention by HRD researchers on the individual, his or her identity as constructed in employment, work and career settings, and on individual gender-based differences. Nord and Fox (1999: 142) spoke of the "individual's disappearance in industrial and organizational psychology and behaviour [literatures]." Brief and Aldag (1981: 75–6) criticized the "relatively passive role" accorded to the individual in models of employee behaviour, calling the "self...one of the most under-researched subjects in the area of job attitudes." The reason for this neglect of the individual was seen by Nord and Fox as a result of the focus of external variables in explaining behaviour in current models and theories. Individual-level research in the organizational sciences over the past 30 years has been dominated by behaviourist and cognitive approaches that have proven unable to provide adequate frames for understanding more complex phenomena, and thus a plethora of latent variables have been postulated, such as flow experiences (Csikszentmihalyi, 2003) and hope (Luthans and Jensen, 2002). Extant research in personality is atomistic rather than integrative. Jung's (1945/1993: 494) vision of a psychology that is "to do with the history of civilization, of philosophy and of religion" has not been realized.

Towards an understanding of persons

With the dominance of an atomistic research in the behavioural sciences and a lost focus on deeper aspects of being, there is a need for increased emphasis on ideographic and qualitative approaches that reflect how individuals view themselves. This renewed focus on the nature of the self is warranted because it can afford a more comprehensive and adequate view of persons – and thus provide theoretical and ethical justification for the undertaking – but also for practical reasons. There is evidence that individuals are seeking deeper understanding of themselves in an age of uncertainty (namely, the strong interest in issues of spirituality and meaningful work), and that social organizations are increasingly concerned with core attributes of being such as creativity, emotions, involvement, trust, citizenship, and psychological ownership. In the empirical research tradition, there was the recognition as early as the Hawthorne studies that people do not "leave their inner selves at the door" when reporting to work and yet the concern with being and qualities of the self have never quite taken hold in the behavioural and cognitive science traditions that have dominated Western academic research throughout most of the past century. The focus on the deeper qualities of persons – so central to philosophy and theology – was still very much at the core of works by early American writers such as Dewey, James, and Royce. With the emergence of empirical social science research and the split between philosophy and psychology, however, the postulation of the self as a central, unifying, and integrating entity was lost. Since the nineteenth century psychologist Wilhelm Wundt's insistence that the new field ought to become a "psychology without a soul" (in Allport, 1955/1968: 25), empirical studies of the persons have focused on observable facet phenomena, and neglected inner states. For a time, humanistic psychology – the "third force" after behaviourism and psychoanalysis – resurrected the idea through notions of self-actualization (e.g. Allport, 1943/1960) but these efforts were overshadowed by experimental positivism and the predominant behavioural, and later cognitive approaches.

The argument here is that experimental and behavioural approaches are insufficient when the goal is to understand persons, and that despite much effort in the social sciences little has been achieved to understand the deeper nature of persons. Subsequently, the influence on individuals or social organizations of atomistic studies of facets of human behaviour has been limited and renewed effort aimed at understanding the nature of persons appears fruitful and interesting. Restoring the central role of the person in organizational practice and in research on individuals and collectives has also been expressed as a major goal of radical humanism (Aktouf, 1992) arguing for a conceptual shift from the presumed passive-obedient role accorded to employees under Taylorism and Fordism towards an active and cooperative one.

Besides ideological barriers responsible for the dismissal of the self in contemporary psychology, epistemological difficulties surround the self-referential nature of the undertaking. For one, with Boulding (1956), it is reasonable to postulate the cognitive limitations in our ability to understand ourselves. Second, attempts to understand the self *qua the self* invites difficulties common to all social sciences expressed in the well-known image of attempting to describe a play in which we, ourselves, perform as actors. Third, as we entertain thoughts about the self, we use our own conscious thought processes to makes statements about the self, inviting dangers not only of reification, but also of solipsism and infinite regress. These problems, however, are not restricted to the topic on hand but, whether acknowledged or not, extend to liabilities of the human and social sciences in general and should not deter but rather invite investigation with an attitude of humility and care.

Historical development of thinking about the self

This section will provide a very cursory outline of major themes that have emerged throughout history related to the self. The coverage will be restricted to Western thought beginning with Greek antiquity and continuing throughout philosophical and theological intellectual history. In Western thought and particularly since the Enlightenment, the self has been treated as an individual rather than collective idea – that is, the self is primarily within an individual and not given from outside; it is unique and not common and thus distinguishes one person from another; it is knowable and accessible to the conscious; and it is substantially secular rather than divine (Kitzinger, 1992). The self is, at least potentially, attainable and the movement in development and maturation is towards the self.

In Socratic thinking the self was seen as identical with the soul and hence not bound by the corporeal body but immortal and a substance in itself. The essential conception of self as a substance was carried forward in history and developed by mystics, such as Meister Eckhart, idealist philosophers such as Descartes and Kant, and pragmatist thinkers like Dewey, Royce, and James. Central to the notion of the self as substance is the idea of the self as independent, a priori, continuous and objective, and this is referred to in the literatures as subject-self, I-self (Harter, 1993), observing self (Deikman, 1982), and experiencing self (James, 1890/1927). The self as substance is contrasted in intellectual history with the self as the object of knowledge and consciousness, referred to alternately as the me-self (Harter, 1993), object-self, and empirical self (James, 1890/1927). These fundamentally different aspects of self are illustrated by Harter (1993: 99) with a simple example:

> Imagine, for a moment, that you are gazing into a mirror and you make the following observation: I see myself, *I see Me*. There are two distinct aspects of self in this rather mundane experience. There is the *I*, the active *observer* and there is the *Me* in the mirror, the Me as *observed*. ... The I-self is the active *observer*, the *knower*, the information processor, as it were, the self that is the architect or *constructor* of knowledge. One such construction is the Me-self. That is the self that is *known, observed*, the self that is *constructed*.

> (emphases in the original)

Critiques of the duality between subject and object self have been based on conceptual and pragmatic grounds. Aristotelian arguments against the existence of universals, such as the soul or self, centered on the idea that universals cannot be known except through particular substantiations of general ideas. Hume regarded the self as a bundle of different perceptions. For Dewey and James, subject and object selves coexisted as aspects of the conscious self. James (1890/1927), for example, describes four constituents of the self: material, social, spiritual, and pure Ego, with the first three representing the me-self, and the last the I-self. Dewey's formulation of the synthetic unity of subject and object neither views knowledge as subject nor object but bound together in the self. The self and the world constitute a "unified universe with no existence apart from this universe" (Dewey, 1890/1969: 57). Since Wundt, as described earlier, academic psychology and personality psychology in particular have dismissed the subject self as a topic of investigation and instead focused on cataloging facets and dimensions of the object self (e.g. London, 1978; Hogan, 1991; Pervin, 2002). Humanistic and existential psychologists reintroduced the topic with the central idea of discovery, realization, and movement toward the actual, authentic self (Allport, 1943/1960; Maslow, 1956). Existentialist writers, in particular Camus and Sartre, spoke about the false self and stressed the consequences of abdicating the freedom to choose an authentic life.

With the dominant role of behaviourally oriented research, however, the vast majority of psychological research has focused on the representational self and, in particular, its facets and dimensions. While the question whether the concept of the self is useful and necessary is recurrent in the personality literature, its discussion most often ends with by referring to the conceptual and methodological barriers to the empirical investigation of the topic. Recent calls for a synthesis between subject and object selves have occurred in psychotherapeutic literatures on Eastern philosophy, spirituality, and mysticism (e.g. Deikman, 1982; Schuman, 1988).

Where even personality researchers contend that the "self will not go away" (Pervin, 2002: 161), philosophical and psychological inquiry into the topic appears in agreement over the outstanding fundamental questions related to the self (e.g. Chatterjee, 1963; Shoemaker, 1963; Gordon and Gergen, 1968; Miri, 1980). These include whether the self should be viewed as a fact or a construct, that is objective and given or (solely) constructed; whether the self should be treated as structure(s) or process(es); and whether the self should be seen as single or multiple.

Classification of theories of the self and work

To provide a focus for the theories of the self and their relationship to work, a three-part model developed by Joanne Martin (1992) to describe theories of organizational cultures will be adapted. Integration theories emphasize the unitary, consensual, and consistent nature of the self; its organization around a single theme or purpose; and the absence of conflict, contradiction, and ambiguity. A metaphor might be the self as an arrow. In contrast, reasoning about the self from a differentiation perspective entails emphasis on multiple and often mutually exclusive priorities, on negotiation and trade-offs between and among themes and purposes, and on the channelling or control of contradictions and ambiguities. A metaphor for the differentiation might be the self as a parliament. Viewed from a fragmentation perspective, the self is characterized by a multiplicity of preferences in the absence of priorities, by shifting definitions, lack of consensus, predominance of ambiguity and complexity, by moving in and out of focus, consistency, and clarity. A metaphor is the self as kaleidoscope.

Following Martin's lead, it should be pointed out that the three perspectives are subjective and inductive; the intent is to clarify and highlight alternative understandings, and the model serves as communicative tool. The use of categories in itself is problematic: categories force dichotomous thinking, oversimplify, and ignore multiple meanings of a given theory. Categorical thinking further invites the danger of reification of the subject and the categories, and implies certainty; it does not allow sufficient focus on the processual, unfolding nature of the subject or the tentative nature of the discussion. With these limitations in mind, however, the model can serve as the starting point for inviting dialogue and thought on an overlooked subject.

Integration perspectives of the self and work

Theories of the self and work written from an integration perspective emphasize unity, harmony, and consistency of the person and his/her relationship to work. Integration theories are simple in the sense that an overriding sense of direction or purpose is implied or described, and that ambiguity, doubt, and uncertainty are absent or are bracketed. This view of self emphasizes "consciousness, autonomy, free will and self-control." Martin (1992: 60). This unitary self might have resulted from a struggle with adversity, often heroic, or a breakthrough in consciousness, the result of a vision or inspiration, often after overcoming adversity. Integration views of the self form the basis of descriptions of legendary figures, such as war heroes or business leaders, and are often idealized in the popular culture. Ambiguity and uncertainty are viewed as inferior detractors from a single and often self-sacrificing pursuit of a goal. Integration conceptions of the self and work can be self-referential (persons' views of themselves) or other-directed (views of the nature of others). Integration views are often normative and prescriptive from a self-development point of view but also specify conditions for group membership. Thus, the manager who informs the job applicant that "hard work and success come first for our people here" not only defines himself or herself with a single focus but also sets expectations for future members of the organization.

Historically, the integration view of the self can be linked to the notion of calling and the formulation of the protestant work ethic. Goldman (1988) describes the history from Hellenistic and Roman thought about the cultivation of one's aptitudes in different disciplines, to Aquinian ideas of inclinations towards specific activities as graces of Providence and commensurate duties by the individual to perfect those talents and place them in the service of humankind. Lutheran and Calvinist notions of *Beruf* (calling or vocation) stress the moral dimension of vocation as commanded rather than selected, and give way, in Weber's words (in Goldman, 1988: 37), to work as the "valuation of fulfilment of duty within the worldly callings as the highest content that the ethical activity of the self could generally receive." As Goldman further suggests (1988: 37), "[O]nly through the fulfilment of one's worldly duties could one live acceptably to God" and thus is provided the moral justification, even duty, for the idea of the "self as worker" and, under advancing capitalism, the Weberian *Berufsmensch*, the worker defined through and defining himself/herself solely through his or her occupational activities. In the North American context, this work ethic was supported by egalitarian notions that "no man ... need be fettered by caste or class, that achievement in the occupation of one's choice is dependent solely on initiative and ability. ... [T]he most heinous sin ... is the admission of failure to achieve, with the concomitant renunciation of the success orientation altogether." (Braude, 1983: 213). The myth of rags-to-riches success available to everyone has been expressed and reinforced in the popular press since the nineteenth century with best-selling books by Horatio Alger, P.T. Barnum and Andrew Carnegie and many more recent and contemporary authors supporting and building, as Wilms (1986) suggests, four core tenets of the "American Dream": First, the belief in free and equal opportunities of success available to everybody; second, the idea that success equals material wealth; third, the notion that unlimited opportunities for success exist; and fourth, the tenet that people are responsible for their own position in life and that the deserving ones rise by their own effort.

These powerful beliefs about the self as worker reflect an integration perspective because of their single and unitary focus, the absence of discussion of competing or alternative goals or aspirations, and of the silence surrounding uncertainty, doubt, or ambiguity over the life lived, the work done, or the goals pursued. This perspective is found in the rhetoric of persons as "human resources" and in corporate pronouncements such as "people as our most important assets" (see Walton, 2003, for an insightful discussion on terminology of HRD). This managerialist view of persons, is also reflected in popular interpretations of humanistic psychology (Maslow, 1965/1973, May 1953) – where self-actualization is interpreted to mean career success and can serve to justify self-management and self-normalization (Deetz, 1992). The integration perspective, however, can also be found in Marxian thinking on alienated labour that enslaves the worker, turning him or her into objects of capitalist modes of production (Marx, 1844/1963) and representing again, though with different value polarity, a unitary (victimized) characterization of personhood. Here, in particular, the bi-directional nature of the perspective becomes apparent: Alienation is both other-directed (capitalists substitute wage labour for meaningful work) and self-directed (workers view alienated work as their own).

Differentiation perspectives of self and work

When the main characteristics of the integration perspective consist of unitary goals, consensus, harmony, and simplicity of purpose, the differentiation perspective broadens the horizon and admits to the discussion the existence of multiple aspects of the self and arrays of priorities and goals. Pluralism and not unitarism is at the core of the self and this pluralism – expressed in multiple and divergent interests, life goals and social roles – requires negotiation, compromise, and choice. Inconsistencies among the various roles, conflict over preferences, and ambiguity of the self are acknowledged in this perspective, but the diversity is channelled and controlled through choices, trade-offs, determination, and maturity. The parliament metaphor employed by Mead to characterize the self, implies rules to manage pluralism and conflict in the service of upholding a common entity. Theories in this perspective assume a basic ability and desire to coordinate and control the various facets of the self, even though this undertaking might be difficult.

Most descriptive research has adopted this perspective. The Meaning of Working research project (MOW, 1987) surveyed employees in many countries and found country-level differences in the role of work in peoples' lives. Work centrality, a core construct in the MOW studies, was also used in Ardichvili's recent project (2003) on employees in post-communist countries. Family commitments and leisure interests competed with work, and pay for work played a less important role than interesting and satisfying work or contacts with interesting colleagues. A similar approach underlies the recent work by Ciulla who argued for increased attention to balance between work and non-work pursuits and for a redefinition of the work centrality (2000).

Two related streams of research and theorizing can illustrate the differentiation approach to understanding the self and work. The first is a series of studies framed in structural development psychology after Piaget and Kohlberg (Armon, 1993; Erdynast, 1990) that position adult conceptions of good work within the larger concept of conceptions of the good life based on social contract philosophy of

John Rawls. Using a stage approach, Armon (1993) described the existence of alternate ideas about the definition and meaning of good work among adults, of movement from one stage to another over time, and of parallel changes in personal definitions of good work and of justice, truth, and beauty.

A last example of differentiation theories is found in Jung's writing on individuation in adult life. Although strongly influenced by ideas of a deep, transcendental, and collective Ego, Jung nonetheless posits the possibility of development in the second half of life that reconciles the various diverging facets of the younger self, including externally imposed roles and moving towards selfhood and true individuality (Jung, 1959; Stein, 1998).

While differing in specific ways of reconciling plurality in the self – through choice and trade-offs, through development along fixed stages, or through ultimate reconciliation of divergent facets – common to theories in the differentiation perspective is the existence of multiple, often contradictory and conflicting aspects of self. In the diversity, however, there is also unity, thus making possible the existence and continuity of the parliament of selves. In the differentiation perspective, the self partakes in different roles, communities and cultures, and is able to accept, function, or manage – through emotional work, compartmentalization, or cognitive manoeuvres – the tensions, inconsistencies, and ambiguities.

Fragmentation perspective of self and work

Whereas the differentiation perspectives presumes a level of unity – however tenuous – among the multiple aspects of self, the fragmentation perspective removes this assumption focusing instead on flux, multiplicity of meaning, discontinuity, and lack of simplicity and predictability in the self. This category is situated in postmodern thought with its critique of the modernist agenda of progress, stability, and order through grand narratives erected to hide complexity and disguise power relationships. Martin (1992) explored postmodern ideas related to an understanding of organizational culture highlighting aspects such as ambiguous and shifting meaning, silenced and preferred views and voices, paradox and uncertainty, domination of grand narratives upheld by power, and suffering, pain, and violence in the normal course of organizational life. Moving to the individual level, Deetz (1992) spoke of resulting self-surveillance and self-domination as individuals accept the dominant mode in organizations as normal and when meaning is fixed or frozen by an over-arching corporate agenda. With respect to the self, notions of authenticity, continuity of self, and agency are seen as fiction and concealment (Deetz, 1992: 291) leading to the fundamental critique of the subject (self) in postmodern philosophy. The anti-subjectivist approach arose in the intellectual and political milieu of the 1950s and 1960s "in reaction to Sartrean existentialism and the extreme capacity for freedom, self-creation, and historical agency with which Sartre credited the conscious ego" (Hengehold, 1998: 197). Foucault, in particular, emphasized the fabrication of the modern self through social institutions and ideologies. With the assumption of the ontological unity of the person removed, the self, and the awareness of the self, become subject to the push-and-pull of multiple societal forces, adrift in a world of hyper-complexity, paradox, contradiction, and inconsistency. Feelings of unity or cohesion by the self, then, are seen not as expressions of the underlying nature or true self, but as part of a societal script. When theories within the differentiation perspective still accord a fundamental capacity for control and unity, the fragmentation perspective perceives this notion as fiction produced by dominant discourses and with the aim of maintaining order and stability of power relations. As Martin (1992: 156) wrote:

> [A] fragmented self constantly fluctuates among diverse and changing identities, pulled by issues and events. … The self is fragmented by a variety of nested, overlapping identities, external influences, and levels of consciousness: The perceiving subject, deluded by imagined notions of its unity and coherence, is in actuality split in such imponderable ways… that it might be conceived as a vacancy mirroring Other(s) whose "space" creates its experience of being a conscious subject.

In the management sciences, postmodern approaches have been used to comprehend the contradictions, paradoxes, and inconsistencies in organizational life (see, e.g. Alvesson and Deetz, 1999; Cohen *et al.*, 1972). At the individual level, the fragmentation perspective has been employed to describe the experience of subordinated groups, such as women and minorities, of middle-class wage earners, and of executives and managers (see Martin, 1992). Individual identity and awareness of the self, in this perspective, are not fixed but arise out of the process of interaction. Shifting from one interaction to another entails shifting to another self. The self, thus, is an ongoing puzzle undergoing continual shifts, change, and discontinuity. This is beautifully expressed in Pablo Neruda's (1990: 363–4) poem, "We are many."

> Of the many men whom I am, whom we are,
> I cannot settle on a single one.
> They are lost to me under the cover of clothing.
> They have departed to another city
>
> . . .
>
> While I am writing, I am far away;
> And when I come back, I have already left…
> I am going to school myself so well in things that,
> When I try to explain my problems,
> I shall speak, not of self, but of geography.

Challenging and extending the model

In this chapter, I have attempted to invite discussion by providing a brief history of ideas about the self and summarizing existing thinking by adapting a tri-partite model borrowed from the organizational culture literature. In the integration perspective, the self might be seen as an arrow: goal directed, assured, fully aware, and in control. The differentiation perspective adds complexity by allowing for multiple and conflicting roles that are nonetheless coordinated and functional, as a parliament with opposing factions might be. The fragmentation perspective removes the assumption of unity of the self and views it in reaction to social forces in constant flux. Carrying forward Harter's image of the self looking into the mirror, the integrated self might appear as a single image, the differentiated self might appear as multiple images, and the fragmented self might appear as a broken mirror – a kaleidoscope. While each perspective highlights specific aspects of being – focus and agency in the first, plurality in the second, ambiguity, and complexity in the third – each is based on specific assumptions about the fundamental nature, or even possibility, of self. Each perspective not only serves to provide a convenient label for different theories and streams of research and writing but also provides an ideology, a normative system of thought about a specific potentiality of self or way of being.

Each perspective requires critique: the spectre of Marcuse's one-dimensional man is inherent in the integration view; the incommensurability of demands of multiple life roles and resultant burden on the individual in the differentiation perspective; and the blurring of the notion of and deep questions about the legitimacy and agency of the postmodern author inherent in the fragmentation view. As with many categorization schemes, a multi-perspective approach to understanding persons and their relationship to work appears appropriate. From a postmodern perspective, however, the three-part model in itself must be critiqued and questioned. As Martin (1992: 193) points out, "the three-perspective framework is a modernist attempt to build a meta-theory. Its tripartite categorization scheme is based on a series of undeconstructed dichotomies that position the perspectives in opposition to each other ... [ignoring] studies that straddle the boundaries ... [omitting] unclassifiable research ... reifying the perspectives and pigeonholing authors." At minimum, research and theorizing on the subject, from whatever perspective, must be self-critical and self-reflective.

Second, the discussion outlined above brackets the question about the identity of the author, the ontological characteristic of the I-self peering into Harter's mirror, and merely describes alternative conceptualizations of the object self. A deeper understanding of the possibilities of essentialist and constructivist views of the self is required to turn the discussion from the image in the mirror to the entity creating and perceiving the image.

Implications for theorizing and practicing HRD

Questioning our thinking about the self, both introspectively and other-directed, should, in this author's view, occupy a central space in the academic and professional communities. The present anaemic and narrow treatment of persons in the HRD and management literatures is insufficient, intellectually untenable, and ignorant of the traditions in philosophy, religion, and wisdom traditions. Allowing the topic greater space and visibility, unfolding the range of possible discourses, and exploring the subject from multiple perspectives would advance the HRD profession and the state of researching, knowing, and speaking. Where research on identity, the person, or self is conducted, this is done almost invariably from an integration perspective with some very limited writing coming from a differentiation perspective, for example in recent feminist research in HRD. Almost no attention has been paid by scholars to an exploration of issues of the person from a fragmentation perspective, and this despite the fact that chaos and complexity theories have been used by organizational sociologists for some 20 years. It is time to broaden the palette of theoretical perspectives in HRD research, and here Martin's classification can serve to inform about alternative research directions.

Institutionally, academic HRD appears to be better positioned for this undertaking than other social and organizational sciences, especially where HRD academic programs are situated outside of curricula of HRM or management. Methodologically, the undertaking will require a focus on phenomenological and other ideographic and in-depth approaches, to focus on self-understanding, language, and personal narrative (see Freeman, 1992; Witz *et al.*, 2001).

With respect to practicing HRD, greater attention on the subject and clarification of the range of possible narratives has the potential to broaden the range of options. Where practice is beholden to a narrow view of persons, advice, intervention, and involvement will reinforce this view and, by definition, fail to address deeper, and more salient aspects of being at work. A fundamental question for HRD practitioners is about the nature of those whose lives we touch in professional practice, and here practitioners face a choice between actions that diminish the self (personal and other-directed) and those that enhance, explore, and broaden the self (again, both personal and other-directed) in daily practice. This should be seen not only as an ethical question of integrity but an imminently practical one. Relevant professional practice must address fundamental aspects and possibilities of being, and herein might well lay a vast area of potential influence and contribution on part of the HRD profession.

This broad view of the possible influence and professional responsibility of HRD, then, affords the possibility to contribute to the creation of humane workplaces (see Aktouf, 1992), reinvigoration of democratic life in society and its social institutions (see Novak, 2002), and a broader conception of the goals of HRD in line with the notion of *Bildung*, the German idea of the general goal of education as subject or self-development in the context of social institutions, such as organizations, corporations, schools, and universities (e.g. Klafki, 2000; Witz, 2000) – ideals that appear to be linked to the contemporary notions of learning and knowledge-intensive organizations. Self-knowledge is never complete, and thus theorizing and practicing with the self in mind will require an attitude of humility, care, and concern for the subject and the process of working – a welcome and much needed balance to the managerialist discourse and practices in our own field and many of today's organizations and other social institutions.

Acknowledgement

This chapter is dedicated to Klaus Witz: with gratitude for his encouragement and admiration for the depth of his insights.

References

Aktouf, O. (1992) "Management and theories of organizations in the 1990s: Toward a critical radical humanism," *Academy of Management Review*, 17, 3: 407–31.

Allport, G. (1943/1960) "The ego in contemporary psychology," in G. Allport (ed.) *Personality and Social Encounter: Selected Essays*, Boston, MA: Bacon, 71–92.

Allport, G. (1955/1968) "Is the concept of self necessary?," in C. Gordon and K. Gergen (eds) *The Self in Social Interaction*, New York: Wiley, 25–32.

Alvesson, M. and Deetz, S. (1999) "Critical theory and postmodernism: Approaches to organizational studies," in S. Clegg and C. Hardy (eds) *Studying Organizations: Theory and Method*, London: Sage, 185–211.

Ardichvili, A. (2003) "Good work, poor pay: The challenge of constructing positive professional self-identities in economies in transition," Unpublished manuscript, Champaign, IL: University of Illinois.

Armon, C. (1993) "Developmental conceptions of good work: A longitudinal study," in J. Demick and P. Miller (eds) *Development in the Workplace*, Hillsdale, NJ: Erlbaum, 21–37.

Barley, S. and Kunda, G. (1992) "Design and devotion: Surges of rational and normative control in managerial discourse," *Administrative Science Quarterly*, 37: 363–99.

Boulding, K.E. (1956) "General systems theory–The skeleton of science," *Management Science*, April, 2, 3: 197–208.

Braude, L. (1983) *Work and Workers: A Sociological Analysis*, Malabar, FL: Krieger.

Brief, A. and Aldag, R. (1981) "The 'self' in work organizations: A conceptual review," *Academy of Management Review*, 6, 1: 75–88.

Burrell, G. and Morgan, G. (1979) *Sociological Paradigms and Organizational Analysis*, London: Heineman.

Chatterjee, M. (1963) *Our Knowledge of Other Selves*, Bombay: Asia Publishing.

Ciulla, J., (2000) *The Working Life: The Promise and Betrayal of Modern Work*, New York: Three Rivers.

Cohen, M., March, J., and Olson, J. (1972) "A garbage can model of organizational choice," *Administrative Science Quarterly*, 17: 1–25.

Csikszentmihalyi, M. (2003) *Good Business: Leadership, Flow, and the Making of Meaning*, New York: Viking.

Deetz, S. (1992) *Democracy in an Age of Corporate Colonialization: Developments in Communication and the Politics of Everyday Life*, Albany, NY: State University of New York.

Deikman, A. (1982) *The Observing Self: Mysticism and Psychotherapy*, Boston: Beacon.

Dewey, J. (1890/1969) "On some current conceptions of the term 'self'," in J. Boyddston (ed.) *The Early Works of John Dewey, 1882–1898*, Vol. 3, Carbondale, IL: Southern Illinois University, 56–74.

Erdynast, A. (1990) "A Rawlsian view of Kohlberg's conception of stage-six justice reasoning," in M. Commons, C. Armon, L. Kohlberg, F. Richards, T. Grotzer, and J. Sinnott (eds) *Adult Development, vol. II: Models and Methods in the Study of Adolescent and Adult Thought*, New York: Praeger, 249–59.

Flew, A. (1979) *A Dictionary of Philosophy*, New York: St. Martin's.

Freeman, M. (1992) "Self as narrative: The place of life history in studying the lifespan," in T. Brinthaupt and R. Lipka (eds) *The Self: Definitional and Methodological Issues*, Albany, NY: State University of New York, 15–43.

Goldman, H. (1988) *Max Weber and Thomas Mann: Calling and Shaping of the Self*, Berkeley, CA: University of California.

Gordon, C. and Gergen, K.J. (eds) (1968) *The Self in Social Interaction*, New York: Wiley.

Harter, S. (1993) "Visions of self: Beyond the me in the mirror," in S. Harter, J. Eccles, and L. Carstensens (eds) *Developmental Perspectives on Motivation*, Lincoln, NE: University of Nebraska, 99–144.

Hengehold, L. (1998) "Postmodern critique of the subject," in E. Craig (ed.) *Routlege Encyclopedia of Philosophy*, London: Routlege, 196–201.

Hogan, T. (1991) "Personality and personality measurement," in M. Dunnette and L. Hough (eds) *Handbook of Industrial and Organizational Psychology*, 2nd edn, Vol. 2, Palo Alto, CA: Consulting Psychologists Press, 873–919.

Honderich, T. (ed.) (1995) *The Oxford Companion to Philosophy*, Oxford: Oxford University.

James, W. (1890/1927) *The Principles of Psychology*, New York: Holt.

Jung, C.G. (1959) "The structure and dynamics of the self," in C.G. Jung, *Collected works*, Vol. 9, pt 2, London: Routlege, 222–65.

Jung, C.G. (1945/1993) *The Basic Writings of C.G. Jung*, New York: The Modern Library.

Kitzinger, C. (1992) "The individuated self concept: A critical analysis of social-constructivist writing on individualism," in C. Kitzinger (ed.) *Social Psychology of Identity and the Self Concept*, Surrey: Surrey University, 221–50.

Klafki, W. (2000) "The significance of classical theories of *Bildung* for a contemporary concept of *Allgemeinbildung*," in I. Westbury, S. Hopman, and K. Riquarts (eds) *Teaching as a Reflective Practice: The German Didactic Tradition*, Mahwah, NJ: Earlbaum, 85–107.

London, H. (ed.) (1978) *Personality: A New Look at Metatheories*, New York: Wiley.

Luthans, F. and Jensen, S. (2002) "Hope: A new positive strength for human resource development," *Human Resource Development Review*, 1, 3: 304–22.

McGoldrick, J., Stewart, J., and Watson, S. (2002) "Postscript: The future of HRD research," in J. McGoldrick, J. Stewart, and S. Watson (eds) *Understanding Human Resource Development: A Research-based Approach*, London: Routledge, 395–8.

Martin, J. (1992) *Cultures in Organizations: Three Perspectives*, Oxford: Oxford University.

Marx, K. (1844/1963) *Early Writings: The Economic and Philosophical Manuscripts of 1844*, New York: McGraw-Hill.

Maslow, A. (1956) "Self-actualising people: A study of psychological health," in C. Moustakas (ed.) *The Self*, New York: Harper, 160–93.

Maslow, A. (1965/1973) *Eupsychian Management*, Homewood, IL: Irwin.

May, R. (1953) *Man's Search for Himself*, New York: Norton.

Miri, M. (1980) *What is a Person?*, Delhi: Shree Publishing.

MOW International Research Team (1987) *The Meaning of Working*, London: Academic Press.

Neruda, P. (1990) *Selected Poems*, New York: Mariner.

Nord, W. and Fox, S. (1999) "The individual in organizational studies: The great disappearing act?," in S. Clegg and C. Hardy (eds) *Studying Organizations: Theory and Method*, London: Sage, 142–68.

Novak, B. (2002) "Humanising democracy: Matthew Arnold's nineteenth-century call for a common, higher, educative pursuit of happiness and its relevance to twenty-first-century democratic life," *American Educational Research Journal*, 39, 3: 593–638.

Pervin, L.A. (2002) *Current Controversies and Issues in Personality*, 3rd edn, New York: Wiley.

Schuman, M. (1988) "The problem of self in psychoanalysis: Lessons from Eastern philosophy," *The American Academy of Psychoanalysis*, 16, 2: 595–624.

Shoemaker, S. (1963) *Self-Knowledge and Self-Identity*, Ithaca, NY: Cornell University.

Stein, M. (1998) *Jung's Map of the Soul: An Introduction*, Chicago: LaSalle.

The American Heritage Dictionary (1982) 2nd college edition, Boston, MA: Houghton-Mifflin.

Walton, J. (2003) "How shall a thing be called? An argumentation on the efficacy of the term HRD," *Human Resource Development Review*, 2, 3: 310–26.

Wilms, W. (1986) "Captured by the American dream," Paper presented at the conference on vocationalising education, University of London, Institute of Education.

Witz, K. (2000) "The academic problem," *Journal of Curriculum Studies*, 32, 1: 9–23.

Witz, K., Goodwin, D., Hart, R., and Thomas, S. (2001) "An essentialist methodology in education-related research using in-depth interviews," *Journal of Curriculum Studies*, 33, 2: 195–227.

13 "To develop a firm persuasion"

Workplace learning and the problem of meaning

John M. Dirkx

About eight years ago, a fierce blizzard swept through the northeast coast of the United States, bringing workplaces to a virtual standstill. With as much as eighteen or more inches of snow piling up in many places, no one seemed to be going anywhere. Airports were closed and most places of employment in the city simply didn't open. In an interview with a reporter from National Public Radio, Jenny, a bank worker who was playing in and enjoying the snows of New York City's Central Park, was asked what she would be doing were it not for the blizzard. With a downcast tone in her voice, Jenny bluntly replied, "Working...bored to death." As she gleefully kicked and slogged through the freshly fallen snow blanketing the Big Apple on a work-free day, I suspect Jenny spoke for many workers.

For a variety of reasons, many people have given up on the possibility of doing what they love and what brings joy. Laden with the responsibilities of being task-oriented and productive, their lives fill with the needs of everyday life. Rather than representing an expression of who they are or what they could become, work has become for many something to get through. In her book, *Working Ourselves to Death*, Diane Fassel observes, "Everywhere I go it seems people are killing themselves with work, busyness, rushing, caring, and rescuing" (quoted in Fox, 1994: 26). Terkel provides a vivid portrayal of working in the United States and how the work we do can and does debilitate the human spirit:

> This book, being about work, is, by its very nature, about violence – to the spirit as well as to the body. It is about ulcers as well as accidents, about shouting matches as well as fistfights, about nervous breakdowns as well as kicking the dog around. To survive the day is triumph enough for the walking wounded among the great many of us.
>
> (1974: xii)

While these are admittedly anecdotal accounts, their message is revealed over and over again in the daily lives of hundreds of thousands of workers in the United States and throughout much of the industrialized world. They reflect the historical experience of work as a primal curse that sentences us to years of painful drudgery (Thomas, 1999). For Jenny and others, work seems a necessary evil needed to achieve other ends far-removed from their daily toil. It often imprisons their sense of spirit and denies who they are as persons. Meaning is found not in their work but in the snowy banks of a work-free day, the freedom of an upcoming vacation, a new level of purchasing power, or the open-ended promises of a pending retirement. They work to live, rather than living to work (Sinetar, 1987).

This sense of alienation and disconnection from what one does for a living has been described by some as a crisis of meaning in work (Pauchant and Associates, 1995) and is perhaps the foundation for the rapid growth of a literature around the spirituality of work (Dirkx, 2000; Wallace, 2001). Clearly, one aspect of this increasingly popular approach to work represents what Wallace (2001) refers to as the "hottest new management theory," a rather elaborate ploy to manipulate workers' energies and commitments. The rapidly escalating number of books, journal and magazine articles, workshops, presentations, conferences, and listservs around spirituality of work provides opportunity for all kinds of shameless charlatans, offering little more than a modern version of snake oil.

Despite this dangerous potential, one has to take account of the degree to which this idea seems to have taken hold. Behind all the schlock, gloss, and new-age hype, a message seeks to be heard (English *et al.*, 2003). With the explosion of technology and computer-mediated forms of communication, the emergence of a global economy, and shifting geo-political realities, our sense of meaning in life is becoming dangerously frayed. We are rapidly losing the traditional social and cultural structures that provide us with the capacity for a sense of understanding, purpose, and coherence in our lives (Morin, 1995). According to Wallace (2001), we can understand the spirituality of work movement as a broad response to the sense of spiritual emptiness that people feel. Although a bandwagon currently being used in the pursuit of many questionable goals (Ciulla, 2000), the idea of a spirituality of work is implicitly giving voice to a deep and abiding search for meaning within the human spirit (Pauchant and Associates, 1995; Dirkx, 2000).

Work is surely not the only way through which we realize meaning in life. Many scholars, however, argue that it plays a critical role in shaping who we understand ourselves to be (Sinetar, 1987; Csikszentmihalyi, 1990; Palmer, 1990; Welton, 1991; Hart, 1992; Fox, 1994; Dirkx and Deems, 1996; Dirkx, 2000; Gallwey, 2000; Wallace, 2001; Whyte, 2001). The field of Human Resource Development (HRD) is charged with the fostering of learning and development of employees and the organizations for which they work. Workplace learning[1] represents a location in which individuals make sense of their experiences (Welton, 1991; Dirkx and Deems, 1996), a notion central to the field of adult learning (Brookfield, 1986; Mezirow, 1991; Jarvis, 1992). Yet, few studies in HRD and workplace learning seek to address the problem of meaning in work. Most conceptions of workplace learning are framed within market economic terms and primarily reflect concern for the organizational "bottom line."

In this chapter I argue for a perspective that grounds the process of workplace learning within the context of the problem of meaning in work. Such a perspective emphasizes the complex, dynamic, and dialogical relationships in workplace learning between our sense of self as worker, the nature of the work we do, and the context in which we do the work. My analysis is framed from the perspectives of organizational existentialism (Pauchant, 1995), vocation (Hansen, 1995; Palmer, 1990; Whyte, 2001), depth psychology (Moore, 1992; Britzman, 1998; Butler, 1999) and the spirituality of work (Palmer, 1990; Fox, 1994).

The meaning of work

For many years, scholars have been concerned about the nature of work and the meaning that it holds to those who perform the work (Thomas, 1999). This concern frequently surfaces in studies of job satisfaction and quality of work life (Freeman and Rogers, 1999; Hyde, 2003; Brown and McIntosh, 2003). The field of organizational existentialism (Pauchant, 1995), however, has systematically focused our attention on the problem of meaning in work and its relationship to organizational effectiveness and development. As Pauchant suggests, this perspective stresses the importance of "understanding the subjective experiences and the actions of the *people* who work in organizations or interact with them" (1995: 3). Of primary concern to many who work in this field are basic issues of the human condition, including loss of personal meaning within people's lives.

The meaning of work is often discussed in rather vague and abstract terms. Indeed, in our modern material culture, we often find it quite difficult to reflect on such unusual questions. Yet, as Victor Frankl learned from his experience in Auschwitz,

> the meaning of life differ[s] from man to man, and from moment to moment. Thus, it is impossible to define the meaning of life in a general way. Questions about the meaning of life can never be answered by sweeping statements. 'Life' does not mean something vague, but something very real and concrete.
>
> (1963: 123–4)

With the loss of traditional social and cultural structures for conferring meaning on our lives, individuals are now more than ever faced with the need to construct meaning within the particulars and concreteness of their own life experiences (Morin, 1995).

But what do we mean by the meaning of work and how might we understand this issue relative to workplace learning and the practice of HRD? Morin suggests that the idea of meaning reflects three broad dimensions:

> If we can agree that work is an object of meaning, we can describe (1) the *significance of work* for the individual as both a definition and a value, (2) the *orientation of the individual work* as defined as the personal objective or purpose of work in his life, and (3) the *coherence of the work experience* as resulting from acts of commitment toward an objective or a cause that allow the individual to transcend himself.
>
> (1995: 46)

In other words, meaningful work reflects activity we understand and grasp, done for particular reasons that indicate a commitment beyond our selves to broader, transcendent values, causes, and issues.

This existential perspective on the meaning of work highlights the spiritual nature of work and its function in our lives in terms of vocation or calling. Scholars have long held that work, closely aligned with a sense of the sacred, is central to what we hold to be the meaning of life (Palmer, 1990; Fox, 1994). This sense of work is not new, however, reflecting an historical ambivalence manifest in views of work as both a primal curse and as sacred duty (Thomas, 1999). Sinetar suggests:

> Work is one of the ways that the mature person cares for himself and others. Through his work and relationships the individual finds a place in the world, belongs to it, takes responsibility for himself and others. Work becomes his way of giving of himself. His work...provides him with a way of dedicating himself to life.
>
> (1987: 162)

Work seems central to who we are as human beings. As such, viewing work in this manner underscores what many have come to recognize as its *expressive* dimension, a notion that differentiates the idea of work from more instrumental approaches inherent in the idea of a "job" (Morin, 1995). The expressive dimension of work is associated with the subjective experience of work, such as interest, vocation, creativity, autonomy, and satisfying human relations (MOW, 1987). In a study of what she refers to as "vital workplaces," Deems (1998) reported that, among the perceptions of her study participants, meaning in work was a dominant theme. In reflections on their work, these participants clearly indicated an awareness of their work as both a caring for themselves and a contribution to the outer world.

In recent years, the idea of work as vocation or calling, as linked to that which transcends the individual, has experienced something of a renaissance. Hansen describes vocation as "work that is fulfilling and meaningful to the individual, such that it helps provide a sense of self, of personal identity" (1995: 3). Work as vocation "describes work that results in service to others and personal satisfaction in the rendering of that service" (Hansen, 1995: 3).

This sense of work as vocation or calling is also reflected within an emerging scholarship of a spirituality of work (Sinetar, 1987; Palmer, 1990; Fox, 1994; Dirkx and Deems, 1996; Mitroff and Denton, 1999; Dirkx, 2000; Wallace, 2001; Whyte, 2001). Expressed through such terms as "right livelihood" (Krishnamurti, 1992), "vocational integration" (Sinetar, 1987), "right work" (Fox, 1994), "flow," (Csikszentmihalyi, 1990), or the "inner game of work" (Gallwey, 2000), this perspective stresses the profound, integral relationship between our work and who we are. In part, the spirituality of work movement seeks spiritual renewal through a deeper, expressive investment in one's work. Work as right livelihood implies a spiritual stance toward one's work, involving matters of both soul and spirit (Moore, 1992; Dirkx and Deems, 1996). David Whyte refers to this perspective as developing a "firm persuasion" in our work, "to feel that what we do is right for ourselves and good for the world at exactly the same time...when we have work that is challenging and enlarging and that seems to be doing something for others" (2001: 4).

While an existentialist and spiritual approach to the meaning of work draws our attention to the subjective experience of work, it does not ignore or deny the objective and instrumental dimensions that are characteristic of much of what we do. Rather, this perspective suggests a dialectic relationship between one's inner, subjective world and experience and the outer, objective conditions of the external world. This last point is an important issue for workplace educators to which I will return in an elaboration of workplace learning from an existentialist and depth psychology perspective.

Loss of meaning in the contemporary workplace

The dilemma that many workers face, and those who seek to foster their learning and development, revolves around this dialectical relationship between our inner worlds and the outer social worlds in which we work. As workers, we experience an inner, existential desire for meaning, ways of acting and being in our work that expresses our sense of identify and creativity. Yet, much of the western world is not supportive of this kind of behavior in our work. Rather, the focus is largely on instrumental and utilitarian aspects of organizational life. The socio-cultural contexts of work do little to encourage or support the kind of commitment to broader causes that this search for meaning requires. As Morin indicates:

> current practices in the areas of mobilization and organizational development emphasize commitment to the organization, more specifically, to the assigned objectives. If these objectives are unrelated to the individual, they do not really call for the individual to surpass or transcend himself or herself.
>
> (1995: 52)

Such practices within the workplace have contributed to what many regard as a deeply disturbing crisis in our individual and collective relationship with work, a fraying of the intimate connection between what we do and our sense of who we are (Sinetar, 1987; Fox, 1994; Whyte, 2001). Within many organizations, work seems to have lost its intrinsic sense of meaning. Organizational and managerial practices often "fragment work to such an extent that it becomes impossible for individuals to do something in their own image, to use their creativity, to make a part of themselves exist" (Morin, 1995: 51), contributing to a sense of a loss of meaning among many workers.

The continuing sense of alienation that many of us experience in our work reflects the absence in our culture of a deep understanding of the spirit, purpose, and meaning of human experience (Moore, 1992). Individuals address this lack of a sense of meaning in their work by other activities that seek to satisfy their need for pleasure or power. For many individuals, the meaning of work is realized primarily in its ability to contribute to their power as consumers. A "good" job is regarded largely as one that pays well or that provides decent benefits. Indeed, economic reward structures figure prominently in many studies of factors that affect perceptions of job satisfaction (Brown and McIntosh, 2003). While I do not mean to imply in any sense a lack of importance to these aspects of work, a focus on the economic rewards of one's work often serves to detract individuals from its deeper, expressive dimensions. Relatively few workers enjoy a sense of passion about their work, and many feel bored, frustrated, constrained, and dulled by what they do. A friend of Howard Cutler expresses the dilemma confronted by many workers who seek a deeper understanding of and meaning in their work. She faces

> an hour-long commute to work. And the minute I step into the office... I have to deal with the pressures, the demands, my boss is a jerk, and I can't stand my co-workers... Things are so hectic I barely have a chance to catch my breath... But I need to work. I need the money. I can't just quit and expect to get another job. So how can I find happiness at work?
>
> (His Holiness the Dalai Lama and Cutler, 2003: 16–17)

Loss of meaning contributes to emotional states of being mainly characterized by loss of interest or lack of initiative (Morin, 1995), and a profound sense of alienation that many individuals feel within their work (Terkel, 1974; Aktouf, 1992; Ketchum and Trist, 1992; Hawley, 1993; Casey, 1995). Violence within the workplace continues unabated, with shootings now commonplace and "going postal" an expression of the dark humor we use to make sense of such horrendous events, perhaps revealing our own thinly disguised sense of rage. Even seemingly high status, highly rewarded corporate and professional work creates powerful feelings of emotional conflict among relatively privileged workers, suggesting important differences between perceptions of work as satisfying and as meaningful, and evoking serious concern for the mental and emotional welfare of these "high status" workers (LaBier, 1986; Pauchant and Associates, 1995; West, 2001).

Those of us involved in workplace learning or organizational development need to acknowledge the critical importance of the expressive dimension of work within the lives of employees. Central to this aspect of work is the search for meaning in work, of finding and doing meaningful work. Because meaning-making is a central dimension of adult learning (Brookfield, 1986; Mezirow, 1991; Jarvis, 1992), this search for meaning should become an integral focus of workplace learning. Learning in and for work is grounded in a broader framework of meaning-making within our life experiences. Such a perspective of workplace learning would reflect a commitment to helping individuals develop a firm persuasion in their work. As we shall see, however, committing the field to such a goal will require a profound shift in the ways in which workplace educators think about work and learning in and for work.

Current approaches to workplace learning and the meaning of work

Several years ago, I had the privilege of talking with a welder who was enrolled in a workplace literacy program. This curriculum was designed to improve performance by enhancing work-related literacy skills. A white man in his late fifties who had worked for this manufacturing company for many years, Harry was required to participate in what many regarded as a state-of-the-art workplace literacy program, based on literacy assessment scores tailored for his work. Shop manuals and other work-related materials were used in the writing curriculum to increase their contextual relevance for the learners. During a break, I asked Harry how it was going in the class. Sitting quietly with his arms folded across his chest, he sighed heavily and replied, "It's okay. I don't really see how any of this, though, has anything to do with my job. If they were teaching me how to read to my grandchildren, now that would be something!"

Harry's gentle comments express a sense of disconnect between his experience of work and efforts to foster workplace learning. This disconnect revolves around how he is making sense of his life experiences, as a welder and as a grandfather. As a context for workplace learning, the problem of meaning draws our attention to the importance of understanding how individuals make sense of their experience. While traditional forms of teaching often stress the meaning intended by the teacher or the text, existentialist perspectives emphasize the ways in which learners as individuals construe the meaning of what it is they are being asked to learn within the particular, concrete nature of their own experiences (Morin, 1995). While learning a particular skill may be critical to improving performance within a given area of the manufacturing process, what acquiring that skill means to the individual worker must be understood within his or her broader understandings, purposes, and commitments. This meaning-making process is shaped and influenced by the learner's biography and reflects both conscious and unconscious influences (Britzman, 1998; West, 2001).

Work and related aspects of learning for work are expressive of the worker's sense of self and identity, of who they are, and how they see themselves in the world. This expressive aspect of work is reflected in perceptions of one's work as interesting and as contributing to a greater cause that is morally important. The search for meaning is expressed through a worker's desire for a sense of agency, participation, authority, and autonomy in their work. These characteristics seem closely aligned with the sense of one's work as vocation or calling. Harry's desire to read to his grandchildren demonstrates the ways in which he seeks to make sense of his workplace literacy experience. The fact that he perceives what he *is* learning as having nothing to do with his work leaves him feeling without authority, power, or agency.

The meaning that workers come to attribute to their work and what they are learning about that work are also influenced by the socio-cultural context in which that work is performed (West, 2001). An organizational context conveys a certain ethos that encourages some kinds of behaviors and beliefs and discourages others. Workplace beliefs, values, and behaviors are also either encouraged or discouraged by prevailing belief systems within the broader culture. Internalization of the so-called "Protestant work ethic" is an example of how the larger society influences and shapes meaning on the shop floor.

The search for meaning in work lays down many challenges for developing and fostering a kind of workplace learning that helps individuals discover or rediscover a sense of calling or vocation, a firm persuasion in their work. While workplace learning is increasingly associated with employment, organizational learning, and development, its relationship to the problem of meaning depends on how educators frame their understanding of learning in the workplace (Garrick, 1999). Different approaches "hold different meanings of workplace learning illustrating the sheer complexity and diversity of factors that directly (and indirectly) shape one's learning including *what counts* in the workplace" (Garrick, 1999: 226).

The performance-based approach

The field of HRD is dominated by conceptions of learning that basically reflect a "bottom-line" perspective to work. Garrick (1999) suggests that "We are getting close to a situation in which what it is to *know* in the modern world appears to have no secure base beyond markets" (1999: 217). Such a view is reflected in the discourses of human capital theory and generic skills and competencies. Human capital theory emphasizes the productive capabilities of human beings. Based on what the organization needs, educators stress helping workers learn that which will enhance their overall performance and value (Swanson, 1999; Swanson and Arnold, 1996). The discourse of generic skills and competencies compliments human capital theory, highlighting the requirement of current as well as future workplaces.

The perspectives of human capital theory and generic skills and competencies stress specific products to be derived from the design and implementation of specific workplace learning activities. This approach to workplace learning has its roots in early twentieth century scientific management (Taylor, 1911) and scientific curriculum-making (Bobbitt, 1918) movements. Grounded in a behavioral psychology, the performance approach understands work as a composite of specific skills and knowledge that, with analysis, can be readily identified. The idea is to specify the knowledge and skills reflected in and needed by "real-world" performance and to select activities most appropriate to yielding these performances (Yelon, 1996). These products are clearly specified prior to the learning experience and serve to guide all phases of the planning, implementation, and assessment of workplace learning (De Jong *et al.*, 2001). The primary intent of such learning experiences is to eliminate deficiencies and contribute to the workers' overall productivity and performance. In this perspective, workers are largely viewed and understood through measures of productivity and performance (Fenwick, 2000).

As Garrick (1999) points out, this approach to workplace learning represents little more than a sub-discourse of a market economics that shapes in powerful ways our understandings of learning in and for work. This performance-orientation to workplace learning renders the worker relatively passive, relative to what it is that comes to be known. Meaning is interpreted as "received meaning." That is, workers are intended to acquire the particular forms of meaning encoded within the predetermined curriculum and the educator's practice. Emphasis is clearly on transmission of an objective set of knowledge and skills that is distinct from the workers who act on it, and not related to the particular socio-cultural contexts in which they work.

Without attention to the expressive dimensions of work, performance-based approaches to workplace learning can only serve to exacerbate, rather than ameliorate, problems of meaning in work. Such perspectives on workplace learning reflect a kind of functionalist rationality (Cervero, 1988) and are highly instrumental in their overall orientation. With their primary commitment to organizational objectives, they create more distance rather than less between the self of the worker and the work itself. Workers are seldom engaged in learning that is intrinsically meaningful to their own experience or that frames an understanding of their work beyond short-term, economic rewards. For the most part, they are simply learning to be more efficient and productive cogs within the greater organizational machine.

The developmental approach

A developmental approach to workplace learning places more emphasis on learning as a developmental process. This approach stresses development, fulfillment, and self-actualization of the worker. According to Bierema, "A holistic approach to the development of individuals in the context of a learning organization produces well-informed, knowledgeable, critical-thinking adults who have a sense of fulfillment and inherently make decisions that cause an organization to prosper" (1996: 22). The developmental approach reflects what Garrick (1999) refers to as a discourse of experience-based learning. This approach focuses on experience as the foundation of and stimulus for learning and constructivist orientations to learning from and through experience. Learning is profoundly influenced by the socio-emotional context in which learning occurs (Garrick, 1999: 230). What workers come to know and understand through the process of workplace learning reflects who they are as persons and how they are making sense of their experiences in the workplace.

The literature on the learning organization (Senge, 1990; Watkins and Marsick, 1993; Watkins, 1996) reflects a concern with learning within a systems perspective and stresses the interconnectedness of all aspects of organizational life, including the overall well-being and development of the individual worker. It is an organic under-standing of wholes and relationships. Proponents of this view seek to recognize the role that context plays in workplace learning and how the various elements of that context serve to ultimately determine the nature of workplace learning.

Developmental approaches to workplace learning attempt to place more emphasis on a sense of human agency within the learning process. They also focus on issues and broader organizational contexts neglected by more performance-oriented approaches to learning (Bierema, 1996). At first glance, developmental approaches to workplace learning seem much more capable of addressing the problem of meaning in work. As we come to understand more deeply the search for meaning and how it unfolds within the workplace, even this approach seems to fall short. Learning is viewed as largely arising from the willful engagement of the individual worker with his or her context and experience, and as a way to foster realization of innate potential or inter-est. There is little recognition within these perspectives of the potentially ambiguous, contradictory, and paradoxical nature of the meaning-making. Although develop-mental views place more emphasis on the subjective and expressive dimensions of workplace learning, the subjective is seen largely as a relatively uncontested arena for expression and actualization of one's interests and calling. Learning is viewed as a conscious, purposeful, and intentional act. As a process of development, learning through one's experience is framed as a positively energized activity, with little atten-tion to emotional conflicts that such learning can precipitate, or the ways in which learning and development themselves might represent a kind of interference within the life-world of the worker (Britzman, 1998; Fenwick, 2001). For all the developmental, experience-based rhetoric, such a view of workplace learning seems little more than a gentler, kinder version of performance-based learning. Concern ultimately remains *primarily* with organizational performance rather than with how individual workers understand and make sense of their work.

In summary, the underlying conceptions of workplace learning reflected in dominant approaches to the practice of HRD do not seem to be well suited to adequately address either the complexities of learning represented by the problem of meaning in work, or the struggle for self-awareness and self-understanding that must be the core of such learning (West, 2001). In fact, they may even circumscribe a practitioner's ability to perceive and address the gnawing existential problems surfacing within the world of work. These approaches suggest a process of learning that is rational, progressive, and linear, and conceive of knowledge as a substance (Felman, 1987). These characteristics, however, do not reflect what we know about the process of meaning-making. A disconnection is evident between the view of workplace learning portrayed by the dominant approaches to HRD, and the nature of learning as it is experienced by workers struggling with the problem of meaning in their work. Clearly, we are in need of a way of thinking about workplace learning that honors and gives voice to the problematic nature of meaning associated with work and its role in the lives of individuals as well as organizations and society.

Helping workers discover meaning in their work

The performance-based and developmental approaches to workplace learning remind us of important but different aspects of the meaning-making process. Within workplace learning, as within work itself, the process of making sense of our experiences reflects the content of what we are being asked to learn, the self of the learner, and the socio-cultural context in which these experiences are taking place (West, 2001). The performance-based perspective stresses the importance of the task itself and the effectiveness with which it is performed in contributing to the overall performance of the organization. It privileges the demands of the outer reality of the work and seeks to address these demands in the most effective means possible. In this sense, the performance-based approach is largely an *instrumental* or utilitarian perspective on workplace learning. This dimension of work is a central focus of workplace learning.

The developmental approach to workplace learning emphasizes the experiences of individual learners and the construction of meaning of their experiences. It draws our attention to the importance not only of what is being learned but how it is that learners are construing and making sense of that which they are being asked to learn. The self of the learner and the socio-cultural context in which they work and learn represent important dimensions of learning as a meaning-making process.

How workers make sense of these reality demands or tasks, however, remains enormously important both to them and to the organization in which they work. In this way, the developmental approach illuminates the *expressive* dimension of the learning process. Students in formal learning situations may interpret their task as memorizing information for little more than reproducing this information on a test and getting a good grade. It is highly unlikely they will retain beyond a few weeks or months much of the information they have mastered. For this information to become more meaningful for the workers, they will have to develop a broader understanding of its significance in their lives as workers, become more clear about the reasons and learning what they are learning and what they intend to use this information for, and how knowing this information in some way relates to broader contexts beyond their immediate situations (Morin, 1995).

As we have seen, however, neither perspective offers an adequate framework for navigating the uncertain, complex, and paradoxical nature of the meaning-making process in work. As Sievers suggests, "The quest for meaning is not an easy venture. It involves becoming aware of the relatedness of our inner worlds, our dreams, hopes, and anxieties, with the outside world and its social constructions" (1995: 291). Despite the seemingly humanistic organizational reforms of the past 25 years, this problem continues to haunt workplace learning efforts (Deems, 1998). In the concluding sections, I want to build on the work of Linden West (2001) to suggest a way of thinking about workplace learning that takes its cue from the problem of the meaning of work. Based on the fields of organizational existentialism and depth psychology, I suggest that the inherently problematic nature of workplace learning itself becomes a locus for ongoing learning and development of self-understanding within the workplace (West, 2001).

A "dialogical" perspective: assumptions about the self, work, and learning

Three important factors emerge for our consideration in a dialogical model of workplace learning: (a) the disciplinary content the worker is expected to acquire (b) the self of the worker, and (c) the socio-cultural context in which this learning takes place (West, 2001). The process of making sense of our work, and learning in and for work, reflects the dynamic and dialogical relationships that exist among these three dimensions of a worker's experience. These relationships represent the matrix in which workers make sense of their work within the broader context of their individual and collective lives. Any foray into existential analysis of work and learning, however, can easily slip into incomprehensible abstracts. To avoid this potential problem, I will ground my discussion in an example of workplace learning from my own background in laboratory medicine.

A case scenario

In my fictitious case example, I have been asked as an experienced clinical microbiologist, to provide training for laboratory technologists to identify a new species of pathological bacteria from clinical material. These technologists work for a large laboratory within Midwestern United States associated with a 400 bed hospital and a medical clinic staffed by over 250 physicians. A new form of bacteria has been reported in clinical material and is suspected of causing significant illness and even death among human populations. Technologists need to be able to recognize this pathological organism from other nonpathological bacteria that may be present in a culture of clinical material, such as a throat swab. They need to know the characteristics of this new species of organism, how it differs from normal bacterial, what it looks like after culturing the clinical material on a petri dish, its appearances and characteristics under microscopic examination, and any biochemical tests that will be appropriate for definitive identification.

The workers in my laboratory setting might be successful in reproducing all this information on an oral or written quiz. Whether they are actually able to use this information to increase the likelihood that this organism will be recognized and identified from clinical material, however, depends on how they are making sense of this information and the broader context in which they are interpreting this information.

The intersecting dimensions of content, the self, and the socio-cultural context

How worker-learners make sense of their learning depends on the nature of the content workers are being asked to learn, their own biography, and the socio-cultural context in which this learning takes place. Despite the existentialist's emphasis on the subjective meaning and understanding of work (Pauchant, 1995), the performance of the particular tasks associated with work usually requires varying degrees of specialized knowledge in particular areas of content. In Harry's case, there is a considerable amount of technical information and numerous, highly technical skills that are required for him to effectively perform his duties as a welder within the plant in which he works. In the case of the laboratory technologists, they cannot identify the pathological bacteria from clinical specimens without particular scientific and technical knowledge.

Virtually all workers face the need to address or meet certain demands of their external reality. Many of these demands are conceptualized as particular tasks that require specialized forms of knowledge and skill. These demands or tasks of the job press in on them in ways that students in formal learning situations are confronted with the need to master certain aspects of the subject matter they are studying (Dirkx and Prenger, 1997). In both cases, if one is to remain a member of the community in which they find themselves, there is work that must be done.

But these tasks and their associated knowledge and skill take on particular meaning within the reality of the concrete lives of individual workers (Deems, 1998; West, 2001) and the particular practice contexts (Wenger, 1998; Daley, 2001). The self of the worker and the biographical influences on its identity figure prominently in the problem of meaning in work and in the process of workplace learning. According to Fenwick, educators who seek to

> help workers thrive and serve a vocational community [confront] workers' struggles to find meaning and purpose in jobs where they seem increasingly to experience anxiety, stress, sadness, and despair. These are fundamental issues of identity related to work and the human quest to understand and unfold self.
>
> (2000: 297)

This sense-making process of the content they are presented and the task they are being asked to perform is significantly influenced by their own biographical situation. Some of our worker-learners may be wondering, after several years on the job, if this is really the work for them. They remain mostly because they need the money and don't know for sure what else to do. Some might have family members who have been afflicted with this infection and who have perhaps suffered or even died from it. In all likelihood, what this knowledge represents for them, how they come to understand it, the reasons they are learning to do these procedures, and the relationship of what they are learning to their broader context will be quite different from those who have no personal experience with this organism and who might think it is highly unlikely that this organism might show up in their laboratory. Some worker-learners might be very uncomfortable with their ability to learn anything new, that such learning tasks pose potential threats to their sense of self-efficacy, and how they see themselves as a worker. Still others might be interested in learning and performing the new procedures because they want desperately to be recognized by their superiors as excelling in their work. They might have little regard for the clinical or medical significance of the new procedures but see the learning of these procedures primarily as an opportunity to further their own careers.

A meaningful understanding of workplace learning and its potential to help workers discover meaning in their work reflects a fundamentally subjective process. Any existential perspective begins with the concrete experiences of the individual person. Thus, the self of the learner significantly contributes to the ways in which he or she comes to understand and make sense of the new procedures they are being asked to learn. We need to attend to the meaning-making process that the learners engage in to conceive and construe the object of their learning (Morin, 1995), in this case particular laboratory procedures. Such a view of learning underscores the felt, organic dimension of the worker's experience. This view of workplace learning stresses the private as well as the public dimensions of learning, the imaginative as well as the rational, that which is concrete and relational.

The study of self and identity strongly suggests that this struggle is integrally bound up with an impulse to learn and develop. The workplace, then, becomes a location for constructing a sense of self in the world (Britzman, 1998). From a psychoanalytic perspective, this human quest involves recognition of the psychic events that make up our lives, the ways in which we often push many of these events – anxieties, fears, disruptions, mistakes, vicissitudes of love and hate – into the background out of conscious awareness (Fenwick, 2000). Learning something new and the prospects of change can bring us face to face with these unconscious aspects of ourselves. While the ego might perceive this learning as a threat to itself and garner defenses against the change, significant learning involves a working through of the "conflicts of all these psychic events and gradually coming to tolerate the self and its desires" (2000: 299). Thus, a dialogical perspective suggests our studies of workplace learning must be grounded in a deeper understanding of the complex relationship that exists between a person's psyche and their experience in the workplace (LaBier, 1986; Moore, 1992; Sievers, 1995; Dirkx and Deems, 1996; Todd, 1997; Britzman, 1998; Butler, 1999; Fenwick, 2001; Whyte, 2001; Kovan and Dirkx, 2003).

Desire and interference are the heart of the meaning-making process in work (Fenwick, 2001). Desire itself surfaces a sense of change, arising from this deep sense of the unfolding self, of wanting something to be different (Butler, 1999). But at the same time desire also evokes a sense of resistance to change and to learning. Recognition of this fact allows for an appreciation of work and workplace learning as a place where profound pedagogical encounters can occur. When we recognize and tap into this paradoxical situation, we often find new energies and enthusiasm emerging for our work. These energies, however, might be running counter to the established order or those purposes prescribed by educators or organizational leaders.

For example, workers may at times subvert explicit efforts to "empower" them or other efforts to shape them in a particular way. They may resist such "learning-centered" approaches, which seek to actively engage the learner within his or her experience. Dominant discourses of workplace learning might lead us to interpret such acts as not going along with the organization's purposes or not wanting to learn and grow. When viewed through a dialogical perspective, however, we might recognize workers as increasingly constructing and regulating their own "human capital." In this sense, workplace learning is interpreted as a form of transgression and resistance (Fenwick, 2001). Through these opportunities for and various forms of resistance, workplace educators seek the possibilities for work, learning, and identity construction.

In our example of the laboratory workers, we can see how these ideas of self, identity, desire, resistance, and interference might shape and influence the learning process. While a developmental perspective might draw our attention to the importance of the learners' experiences, our analysis suggest that the ways in which learners make sense of these experiences reflects more than rational, progressive, and linear processes. Within a group of ten workers, several different frames of reference might be present, each offering different interpretations of how the learners construe the new information and skills within their own concrete experiences. These different frames of reference lead to different understandings of this knowledge, its intended purposes, and how it might relate to broader contexts beyond oneself.

Finally, the process of meaning-making reflects the influence of the particular socio-cultural contexts in which the individuals work and learn (Deems, 1998; Wenger, 1998; Daley, 2001). This context is both narrow, in the sense of the organizational context, and broad, in the sense of professional and societal influences on the work. In a wide variety of professions, reflective practitioners who think carefully about their work (Schön, 1983) have suspected there is more to their knowing than the technical subject matter in which they were trained (West, 2001). Their evolving expertise, learning, and change reflect not only the shifting peculiarities of their subject matter but also the dramatic currents associated with the contexts in which their practices are located.

Context refers to socio-cultural characteristics and attributes of the particular, organizational settings in which we work. The process of constructing knowledge and transforming experience occurs within and is responsive to these contexts. For example, the extent to which performance or productivity is understood as a responsibility of the individual or the group will significantly shape the meaning that individuals construct with regard to any new learning about their work. Beliefs about gender relations and how they relate to the particular work context also have a significant influence on the particular meaning that individuals come to hold about their work. Organizational beliefs about the role of ambiguity, uncertainty, or failure in work also represent powerful shapers of the meanings that learners come to hold about their work. Finally, the meaning of one's experience in work and learning is molded by the broader cultural, economic, and political contexts of society. The emphasis within many companies on remaining globally competitive often results in processes of exporting jobs, automating previously high prestige, high paying jobs, and fostering other processes of lean "production." When individuals consider possible career choices or their future with their present employer, these broader social processes significantly shape the meaning they develop around such decisions.

In a broader sense, however, context also refers to the cultural ethos of one's profession and the particular value it places on particular aspects of one's practice, such as the role of feeling and emotion in one's work or the various ways in which our practice may implicitly support sexist or racist perspectives in society (West, 2001). Local interpretations and understandings of gender, race, class, sexual orientation, and power manifest themselves within the particulars of practice, within the feelings and emotions that practitioners have about their work, their clients, and themselves. For example, professional associations and societies may proscribe certain actions, attitudes, or behaviors, despite a professional's perceived need to address them in some way. These contexts, as with their particular areas of professional expertise, contribute to the uncertainty and ambiguity that practitioners come to recognize as essential dynamics of professional practice.

Conclusion

The problem of the meaning of work, of doing meaningful work, and finding the work that one does as meaningful, manifests itself across the life span. Community colleges and universities are filled with young adults "career surfing," going from program to program looking for areas that interest them. Many middle-age adults find themselves seemingly trapped in jobs that have long become boring and meaningless. Frustrated with the lack of connection between what they do and who they are, many workers turn to alternative ways of finding their work meaningful, such as increased power to consume, status, prestige, planning for retirement, or unhealthy lifestyle behaviors.

Education for work and workplace learning programs, such as those delivered by HRD practitioners, have continued to conceptualize their efforts within functional, performance-based, and instrumental frameworks, largely ignoring the expressive needs reflected in this growing problem of meaning in work. A few scholars and practitioners have argued for an alternative, more developmentally oriented approach to workplace learning but, for the most part, their efforts remain marginal both with the research and practice. When taken seriously, they are often assimilated within a pervasive performance-based, bottom-line framework. Despite numerous efforts over the last 20 years to change the way work is structured and organized within the workplace, the growing spirituality of work movement reflects increasing attention to the search for meaning in one's life, and suggests these "reform" efforts have done little to help workers discover work that is meaningful to them and to the world.

In this chapter, I have argued that the practice of workplace learning represents a major resource for assisting workers with discovering and developing meaning in their work. This premise suggests that work and the workplace represent primary locations for adult learning and development (Palmer, 1990; Welton, 1991; Hart, 1992). If we take this idea seriously, it has profound implications for the ways we conceptualize, develop, and deliver workplace learning. While a detailed analysis of the implications of this analysis for the practice of HRD is beyond the scope of this chapter, I will close with several implications that are suggested by the lens explored here. The ideas presented here reflect many concepts of practice already present within the field of adult learning.

When the meaning of work is considered central to workplace learning, practitioners and learners must confront and foster the dialectic relationship referred to earlier between the workers' inner worlds and the outer world in which their work is performed, between their sense of self, what they are expected to learn and to do, and the particular socio-cultural contexts in which this work is performed. To help sustain this often complex and contradictory relation, workplace learning needs to be viewed through constructivist perspectives. Workers need to be participating more fully in determining what they need to learn and how they will learn it, to have more of a sense of agency not only in their work but in their learning. At times, it may be more appropriate to incorporate the worker's interests beyond that specifically represented in the tasks performed on the job, such as improving a worker's reading skills by focusing on how he or she wants to use these new found skills.

Meaning-making occurs within particular contexts. For this reason, workplace educators need to consider plans, activities, and learning experiences that provide for a more holistic sense of one's work and how particular tasks being learned relate to the broader context of one's work, of the organizational culture, and ultimately to that which is morally good within society. Attention needs to be given to the expressive as well as the instrumental dimensions of work and the learning process. The expressive dimension is manifest through the workers' desires and interests, and the images, emotions, and feelings that animate their experiences in the workplace.

When formal programs are used, educators should employ problem-based and case-based learning that provide for ill-structured problems and situations within collaborative learning structures. These processes provide workers with opportunities to not only master the particular content to be learned but also to use the process itself to address other aspects of their learning, such as working across difference, communication, and teamwork. As West (2001) and others have demonstrated, when designed and facilitated appropriately group work can significantly contribute to making and sustaining connections between the worker's inner life and the demands and contradictions posed by the outer world.

Grounding workplace learning within the idea of the meaning of work also calls for more emphasis within the workplace on informal and incidental learning (Marsick and Watkins, 1990, 2001; Garrick, 1998; Marsick and Volpe, 1999). We may very well determine that most significant and meaningful learning takes place outside of formal HRD programs and within day-to-day experiences and relations of individual workers and groups of workers. Such an approach will place more emphasis on structures and organizations of the workplace that are consistent with meaningful work (Deems, 1998).

When conceptualized from the perspective argued here, workplace learning provides workers with a rich opportunity for lifelong learning, for learning about themselves and their relationship to their world. A sense of firm persuasion represents a kind of self-knowledge, an outcome of attending more closely to our world and how we each make it different (Whyte, 2001). "To have a *firm persuasion*, to set out boldly in our work," Whyte suggests, "is to make a pilgrimage of our labors, to understand that the consummation of work lies not only in what we have done, but who we have become while accomplishing the task" (2001: 5). I am under no illusions about the difficulties associated with such shift in our thinking and practice. Enormous political and economic interests make this an up-hill struggle. But the struggle for meaning in work has already been going on for many years. Our existential need for it demands nothing less.

Note

1 For purposes of this chapter, I use the term "workplace learning" broadly to refer to formal and informal experiences within the workplace, as well as experiences intended to prepare individuals for particular forms of work and workplace settings.

References

Aktouf, O. (1992) "Management and theories of organizations in the 1990s: Toward a critical radical humanism," *Academy of Management Review*, 17, 3: 407–31.

Bierema, L.L. (1996) "Development of the individual leads to more productive workplaces," in R.W. Rowden (ed.) *Workplace Learning: Debating Five Critical Questions of Theory and Practice*, New Directions for Adult and Continuing Education, No. 72 (Winter), San Francisco, CA: Jossey-Bass, 21–8.

Bobbitt, J.F. (1918) *The Curriculum*, Boston, MA: Houghton-Mifflin.

Britzman, D.B. (1998) *Lost Subjects, Contested Objects: Toward a Psychoanalytic Inquiry of Learning*, Albany, NY: SUNY Press.

Brookfield, S.D. (1986) *Understanding and Facilitating Adult Learning*, San Francisco, CA: Jossey-Bass.

Brown, D. and McIntosh, S. (2003) "Job satisfaction in the low wage sector," *Applied Economics*, 35, 10: 1241–54.

Butler, J. (1999) *Subjects of Desire: Hegelian Reflections in Twentieth-Century France*, New York: Columbia.

Casey, C. (1995) *Work, Self and Society: After Industrialism*, London: Routledge.

Cervero, R.M. (1988) *Effective Continuing Education For the Professions*, San Francisco, CA: Jossey-Bass.

Csikszentmihalyi, M. (1990) *Flow: The Psychology of Optimal Experience*, New York: Harper Perennial.

Ciulla, J.B. (2000) *The Working Life: The Promise and Betrayal of Modern Life*, New York: Times Books.

Daley, B. (2001) "Learning and professional practice: A study of four professions," *Adult Education Quarterly*, 52, 1: 39–54.

Deems, T.A. (1998) "Vital work: Adult development within the natural workplace," *39th Annual Adult Education Research Conference Proceedings*, San Antonio, TX: University of the Incarnate Word.

Dirkx, J.M. (2000) "Spirituality of work: The new opiate or a postmodern search for meaning in life?," *Working Knowledge: Productive Learning at Work Conference Proceedings*, Sydney, New South Wales, Australia: UTS Research Centre Vocational Education and Training, University of Technology Sydney, Working Paper 16.

Dirkx, J.M. and Deems, T.A. (1996) "Towards an ecology of soul in work: Implications for Human Resource Development," in E.F. Holton III (ed.) *Academy of Human Resource Development 1996 Conference Proceedings*, 11–4, Minneapolis, MN: University of Minnesota.

Dirkx, J.M. and Prenger, S.A. (1997) *Planning and Implementing Instruction for Adults: A Theme-Based Guide*, San Francisco, CA: Jossey-Bass.

De Jong, J.A., Thijssen, J.G.L., and Versloot, B.M. (2001) "Planned training on the job: A typology," *Advances in Human Resource Development*, 4, 3: 408–14.

English, L.M., Fenwick, T.J., and Parsons, J. (2003) *Spirituality of Adult Education and Training*, Malabar, FL: Krieger.

Felman, S. (1987) *Jacques Lacan and the Adventure of Insight: Psychoanalysis in Contemporary Culture*, Cambridge, MA: Harvard University Press.

Fenwick, T. (2000) "Putting meaning into workplace learning," in A.L. Wilson and E.R. Hayes (eds) *Handbook of Adult and Continuing Education (New Edition)*, San Francisco, CA: Jossey-Bass, 294–311.

Fenwick, T.J. (2001) "Transgressive possibilities in post-corporate enterprise culture," in R.O. Smith, J.M. Dirkx, P.L. Eddy, P.L. Farrell, and M. Polzin (eds) *AERC 2001: Proceedings of the 42nd Annual Adult Education Research Conference*, East Lansing, MI: Michigan State University, 131–7.

Fox, M. (1994). *The Reinvention of Work: A New Vision of Livelihood For Our Time*, San Francisco, CA: Harper.

Frankl, V.E. (1963) *Man's Search for Meaning: An Introduction to Logotherapy*, Boston, MA: Beacon Press.

Freeman, R.B. and Rogers, J. (1999) *What Workers Want*, Ithaca, NY: Cornell University Press.

Gallwey, W.T. (2000) *The Inner Game of Work*, New York: Random House.

Garrick, J. (1998) *Informal Learning in the Workplace: Unmasking Human Resource Development*, London: Routledge.

Garrick, J. (1999) "The dominant discourses of learning at work," in D. Boud and J. Garrick (eds) *Understanding Learning at Work*, New York: Routledge (pp. 216–231).

Hansen, D.T. (1995) *The Call to Teach*, New York: Teachers College Press.

Hart, M. (1992) *Working and Educating for Life: Feminist and International Perspectives on Adult Education*, New York: Routledge.

Hawley, J. (1993) *Reawakening the Spirit in Work*, San Francisco, CA: Berrett-Koehler.

His Holiness the Dalai Lama and Cutler, H.C. (2003) *The Art of Happiness at Work*, New York: Riverhead Books.

Hyde, A.C. (2003) "What federal employees say: Results of the 2003 federal human capital survey," *Public Manager*, 32, 2: 62.

Jarvis. P. (1992) *Paradoxes of Learning: On Becoming an Individual in Society*, San Francisco, CA: Jossey-Bass.

Ketchum, L.D. and Trist, E. (1992) *All Teams Are Not Created Equal*, Newbury Park, CA: Sage.

Kovan, J.T. and Dirkx, J.M. (2003) "Being called awake: The role of transformative learning in the lives of environmental activists," *Adult Education Quarterly*, 53, 2: 99–118.

Krishnamurti, J. (1992) *On Right Livelihood*, San Francisco, CA: Harper.

LaBier, D. (1986) *Modern Madness: The Emotional Fallout of Success*, Reading, MA: Addison-Wesley.

Marsick, V.J. and Volpe, M. (eds) (1999) *Informal Learning On the Job*, Advances in Developing Human Resources, No. 3, Baton Rouge, LA and San Francisco, CA: Academy of Human Resource Development and Berret Kohler.

Marsick, V.J. and Watkins, K.E. (1990) *Informal and Incidental Learning in the Workplace*, London: Routledge.

Marsick, V.J. and Watkins, K.E. (2001) "Informal and incidental learning," in S.B. Merriam (ed.) *The New Update on Adult Learning Theory*, New Directions for Adult and Continuing Education, No. 89, Spring: 25–34.

Mezirow, J. (1991) *Transformative Dimensions of Adult Learning*, San Francisco, CA: Jossey-Bass.

Mitroff, I.I. Denton, E.A. (1999) *A Spiritual Audit of Corporate America: A Hard Look at Spirituality, Religion, and Values in the Workplace*, San Francisco, CA: Jossey-Bass.

Moore, T. (1992) *Care of the Soul*, New York: HarperCollins.

Morin, E.M. (1995) "Organizational effectiveness and the meaning of work," in T.C. Pauchant and Associates (eds) *In Search of Meaning: Managing For the Health of Our Organizations, Our Communities and the Natural World*, San Francisco, CA: Jossey-Bass, 29–64.

MOW International Research Team (1987) *The Meaning of Working*, San Diego, CA: Academic Press.

Palmer, P.J. (1990) *The Active Life: A Spirituality of Work, Creativity, and Caring*, San Francisco, CA: Jossey-Bass.

Palmer, P.J. (1998) *The Courage To Teach: Exploring the Inner Landscape of a Teacher's Life*, San Francisco, CA: Jossey-Bass.

Pauchant, T.C. (1995) "Introduction: Toward a field of organizational existentialism," in T.C. Pauchant and Associates (eds) *In Search of Meaning: Managing For the Health of Our Organizations, Our Communities and the Natural World*, San Francisco, CA: Jossey-Bass, 1–25.

Pauchant, T.C. and Associates (1995) *In Search of Meaning: Managing For the Health of Our Organizations, Our Communities and the Natural World*, San Francisco, CA: Jossey-Bass.

Schön, D.A. (1983) *The Reflective Practitioner: How Professionals Think in Action*, New York: Basic Books.

Senge, P.M. (1990) *The Fifth Discipline: The Art and Practice of the Learning Organization*, New York: Doubleday.

Sievers, B. (1995) "Organizational culture and its discontents: Life in a spiritual community," in T.C. Pauchant and Associates (eds) *In Search of Meaning: Managing For the Health of Our Organizations, Our Communities and the Natural World*, San Francisco, CA: Jossey-Bass, 271–92.

Sinetar, M. (1987) *Do What You Love, the Money Will Follow: Discovering Your Right Livelihood*, New York: Paulist Press.

Swanson, R.A. (1999) "The foundations of performance improvement and implications for practice," in R.J. Torraco (ed.) *Performance Improvement: Theory and Practice*, Advances in Developing Human Resources, No. 1, Baton Rouge, LA and San Francisco, CA: Academy of Human Resource Development and Berret-Koehler Communications, 1–25.

Swanson, R.A. and Arnold, D.A. (1996) "The purpose of Human Resource Development is to improve organizational performance," in R.W. Rowden (ed.) *Workplace Learning: Debating Five Critical Questions of Theory and Practice*, New Directions for Adult and Continuing Education, No. 72, Winter, San Francisco, CA: Jossey-Bass, 13–19.

Taylor, F. (1911) *The Principles of Scientific Management*, New York: Norton.

Terkel, S. (1974) *Working: People Talk About What They Do All Day and How They Feel About What They Do*, New York: Ballantine.

Thomas, K. (ed.) (1999) *The Oxford Book of Work*, Oxford: Oxford University Press.

Todd, S. (ed.) (1997) *Subjects of Desire: Perspectives on Pedagogy, Culture and the Unsaid*, New York: Routledge.

Wallace, C.M. (2001) "The 'spirituality' of work," *Anglican Theological Review*, 83, 1: 183–8.

Watkins, K.E. (1996) "Of course organizations learn!," in R.W. Rowden (ed.) *Workplace Learning: Debating Five Critical Questions of Theory and Practice*, New Directions for Adult and Continuing Education, No. 72, Winter, New York: Jossey-Bass, 89–96.

Watkins, K.E. and Marsick, V.J. (1993) *Sculpting the Learning Organization*, San Francisco, CA: Jossey-Bass.

Welton, M.R. (1991) *Toward Development Work: The Workplace As a Learning Environment*, Geelong, Australia: Deakin University Press.

Wenger, E. (1998) *Communities of Practice: Learning, Meaning, and Identity*, New York: Cambridge University Press.

West, L. (2001) *Doctors On The Edge: General Practitioners, Health and Learning In the Inner-City*, London: Free Association Press.

Whyte, D. (2001) *Crossing the Unknown Sea: Work As a Pilgrimage of Identity*, New York: Riverhead Books.

Yelon, S.L. (1996) *Powerful Principles of Instruction*, White Plains, NY: Longman.

14 Sense or sensibility?

A reflection on virtue and 'emotional' HRD interventions

Linda Perriton

Introduction

The field of Human Resource Development (HRD) has never seemed overly concerned with questioning the ethics of its policies and practices. Because learning is seen as intrinsically 'good', organisations that provide training and development are seen as automatically virtuous (Woodall and Douglas, 2000) and the facilitators of such events are, by association, virtuous also.

Virtue is acknowledged as an area of ethics that has been neglected by moral philosophers. This is a fact that is not only a matter of regret to philosophers but also some embarrassment because there is no doubt that a fully developed concept of virtue is needed (Becker, 1975). Becker observes that, as a result, there are very few philosophical tools that can be used to determine the morality of an agent, as opposed to the morality of a situation. And it also leads to the situation where a profession, such as HRD, can afford itself the title of 'virtuous' based on its own high self-esteem, rather than any objective argument of its intrinsic worth. The problem is that:

> Self-esteem is very often the crux of the matter in evaluations of one's conduct. And self-esteem is not built entirely on estimates of the value or dutifulness of one's performance. No matter how many successes some people have, they still feel they 'are' failures; no matter how many lies some people tell, they still feel they 'are' fundamentally honest.
>
> (Becker, 1975: 112)

This chapter looks at a particular form of HRD practice and asks whether the high self-esteem in which we hold our own profession doesn't perhaps blind us to conduct within it that is worthy of challenge. My argument is based on the consideration of data collected as part of a research project I was undertaking into forms of 'alternative' training approaches. In the course of this research I became interested in the teaching approach of the women I met who, although they identified themselves as opposed to the orthodoxy of management education (rationalist, goal oriented, measured and evaluated) and as having broadly feminist sympathies were not teaching in any identifiably feminist way. Instead of politicising their teaching spaces and engaging with feminist issues they were creating spaces for emotional expression and feelings and claiming this to be a distinct contribution to management pedagogy.

For centuries individuals have made judgements about what is a desirable attitude – we could refer to it as posture or, if we wanted to be more contemporary, identity – to adopt in relation to emotion. And so it is to questions of emotion, reason and virtue that I wish to turn in this chapter. I believe that by examining these key concepts in relation to HRD that we can critically engage with some contemporary practices within the field and re-examine their claims to being intrinsically 'good'. I do this by framing the discussion of some contemporary HRD interventions within a much broader and theoretical debate around the idea of 'sensibility'. Sensibility, because of the way that it elevates emotional response to a form of 'truth', is central to an understanding of eighteenth century radicalism and in the twenty-first century is a useful heuristic for examining the claims to radicalism by the HRD practitioners in my research study.

The chapter is structured in the following way. In the first section I look at the research context for this argument – an investigation of 'alternative' training and development practices. The second section examines the eighteenth century conceptualisation and reaction to sensibility. The relationship that women, in particular, have had historically with sensibility is particularly relevant to its current incarnation within the HRD context. The third section draws parallels between the faith in emotion and sentiment in past centuries and its reappearance in contemporary HRD practice. I argue that far from being a new phenomenon the faith shown in the 'truth' of emotion and emotional responses is a reworking of sensibility in modern settings. I argue that these pedagogical approaches ignore, and sometimes actively reinforce, inequalities in the workplace in the pursuit of 'development' borne out of emotion. The final section concludes that the time is right for a reconsideration of some of the practices we see as inherently virtuous because they value emotion over reason, and suggests that a proper balance needs to be struck between sense and sensibility.

The research context

In 1999/2000 I interviewed management development practitioners working within industry as part of a project on 'alternative' pedagogical approaches. The orthodox management development practice in industrial settings was designed to fulfil the educational priorities of the organisation, not those of the individual (whatever the 'learning organisation' rhetoric might have promised). Most 'alternative' educators saw themselves as challenging the primacy of the organisational objectives for education and instead saw themselves as developing distinct pedagogies. These pedagogies took as their central faith the idea of the limitless developmental potential of the individual and the focus on the espoused needs of the employee.

My research led me to four women working within industry in this humanist tradition. What was striking about my conversations with them was the tales they shared of their professional and personal journeys to this point in their careers. These women were funny, articulate and very aware of the struggles that they had faced as women in their professional lives in order to gain credibility within larger organisations and then in establishing their own businesses.

One respondent's description of her educational practice made a lasting impression on me. Although, on the continuum of management development practice her pedagogy is in no way strange or particularly extreme, it has always troubled me. I have framed previous analyses of her practice by drawing parallels with the New Age movement as the contemporary incarnation of the Human Potential Movement (Perriton, 2000). And in this chapter I want to consider her practice from the vantage point of a historical debate on the 'proper' deployment of emotional response.

It doesn't seem particularly surprising to see women at the centre of a movement towards an emotionally based development pedagogy. Throughout history women have shown themselves willing to artificially raise and lower the stocks of 'emotion' and their claims to it as a political tactic (Rendall, 1985). The much debated and discussed dichotomous attribution of Female and Emotion versus Male and Reason has been enthusiastically reinforced over many generations – not as the result of the all-seeing, all-powerful hand of Patriarchy but also by individual women seeking social and political ground – so why not those seeking educational ground also?

Giving employees their emotional space

This following sub-section explains the HRD practice that I wish to critique. The main emphasis in the development interventions used by the management development practitioner – let's call her Morven, for convenience's sake – is on improved communication. In this sense Morven's practice is based on one developmental idea, that if people were more practiced in sharing their essential humanity with each other the workplace would be less 'toxic' and more productive. To create an environment where this development work can take place it has to, above all, look different to the workplace. To that end Morven creates an environment that is visually stimulating and includes the use of primary colours, wall charts, soft furnishings and flowers. Participants are encouraged to – in the early stages of the development intervention – avoid the use of language and 'speak' instead through drawings and paintings that they create in the workshop. Music is played in the background and soft toys and sweets are often left on participant's chairs to reassure them. The 'serious' and colourless world of business is banished in favour of a return to the riotous colour of the kindergarten and an invitation to play.

The role of the facilitator in this process is a deliberate 'feminine' and nurturing one. Her contribution is one of play organiser and interpreter, she gently invites people to 'open up', supervises naps (reflection) and mops the occasional tear. The discourses allowed within this space are actively policed – Morven only allows 'positive' language to be used. For example she rejected one exercise on the grounds that it would introduce negative thoughts:

> one of the exercises that has been recommended to us is an exercise which actually shows how awful people get in negotiation situations, they really start bitching at each other. We can't use that exercise because it's creating the sorts of behaviours that we don't want to have, so we work not to create the negative experiences, we want to create the positive experiences. Then we have people reflect on

them to reinforce them and build on the strengths there, so we don't do 'let's do it all the wrong way and then the right way', we say, 'let's do it the right way and then reflect on how we made it work'.

By the use of the specific games and exercises Morven also encourages self-disclosure and a type of communication that, because it is not heard often in the workplace or often thought to be an appropriate discourse, is interpreted as 'deeper', 'better' and 'more authentic' communication. The use of reflective exercises helps to reinforce this message of deep learning and of a shift in perceptions. This practice is legitimised through recourse to a discourse of spiritual wholeness and healing that is held out as a reality both for the individual and for the (economic) good of the organisation.

Sensibility

The choice of the facilitation of emotion as a conscious intervention is interesting to me. Communication and emotion appears, in HRD practices such as Morven's, to be viewed as important tools for organisational (and socio-economic) change and regeneration. But at the same time this sort of HRD intervention shuts out non-emotional discourse from its educational space and can *only* carry the subject matter of emotion. As such it is strangely reminiscent of the eighteenth century idea of sensibility.

The roots of sensibility have been traced back into the seventeenth century religious sermons of latitudinarians who preached the following tenets: the identification of virtue with acts of benevolence, the assumption that good affections are natural, an anti-stoical praise of sensibility and self-approving joy (Conger, 1990). This early identification of sensibility with benevolence enabled it to gain a popular foothold in society. It laid proper Christian emphasis on the need to cultivate a sense of responsibility towards others and a desire to do good but added to it a permission for the pleasure that comes from knowing that you have done good works to be expressed and to be felt. Whilst these two things were kept in balance 'sensibility' was a modest step on the path to self-consciousness and indulgence of the 'feel good' factor. Later it would become uncoupled from the virtue of benevolence and become what many considered mere mawkish sentimentality and an escape into excessive displays of emotion.

Todd (1986) has commented that 'sensibility' should perhaps be considered the key term of the eighteenth century – although it came in and then out of popular use only in the second half of that century. A word that was rarely in use until the middle of the century, by the end of the 1700s had become, in Conger's words, 'an over-determined linguistic sign' (1990: 14) struggling under the weight of incompatible values that had been attributed to it. But this is to look ahead at its demise – at its height of use the term came to denote the faculty of human feeling, the capacity for refined emotion and a readiness to display compassion when confronted with suffering (Todd, 1986). Warren (1990) notes that whether one sees sensibility as an ethical or a psychological concept the emphasis is on the individual. And as such he sees sensibility as referring to the system through which an individual responds to experience. Sensibility is a concept that starts us on the path to our own understanding of identity and self-awareness because, as Warren further notes, it is 'an attribute that exalts the self' (1990: 28).

In fiction the 'cult of sensibility' lasted from the 1740s until the 1770s. Above all it was a didactic form of literature – albeit with a single focus, how to behave properly in the realm of emotion. In the early years of sentimental fiction the emphasis was on the expression of friendship and how to respond decently. Later it prided itself more on making its readers weep and teaching them when and how much to weep (Todd, 1986).

> [This] literature is exemplary of emotion, teaching its consumers to produce a response equivalent to the one presented in its episodes. It is a kind of pedagogy of seeing and of the physical reaction that this seeing should produce.
>
> (Todd, 1986: 4)

Sensibility as a discourse equates intellectual authority with the ability to either display emotional susceptibility or to elicit it from others. Its appeal to emotional spontaneity is an important feature of how it 'works', because the authority that it claims from the authenticity of emotional response was a substitute for careful analysis of fact and application of reason (Cox, 1990).

Women were considered to have a special and increased capacity for sensibility in comparison to men. This was, of course, seen as a feature of their sex and was reinforced by the changing perceptions of the importance of gender in the concept of the 'Christian self' evident in the church at this time (Taylor, 2003). Although the soul was considered sexless it couldn't be denied that the bodies they inhabited whilst on the earthly plane were male and female. Again, from the mid-century onwards there was an increasing belief that the female religious feeling was inherently more powerful than that of men (Taylor, 2003). Women were seen as having a greater capacity for pity and empathy for the suffering of others given to them by nature. So whilst men came to religion through the exercise of reason, women's religious belief was as a result of emotional sensitivity. Taylor notes 'Women may be men's inferiors in social and political life, but in matters of the spirit they are pre-eminent' (2003: 100).

Even Mary Wollstonecraft, a trenchant critic of sensibility in later contexts – she believed it to be a manipulative doctrine designed to keep women subservient and silly (Conger, 1990) – was not above writing sentimental fiction. Her heroine in *Mary: A Fiction* is the epitome of sensibility as she tends tearfully to the needs and sufferings of others whilst having greatness upon her soul as a result of performing good deeds (Taylor, 2003). Part of the imperative of those in the grip of sensibility was the need to speak from the heart and soul. As a result sensibility in the eighteenth century saw all kinds of women – not just those who were campaigning for women's rights but also those who opposed such ideas – united in piety and the belief that women's moral superiority must be used to good effect. It was a belief that saw women campaign against the slave trade because they saw an opportunity to demonstrate moral and not political or economic leadership (Taylor, 2003).

Feminists, from contemporaries of the cult of sensibility like Wollstonecraft, to Poovey in our own generation have found much to critique in this philosophy.

Conger (1990) notes that Poovey sees sensibility as part of a reactionary and not revolutionary impulse that works to stifle women.

> It encouraged them to cultivate their emotions at the expense of their physical, moral, spiritual, and intellectual growth; and it trapped them in a paralyzing paradox: they were acknowledged freely to be men's superiors in the exercise of feeling, but at the same time they were reminded that excess exhibition of feeling demonstrated weakness of character and inferiority to men.
>
> (Conger, 1990: 15)

But in the end it was not feminist critique that was fated to loosen the grip of sensibility on British society – it was the political situation (Todd, 1986). At the close of the eighteenth century the English were transfixed by the political situation across the channel and the threat it posed to its own government. Conservative opinion in the form of 'The Anti-Jacobin Review' was hard at work implicating and allying sensibility with radicalism – hoping to dampen any reformist zeal (whether its origins were religious or political). Todd notes that supporters of the revolution had also written of events in France in highly sentimental ways and given effusive emotional support. When reports of the Jacobin Terror became widespread attention was turned to sensibility itself as many wondered whether excessive feelings of benevolence and the desire to benefit humanity wasn't always destined to end up as excess of another form altogether. Sensibility was now seen as not only self-indulgent but also dangerous (Todd, 1986).

Whatever we may think of sensibility in retrospect, Conger (1990) makes the point that it ushered in a new era of consciousness – a consciousness of the self that forms our own modern understanding of who we are. It is my argument in the next section that there are enough similarities between the eighteenth century philosophy of experience and the emotion-based practice of HRD professionals such as Morven to suggest that sensibility is still with us today.

Resurrecting sensibility

The examples of 'new' or 'radical' HRD pedagogies I came across in my research all had the espoused aim of 'improving communication' between individuals in organisations. Morven's emotional HRD interventions are no different in this respect – although in interview she did go further, insisting that the ultimate goal was to 'talk to people about putting love back into the workplace'. But the objectives of the individual workshop or training event were to create the environments in which people came to know each other better through opening themselves up and speaking from the perspective of feeling, rather than thought or, as we might characterise it in a more philosophical argument, from the perspective of Emotion as opposed to Reason.

The aim of better communication between individuals is a common goal in many team building and other organisational training interventions. What differs between HRD practitioners is the choice from the range of training approaches available – from outdoor training events to T-Group approaches. But whatever the approach taken the 'better communication' aspect usually comes down to the individual skill of the facilitator in drawing 'appropriate' responses from the participants. As such the skill of the HRD practitioner – however they might want to view other tools that they use in development interventions – is the skill of purposeful conversation.

The association of sensibility with conversation in the eighteenth century has been highlighted by Warren (1990). By identifying himself or herself with a withdrawal from the active world to one of refined emotional response the person of sensibility can convey a form of authoritative objectivity. Or, as Warren puts it, 'Free of ... the desires that dominate the masculine world of social action, the man or woman of sensibility sees clearly and speaks with utter sincerity' (1990: 34). This is surely the conviction that is behind the faith shown by HRD practitioners such as Morven in the 'truth' of speaking from your emotions. She does not allow the trappings of the 'masculine world of social action' in her training environment but instead insists on emotional conversations in order to 'improve' communication.

Of course, by subtly policing *how* things can be expressed in the training environment, this practice can never be judged to have failed. Participants receive very strong non-verbal instructions as to what the permitted discourse will be both from the environment that Morven creates and from early exercises in the workshop that only allow them to express themselves through drawing, rather than verbally. Given the policing of the discourse and the public identification of those who resist such pedagogical manoeuvring as 'bringing a lot of anger to the event', often with the effect of silencing them, it is true that participants *will* speak 'from their emotions'. We are the generation, as Dineen (1999) sees it that has been raised by the psychology industry and are thus perfectly competent in the discourse of emotional distress. Workshops and seminars and self-development (or development done unto us) are part of the dominance of this discourse in contemporary life and the prize they hold out is the one of the possibility of fulfilment. The question that we need to ask, however, is why a self-consciously emotional discourse is considered more authentic or qualitatively better than one based on reason.

My argument is that HRD practice based on the privileging of emotional discourses are a contemporary expression of sensibility. So the answer to the question posed in the previous paragraph would be obvious to a woman of sensibility such as Morven. Emotional refinement and being able to speak directly from one's feelings are the best routes to knowledge – not for those of sensibility the 'laborious processes of reason or the long round of experience others need' (Warren, 1990: 34) – emotion is not only the more authentic expression of one's humanity but also a short-cut to Truth. If nothing else this is certainly a handy marketing tool for the freelance HRD practitioner when pitching for business to an organisation – emotion is the faster way to better communication, especially if you define better as 'emotional'.

It is only a short journey for a facilitation style that is based on the ability to elicit emotional responses from participants to attain the status of ideology. Warren has noted the tendency for those who embrace sensibility to think of conversations as a sort of genuine secular communion:

> sensibility makes it possible for a certain conception of conversation to assume the force of an ideology. Conversation was extolled as the way an entire society could participate in defining a workable reality, a social context in which all could have a voice and upon which all could draw, but no writer could explain how such a discourse could emerge or function.
>
> (Warren, 1990: 34)

The belief in the power of conversation by those who subscribe to a philosophy of sensibility is also sometimes presented, as with Morven, as a belief in emotion's potential as a radical force in organisations, removing their capacity to be 'toxic' to individuals who work in them through authentic communication and transforming the organisation in the process.

The next section of this chapter therefore examines the case for an ethics of emotion and care for others being thought of as 'new', 'radical' or 'critical'.

Questioning the ethics of care and emotion

In the last section I argued that contemporary HRD practices that privileged emotional discourses and were designed to elicit them from participants were essentially a reworking of sensibility. There are also, I think, parallels that could be drawn between the women of the eighteenth century, attracted to human rights projects because of a belief in their moral leadership as a result of their superior quality of emotional response, and women such as Morven who wish to transform organisations not out of political radicalism but a belief in emotional truth. We have seen how the facilitative act – the skill of purposeful conversation in a development context – can, according to the tenets of sensibility, also be an act of secular communion that is capable of bringing about change. But what are the radical possibilities of this pedagogical method? This section critiques the idea that sensibility can be thought of as anything but an inherently conservative philosophy and practice – leaving to one side (for now) questions of whether it could be thought of as a good or virtuous activity.

As feminist historians have noted, when women find themselves outside of the political arenas where they are afforded influence they are often told to develop their own best qualities 'those of heart and moral feelings, while also fitting themselves, by patience, industry, frugality and piety, to be the wives and mothers of citizens' (Rendall, 1985: 20). I believe that the retreat from Reason into Emotion in the field of HRD is also an example of a response to lack of influence and presence in organisational politics. Forced to make a virtue out of necessity HRD practitioners are increasingly promoting the idea of their own 'special' skills of empathy and compassion. They seek to develop in themselves and those they teach the 'best qualities' of heart and moral feeling. By choosing to remain outside of (or being forced out of) the decision-making arena, the pedagogy many women practitioners turn to is one that seeks a 'domestic' influence by acting in the role of organisational wives and organisational mothers to participants attending these development events.

As Mendus (2000) notes, there are only two possible responses to the exclusion of women from the political sphere. The first – demonstrated in Morven's approach – is a call for the state (or, in this case, organisations) to find room for love and compassion. The second response is to argue that there is nothing at all in women's nature that precludes them from political life and if educated in a similar way they will temper emotion with reason and be able to assume the full political rights afforded to men. This second response is that most closely associated with liberal forms of feminism and – although feminist voices are heard rarely in HRD – is the one most commonly pursued in Human Resource Management approaches.[1]

In the wider political sphere, the cause of sensibility has been subsumed under the 'ethics of care' argument. I have argued elsewhere at some length about the way that a feminist 'ethics of care' impacts on women educators in the field of management education (Perriton, 1999) and it is not my intention to reprise those arguments in this chapter. I am, however, interested in looking at the claims that sensibility and the ethics of care have to being a radical form of the way that women engage with organisations.

Mendus argues that western political philosophy is full of arguments that move seamlessly from the assertion of women's caring and emotional nature to the conclusion that she is unfit for public life. An 'ethics of care' is characterised as having two distinct features.

> The first is its emphasis on the differences which divide people rather than the similarities which unite; the second is the centrality it accords to small-scale, face-to-face relationships.
>
> (2000: 101)

At the level of educational practice this understanding of difference has been individualised so that educators working within this tradition in industry instead refer to the differences *between* individuals, which are more often framed as ones of personality than race or gender. Workshops designed to elicit emotion bring participants (who will also be work colleagues) into contact with the 'individuality' of each other. So, for example, participants may be invited to find items in the natural environment that describe them metaphorically (e.g. 'I've returned with a pine cone because I feel that I am the sort of person who opens and is more expansive when showered with warmth'). Participants are also invited to share with their colleagues vignettes from their non-work lives in order to focus on the individual identity and differences that people bring to their work. Differences are things to be celebrated and diversity something to embrace. Race and gender are not things to be tackled in the abstract but instead become part of the *individual's* difference and therefore cannot claim a status different in nature or magnitude to an individual's hobby of stamp collecting or their love of opera. When treated as part of the individual then all individual difference becomes fetish.

The emphasis on face-to-face relationships is obvious within this educational practice. Not only is it the ostensible subject matter but, as I have claimed in the previous section, it is also the unique skill that the educator brings to the event. Mendus, however, claims that it is impossible when working with the micro level of individual relationships to consider this as *political* transformation:

> emphasis on small, face-to-face relationships compounds the difficulty [of political exclusion] when once we recognize that political problems are characteristically large-scale. Typically they do not arise at the level of individual relationships, and therefore an ethic which concentrates on the small scale may have little to contribute to their solution.
>
> (Mendus, 2000: 101)

Warren (1990) is similarly sceptical about the possibility that conversations of sensibility can ever bring about wider social change. For, as he states:

> The ideal conversation always depends upon openness and equality among its participants, but that openness requires admitting very few into the exchange. Consequently, the values of this discourse will actually reflect the needs of the small, self-conscious group that accepts this notion of conversation. Making sensibility as part of this idealized talk masks the exclusiveness that conversation both requires and nourishes.
>
> (Warren, 1990: 35)

HRD interventions of this kind will only ever be able to effect change through communication within very small groups. And whilst all might be equal when speaking from the heart, outside of the training event material realities such as power, hierarchy and status (that 'masculine world of social action' again) will soon reassert their dominance.

An educational practice based on an 'ethics of care' by its nature ignores questions of dictates of universal reason in order to concentrate on the particularities of individual relationships. Mendus notes that this is quite different from political philosophy based on reason – that starts with a moral agent separate from others independently electing principles to obey. In contrast the 'ethics of care', and the view of the individual and the workplace which this pedagogy promotes, places the individual within a network of others and the moral deliberations of the individual are aimed at maintaining these relations (Mendus, 2000).

This form of education in industry is taking feminist ethics into labour relations in ways that distorts its links to a philosophical tradition of rights and the independent moral agent. Instead it is trying to transform the workplace through its rehashing of much older philosophical arguments concerning the possibilities of regeneration of the social and economic sphere through (women's) emotional qualities. In effect it is making quite explicit links between maternal virtues and organisational virtues. It is being helped in this by contemporary discourses of 'strategic' human resource management, which suggests that traditionally female communicative methods are missing in organisational life (i.e. the recent trend towards measuring 'Emotional Intelligence' and latterly 'Spiritual Intelligence').

Family life is not replicated in organisational life any more than it is recreated in political life. Improving family communication is just that – it does not tackle the remaining inequities for women in the economic sphere, nor does it tackle race and sexual orientation at the policy and legislative level. It removes the possibility of educational spaces within industry to be harnessed as spaces where change can begin and similarities understood because it promotes the idea of difference as defining of individuality. It also pretends that in authentic individual communication all the ills of the world can be solved. It is such an emphasis on the endless possibilities of individual influence that Smail (1994) maintains removes from people the recognition of systemic failure and therefore the possibilities for solidarity and impetus for change.

Mendus sums up the *cul-de-sac* that an 'ethics of care' and sensibility represents for the possibility of change.

> By urging the centrality of face-to-face relationships, proponents of the ethics of care hope to render political life an extension of family life. This may be an appropriate aim in societies which are small-scale, and where face-to-face relationships are the norm. But in large, anonymous, post-industrial societies the analogy becomes diminishingly useful or plausible. In brief, an ethic of care seems best suited to small-scale societies where face-to-face relationships are the norm, but these societies are not the ones which we now have. Modern society is large, sprawling and anonymous, and whilst we might wish that it were not so, the insistence on an ethic which emphasizes actual relationships may nevertheless appear nostalgic and untrue to the realities of modern life.
>
> (Mendus, 2000: 105)

The question for this pedagogy, which purports to be about positive change within organisations, is whether it is aware of the conservative nature of its practice? By anchoring morality and organisational virtue in the emotional authenticity and care displayed in relationships the possibilities for change become self-limiting. Ignatieff has observed that we cannot extend care beyond those we know and that care itself may not be a obvious 'good' when extended beyond the small circle of acquaintance (Mendus, 2000). Mendus observes that the substitution of compassion for justice was, after all, at the heart of some of the most unpalatable aspects of the Victorian Poor Laws. Such a substitution for justice at the heart of organisational life is hardly a guarantee against a contemporary form of moral Victorianism in the economic sphere. Nor will it deliver justice for those discriminated against on the grounds of gender, race or sexual orientation.

A 'pedagogy of sensibility' may in the future be judged on very different terms than those that its proponents would wish it to be viewed today. For educators such as Morven the pedagogy is a force for change and good and for the promotion of a positive moral evolution in organisations. Viewed from outside the rosy glow cast by the philosophy of sensibility – that is, from the realm of Reason – the pedagogy looks distinctly conservative rather than radical.

Conclusion

> Virtue requires habit and resolution of mind as well as delicacy of sentiment, the former qualities are sometimes wanting where the latter is in the greatest perfection.
>
> (Adam Smith)

I started this chapter with a question concerning virtue and it is to the judgement of virtue that I wish to return to at the end. There is an undoubted tendency within HRD to consider that because it means well and is involved in projects of development and improvement its actions are virtuous. However, as the earlier quote by Adam Smith reminds us, it is not enough to have delicate sentiments to earn the title of virtuous. Emotion and sentiment alone are not a guarantee of virtue – the exercise of Reason is required as well.

Virtue, as Becker (1975) noted, has been a relatively neglected concept. We are more familiar with talking in the language of ends and means, utility, values, duties, rules, obligations and responsibilities. In HRD we too are more familiar with the concepts of evaluation of utility, of the establishment of end points and design of the appropriate means of achieving them, of discussions of professional rules and of the placing of responsibilities upon learners. We too rarely stop to ask if our actions and interventions are virtuous or whether what we hold to be virtues are always viewed as such by those who are placed in our professional care.

The focus of this chapter was a form of HRD intervention that is by no means unusual in the spectrum of development approaches used in contemporary organisations. Its principle aim was to promote 'better', that is, more emotionally authentic communication between individuals. A process that, in effect, narrowed the possible discourses available to only those that allowed the expression of feeling rather than reasoned argument. Those that resisted the discourses could be silenced by categorising them as individuals who acted inappropriately by bringing 'anger' to an otherwise positive event or by pedagogical tools that narrowed their scope to speak outside the privileged discourse. My argument was that the moral force behind this sort of training and development practice was a resurrection of the eighteenth century idea of 'sensibility', which afforded those of superior emotional refinement a claim to speak the truth. But in the training and development context this reverses the realm of the private and the public. Emotional discourses belong to the realm of the domestic and the private and are rarely seen as valid in organisational (public) arenas. Sensibility promoted to a HRD philosophy – Warren (1990) would suggest 'ideology' was more apt – seeks to domesticate the organisation.

We should not be surprised at the ease with which the workplaces can be transformed from public to domestic spaces. The United Kingdom has an acknowledged culture of long working hours, which have caused many to comment on the amount of our previous leisure time now devoted to work. In addition, contemporary theorists have noted how the personal has become economic (e.g. Abercrombie and Longhurst, 1998; Adkins and Lury, 1999; Thompson and Warhurst, 1999). Work is something that we now have a 'psychological' and personal relationship with as if it too is part of the web of natural law that exists alongside familial obligations.

The domestic has its place, as does emotion, but our continued failure to challenge overly sentimental practices within HRD are hardly a sign of virtue. We have afforded too much credence to practitioners who use their facilitative skills in order to promote better communication by *restricting* the ability of individuals on development programmes to give voice to challenges to the appropriateness of the pedagogy or its application to their own context. In this view, HRD practitioners are not virtuous – they are merely the (self-appointed) overseers of a morally unclear project of the self.

Note

1 That is, most HRM responses to issues of discrimination are made from an 'equal opportunities' standpoint. This approach emphasises training and encouragement for women to enable them to take their place alongside men in the management of organisations. There is no assumed lack of ability keeping women from assuming their full organisational rights. The Equal Opportunities Commission's checklist for effective management of EO in the workplace asks questions under six headings. None assume that women are excluded from a full organisational life because of their 'nature', rather the checklist focuses on commitment, awareness, information and monitoring, implementation, policy and procedures, reviewing and updating (Dickens, 2002).

References

Abercrombie, N. and Longhurst, B. (1998) *Audiences*, London: Sage.

Adkins, L. and Lury, C. (1999) 'The labour of identity: performing identities, performing economies', *Economy and Society*, 28, 4: 598–614.

Becker, L.C. (1975) 'The Neglect of Virtue', *Ethics*, 85, 2: 110–22.

Conger, S.L. (ed.) (1990) *Sensibility in Transformation*, Cranbury, NJ: Associated University Presses.

Cox, S. (1990) 'Sensibility as argument', in S.L. Conger (ed.) (1990) *Sensibility in Transformation*, Cranbury, NJ: Associated University Presses.

Dickens, L. (2002) 'Still wasting resources? Equality in employment', in S. Bach and K. Sisson (eds) *Personnel Management*, 3rd edn, Oxford: Blackwell Publishing.

Dineen, T. (1999) *Manufacturing Victims*, London: Constable.

Mendus, S. (2000) *Feminism and Emotion*, Basingstoke: Macmillan Press.

Perriton, L. (1999) 'Paper dolls: the provocative and evocative gaze upon women in management development', *Gender and Education*, 11, 3: 295–307.

Perriton, L. (2000) *The Crime of Miss Jean Brodie? Women, the New Age and the Fast Track Out of Management.* Paper presented at the US Academy of Management Conference, Toronto, 3–9 August.

Rendall, J. (1985) *The Origins of Modern Feminism: Women in Britain, France and the United States, 1780–1860*, Basingstoke: Macmillan Press.

Smail, D. (1994) 'Community psychology and politics', *Journal of Community and Applied Social Psychology*, 42: 3–10.

Taylor, B. (2003) *Mary Wollstonecraft and the Feminist Imagination*, Cambridge: Cambridge University Press.

Thompson, P. and Warhurst, C. (1999) 'Ignorant theory and knowledgable workers: myths and realities of workplace change', in D. Robertson (ed.) *The Knowledge Economy*, London: Macmillan Press.

Todd, J. (1986) *Sensibility: An Introduction*, London: Methuen.

Warren, L.E. (1990) 'The conscious speakers: sensibility and the art of conversation considered', in S.L. Conger (ed.) *Sensibility in Transformation*, Cranbury, NJ: Associated University Presses.

Woodall, J. and Douglas, D. (2000) 'Winning hearts and minds: ethical issues in human resource development', in D. Winstanley and J. Woodall (eds) *Ethical Issues in Contemporary Human Resource Management*, Macmillan: Basingstoke.

15 Pedagogies of HRD

The socio-political implications

Sharon Turnbull and Carole Elliott

In this chapter we wish to argue for a more vigilant approach to the unintended outcomes of HRD pedagogies. We will seek in particular to understand the identity-shaping role of learning in organisations, the politics of pedagogical practices and the implicit as well as explicit assumptions framing our decisions to introduce HRD practices and make learning interventions inside organisations. We seek to inquire into our pedagogical practices as educators, developers and designers of programmes – ranging from internally focussed customised courses to university accredited qual-ifications. We suggest that we may be neglecting in practice a number of unintended outcomes that impact upon both the individual and the organisation.

In order to explore these issues further we have identified a number of discourses and trends within lifelong learning and continuing professional education. We ask how these are influencing the HRD profession, and the assumptions and expectations of HRD practice inside organisations. We are interested in this chapter in a full spectrum of HRD interventions, whether initiated inside organisations by HRD professionals, or provided outside by training, development or education institutions. We are particularly interested in the role of higher education as regulator of profes-sional and managerial practice since this is a relatively unexplored topic. We hope that in drawing attention to these issues, which we argue are central to HRD, we will be able to influence the debate about the future of HRD.

The future of HRD

The future of HRD is much debated in the HRD academic literature, and is often conceptualised in terms of changing world events, for example, global competition, the technological explosion and organisational knowledge (Chermack *et al.*, 2003).

Bing *et al.* (2003), for example, identify a number of challenges which they suggest will face the HRD profession in the future, such as responding to multiple stake-holders, measuring impact and utility, orienting toward the future, focusing on problems and outcomes and achieving status as a profession. Relatively few com-mentators, however, acknowledge the social and ethical roles to be played by HRD in influencing workplace behaviours, or the role of HRD as moral conscience of the organisation (see Elliott and Turnbull, 2003).

Russ-Eft and Hatcher are the exception to this, acknowledging the critical role of HRD in defining ethical principles in the workplace. They state:

> We will have a future only if we start to acknowledge our role in developing sustainable workplaces/organizations. If we as HRD professionals continue to assume a subordinate role in organisations that are unethical and socially unresponsive then we are complicit.
>
> (2003: 302)

Chris Mabey has suggested that HRD probably 'incorporates the multiple threads of organizational existence most quintessentially' (2003: 430). He criticises those who take a single perspective of HRD, such as Swanson (2001), who focuses primarily on performance measures, or those who focus exclusively on the way that HRD reinforces unequal power relations whilst ignoring the potential of HRD to produce more empowering outcomes. He also criticises those who focus exclusively on HRD as individual development whilst ignoring learning as discourse (Fairclough and Hardy, 1997) or HRD as organisational learning. This fragmentation of HRD, as Mabey perceives it, leads him to propose that we need an 'interplay of multiple lenses', and that we will benefit from confronting the tensions and contradictions that appear in the HRD literature. This chapter applies the lenses of identity and the politics of pedagogic practices to examine HRD practice in the domain of management development, and asks what further questions and concerns the application of these lenses raises for the future of HRD.

The identity-shaping role of HRD

The starting point for this chapter is to examine the role of identity in professional development programmes. It is a question rarely raised by programme designers, since the espoused outcomes of most professional development programmes tend to focus more often on the less contentious domain of knowledge, competencies, skills and expertise. Since it is professional competence which is often perceived to be an important 'driver' for organisational performance, it is not surprising that for a long time now the HRD agenda has emphasised knowledge management and organisational learning, devoting considerable amounts of research money and time to the capture and retention of organisational 'know how' for competitive advantage.

Whilst this agenda is still as alive and important today, a focus on knowledge creation is not the only aspiration on an HRD practitioner's horizon. Alongside this, there has arguably been an equal emphasis on organisational culture and values. This focus has led, since the eighties, to an interest in designing professional development programmes, which enhance, shape or radically change the culture and values of the workforce. Like the 'knowledge' agenda, the rationale for this is competitive advantage.

Having reached its peak in the eighties and nineties when cultural change programmes were the most prolific form of management development, the vogue for cultural management is now waning. However, this has been replaced by similarly focussed 'Values' programmes which seek to instil company or organisational values into their employees. HRD practitioners have often found themselves at the helm of such initiatives, but frequently with little understanding of the impact they have on those who are targeted by them. We will provide some illustrations for this in the following paragraphs.

In this second important agenda for HRD professionals – the management of culture and values, it is the management of meaning and identity that takes the foreground and becomes prioritised, above the knowledge, skills and competencies agenda. However, whereas we as programme designers have numerous techniques and tools for measuring the enhanced skills produced by a knowledge-based training programme, we know much less, and have focussed very little, on how to identify, measure and evaluate the managerial and professional identities resulting from these values-based development programmes. This apparent neglect is of some concern. Twenty years on, it is timely to ask what is the legacy of the cultural change programmes of the eighties and how those managers targeted by the change initiatives are surviving in the ambiguous, fragmented and increasingly virtual organisations of the twenty-first century.

Much HRD is concerned with identity shaping – transforming managers into leaders, administrators into change agents and workers into quality experts. Organisations invest millions in transforming their employees into company people who will represent their 'core values', symbols to their customers of their ethos. Training and development play an essential part in this identity-shaping process. Little thought, however, has been given to the short- and long-term effects of training and development on the identities, emotions and well-being of those who participate in training programmes with powerful identity messages. This applies to many organisational programmes, but we are particularly concerned here with management and leadership programmes which often contain at their core models of certain ideal identities to which the participants are encouraged to aspire. We are also concerned that many of these same individuals are asked to undergo multiple development programmes throughout the course of their careers, and that these may be based on different and conflicting identity models, constituting multiple assaults on their identities.

As researchers, we may be open to accusations that at best we are missing an important element of the role of HRD, particularly in its role as providing professional development, and at worst that we are tacitly supporting a hidden and unacknowledged agenda of organisational control. To address this criticism, and to raise awareness of our role as moral agents, we need to ask some important questions about the implications of the identity-shaping role of HRD and the moral as well as social repercussions of this role.

We suggest that HRD professionals should be challenged to consider the models of professional identity that are implicit in their HRD programmes, and of course, the alternative identities that have already been silenced by the design of the process. The answers to these questions are not always evident, since many of the assumptions made inside today's organisations are the product of the socio-political climate and agenda in which they are situated. They have become so taken for granted that they are no longer visible or questioned – making our critique a difficult and not straightforward task.

Imbalances of power are inevitably implied by our questions, since in making assumptions around questions of professional identity, and in recognising some values above others, some behaviours above others, it is inevitable that certain voices, groups and identity roles will be heard above others. Issues of gender, class, ethnicity and belief, which often serve to differentiate those with power from those without, are likely to be hidden from view in many forms of continuing professional development. Whilst it is not within the purpose and scope of this chapter to seek to remove these inequities, we believe it to be important to uncover them, to spotlight the impact of them as sources of power imbalances, to recognise them as inevitable part of the HRD process and to ensure that they may no longer remain hidden from view.

This leads us to raise further questions of identity. Like power, identity issues are rarely the focus of research into the theory and practice of HRD. Yet identity is at the heart of all that we do, and identity shaping is an inevitable, yet under-recognised, aspect of continuing professional development, management education and all other HRD processes.

The management of the self, and self-identity, has been increasingly the concern of organisational scholars seeking to understand how work roles and relationships are continuously shaped and reshaped through work. Rose's (1989) seminal work, for example, raised the profile of identity work in his Foucauldian discussion of the technologies of self-monitoring, self-inspection and confession, and the therapy and techniques designed to govern the soul.

Identity construction is at the heart of the organisation, and has been studied quite widely amongst middle managers in particular (Kunda, 1992; Watson, 1994; Casey, 1995; Thomas and Linstead, 2002; Wajcman and Martin, 2002). Many of these studies have taken the form of deep ethnographies of managers in their workplaces, and have led to some important insights into the experiences of doing identity work. Wajcman and Martin (2002), for example, have analysed the construction of identity in modern management in the context of the reflexive modernisation thesis. This thesis has suggested that there is a social trend toward the freeing of individuals from institutional constraints to take ownership of the lifelong project of constructing their own career identities. However, Wajcman and Martin question the validity of this thesis, contrasting its portrayal of individuals as being in control of their career choices with Sennett's (1998) account of lost employees with unclear identities. They conclude that both models of the relationship between identity and work are limited, in particular in their gender neutrality. They suggest the analysis of narrative as a useful and rigorous technique for exploring people's conceptualisation of their own identities and the relationship between this and action.

How might we interpret the longer term impact of 'identity-shaping' development programmes on the individuals themselves, their home and work lives and their relationships? Before considering this question, we must first support our claim that identity management is embedded in corporate and academic HRD programmes, and that this phenomenon is closely related to the political processes which are inevitably present within all HRD interventions.

The politics of pedagogical practices

The politics of pedagogical practices in education and development interventions, such as those employed on the programmes described above is an issue rarely considered by HRD practitioners. Whilst more recent critical perspectives question the ethical implications of HRD practices in organisations, and across adult and professional education, generally, educators demonstrate little appetite for a critically reflexive examination of their own pedagogic methods and processes. Ellsworth's (1989) challenge to critical pedagogues for example, is a discussion that has yet to occur within management education (Perriton and Reynolds, 2004) and development. Yet, a political analysis of pedagogy reveals its significance in shaping individuals' experiences of, and approaches to, learning.

HRD's general refusal to examine the political nature of its role is better understood by placing it in the context of discourses and trends contained within lifelong learning and continuing professional education.

Over the last 15–20 years in the UK, government initiatives with regard to the education and training of adults have been designed to encourage individuals to take greater responsibility for the direction and pace of their own learning (Harrison, 2000). These assumptions concerning the configuration of the relationship between education, training, and the individual, as well as the role to be played by state-funded education within this, arose contemporaneously with broader debates about the adequacy of the nation's skills base to compete in the global economy.[1] This has led to a discourse that encourages individuals to follow a process of 'lifelong' learning as a means to increase autonomy and control over their status within the workforce. The individualisation of educating and training oneself for work, through techniques such as personal development planning and continuing professional education, is seen as a departure from 'progressive, ethical and liberatory' sentiments that have previously driven learning policies. Now the increased presence of the lifelong learning discourse is interpreted to be a product of economic determinism (Bagnall, 2000), one that is placed within a contemporary social and economic order that 'highlights instability and change as core conditions' (Harrison, 2000: 312). Wain (2000) makes the explicit link between lifelong learning and the concept of performativity, tracing its emergence back to the 1970s within the language of human capital theory and human resource investment. In arguing that the student-centred approaches to education and training that are common in professional education are advocated within a context of economic need for adult learning, Edwards observes the contradiction that this approach has as unquestioned orthodoxy the meeting of individual learning needs, so they 'are able to learn what is relevant for them in ways that are appropriate' (1991: 85).

Within the professions the emphasis placed on individuals to become lifelong learners has led to the development of systems of continuing professional education. Over the past 20 years such systems have increasingly come to regulate professional practice, in addition to relying more and more on universities to provide professionals' educational updates (Cervero, 2001). The trend for systems of continuing professional education to regulate practice has led to the incorporation of accountability systems for professional workers. This is despite a lack of evidence to demonstrate a connection between competence in professional practice and continuing education. In North America at least, continuing education in many of the professions is now a pre-requisite for re-licensure, a movement that Cervero (2001) sees as having arisen from clients' challenges to the professions in the form of litigation.

Awareness of the knowledge forms privileged through methods and processes of learning and assessment is conducive to an appreciation of their subsequent impact on the learner's experience. A Habermasian perspective on HRD pedagogies' cognitive interests illustrates further that even when HRD ostensibly focuses on the needs of participants, by employing less hierarchical practices for example, or when it seeks to take an ethical standpoint on HRD practices, there are nevertheless limitations to the extent to which we can influence wider discourses and trends, such as those identified here.

Habermas's work, specifically his theory of communicative action, has been influential in developing more participatory adult and professional education forms, and is generally acknowledged as being 'of central importance for critical educational theory and practice' (Welton, 1995: 136, quoted in Gosling, 2000; see also Reynolds, 1997). Examining the knowledge-constitutive interests of pedagogical methods provides a heuristic to illuminate their respective purposes, foci, orientations and projected outcomes. In doing so, this subsequently offers the possibility of formulating approaches to HRD pedagogies that work towards a more critical awareness.

Habermas's knowledge-constitutive interests arise from a challenge to science to remember the particular social needs or interests linked to the different knowledge and research traditions (Usher *et al.*, 1996). According to Habermas, three cognitive interests 'underpin the production of distinctive forms of knowledge (and associated types of science): a technical interest in production and control; a practical (historical-hermeneutic) interest in mutual understanding; and finally an interest in emancipation' (Willmott, 2003: 94). In seeking an understanding of 'how human interests are constitutive of different kinds of knowledge' (ibid.), the identification of cognitive interests facilitated 'a reflection on the conditions of the possibility of emancipation from ideologies and power structures' (Ottman, 1982: 79).

Illustrative case studies

In the following case studies we seek to illustrate both the political and identity-shaping nature of HRD practices through our recent empirical research.

Case study 1: the Aeroco Values programme

The managers of a large engineering company studied by Turnbull (1999) were extremely affected by a corporate Values programme that sought to change the culture from a macho, competitive, aggressive culture to one where partnership, collaboration, empowerment, sensitivity to others and the unity of the organisation were core values. The programme produced a variety of responses from the managers, ranging from scepticism to evangelism. However, it consistently evoked hope of success, fear of failure and the desire to believe in a dream that would subsequently prove to be elusive. The managers who did engage early on in the process, quickly took on board the new managerial identity expected of them, despite some difficulties discarding the identities with which they had previously been successful in their careers (Turnbull, 1999). A new language was adopted, first with humour, and later with serious intent to portray the new form of manager that they had been asked to become. Some found that this identity work conflicted with other non-work identities, and struggled with the consistency of their whole selves. Others found that the new identity was much more congruent with the selves that they recognised outside of their work persona, so slipped easily into a new work-based identity. The fear of most was that having brought their identities into line with what was asked of them by senior managers, this programme would be short lived, and change would once again be imposed upon them.

Their fears were well founded. Only twelve months after this programme had been rolled out to all one thousand five hundred middle managers targeted, the company merged with another company equal to it in size, became preoccupied with the merger, and the business demands that this entailed, and gradually the new corporate Values slipped off the agenda, and the new identities became redundant. The managers once again found themselves in a competitive arena where they were required, literally, to fight for their jobs, their departments' survival and to reclaim the combative identities that had preceded the programme.

In this case, the HRD function was expected by senior management to respond to the shifting demands of the business, and to comply with the demands of the present. However, they were not asked to, nor were they able to quantify, the emotional distress and dissonance caused by conflicting and ambiguous identity messages that they had been asked to convey. HRD was expected to enact the messages required by the present as it changed focus, but to disregard the past as it became considered obsolete. The mistaken belief of senior managers that the past had no power to shape the present caused confusion, disappointment and resulted in a legacy of cynicism and mistrust. In this case, as well as a significant impact on these managers' sense of self and managerial identity resulting from the programme, we also see political processes at play. Significantly, the technical interest of control that is apparent in the design of the programme clearly conflicts with the emanciptory language of the core values.

Case study 2: leadership development in the UK National Health Service

The second of our illustrations is a public sector organisation engaged in developing senior leaders through a bespoke programme, designed and delivered at a UK Management School. In this case, the aim was to re-energise a group of experienced leaders many of whom had become burned out, tired, trapped and low in energy as a result of the intractable problems that they faced every day. Their identities as Chief Executives and leaders were confused and ambiguous, and few of them had clarity about what it meant for them to be leaders, since they were responding on a daily basis to targets and measures set for them through the political agenda. They found themselves primarily in the role as buffers, interpreters, protectors and nurturers of those below them, and could speak only of their leadership identities in this way. Prior to the Leadership programme, few of them could articulate a clear leadership identity for themselves, and few could say much about leadership beyond the ideas that they read in popular airport bookshop literature. Instead, their identities were shaped by their vocation. They had joined the sector to serve others, and had strong views about the nature of the service they were delivering. They saw their roles as having increasingly become detached from the realities of this profession, driven instead by paper trails, protecting themselves and their followers from blame and punishment. Furthermore, they found their work roles to be directly competing with their home lives, since they were able to find fewer and fewer times in their working week for recreation or relaxation with their families.

The outcome of the leadership development programme designed and run for them was complex. They reported a clearer sense of self-worth as leaders, increased self-confidence, a greater sense of shared identity with the other leaders on the programme and a reduced sense of isolation. However, they also reported feeling alienated from aspects of their role which they felt did not make a difference, frustrated with meaningless targets and measures and some decided to leave the Service to pursue alternative roles. This is clearly a double-edged sword for HRD. In terms of an identity-shaping role the programme was clearly emancipatory for the leaders, however, when viewed as a political process the programme had destabilising effects on their working and home lives which the design of the programme was unable to address.

Case study 3: accredited management education programme, UK university

The findings emerging from a longitudinal study of managers following a part-time MBA show the unintended impact of pedagogic practices on individuals' approaches to learning and on their identity. The learning methods adopted by the programme were largely student-centred in intent, predominantly conforming to the experiential forms commonly used within management education (Vince, 1996). The programme design incorporated an Action Learning approach to facilitate individual learning, and encouraged participants to adopt an Action Research methodology when undertaking assessed work. In addition to the five 5,000 word assignments and the dissertation, students were assessed by case-study-based examinations. Individuals' expectations held at the start of the MBA were found to contradict their approach to MBA work as they progressed through the programme, and their responses illustrated the tensions between their expectations and programme aims. For example, when managers were first interviewed they placed importance on the learning and skills enhancement they saw the MBA providing. At a later stage, once they had received their first mark and tutors' comments, it was their own assessment that dominated responses to their MBA experience. Assessment was referred to continuously by participants throughout the 30-month period of the study, extending to 6 months after the programme's completion.

Action learning's cognitive interest

Examined within Habermas's framework of knowledge-constitutive interests, the action learning principles underpinning the programme can be understood to lead to a design that is guided by two cognitive interests. Underpinned by a conception of the individual that views her/him as capable of instituting some form of change, the action learning model implies that individuals can gain a measure of control over an aspect of their working lives. Its principles appear driven by a humanistic intent to empower individuals to take authority over a situation, and therefore might be considered emancipatory. The ways in which individual students might harness that power, in relation to the nature of the organisational intervention they initiate prompted by this model, is a separate consideration. That is, they may use the intervention itself in a more or less 'emancipatory' way. For example, it might initiate them to expose and rectify pay discrepancies between male and female workers. Alternatively, the intervention might lead them to introduce conditions of employment that reduce workers' rights to wage bargaining. As employed within management education programmes, the level of control implicitly made accessible to students by the action learning model mirrors characterisations of managers that view them as equally subject to the same processes they visit on others, as

> victims and not just agents of a rationality that inhibits critical reflection upon, and transformation of, a structure of social relations that systemically impedes and distorts efforts to develop more ethically rational, morally defensible forms of management theory and practice.
>
> (Alvesson and Willmott, 1996: 36)

Given this understanding of managers' positioning within social and organisational frameworks, the action learning model affords them at least the illusion of a degree of power and control within the moment of management education.

Assessment's cognitive interest

The anxiety apparent in interviewees' responses to the MBA, particularly with regard to the assessment of their assignments as it occurs within the programme's overall action learning framework, illustrates tensions contained with an experiential, student-centred, educational design. This correspondingly serves to reveal the dual nature of the cognitive interests driving the MBA. Interviewees' responses to the tutor-dictated framework placed on the assignments illustrated that in many instances they viewed it as an inhibitor to learning. Jo, for example, stated she found it difficult

> to always fit the work into the plan given to us, it has to be done in a certain way. Sometime I spend more time worrying about whether I have got information in the right parts than I do about the actual content.

Richard viewed the assignment structure as irrelevant when placed in an organisational setting:

> I now see, certainly within our own organisation how, if you're wanting to influence opinions, how you do it ... and it's not by writing 5,000 word essays.

Nevertheless, as soon as they registered for the MBA interviewees recognised that they must at least attempt to accede to the MBA's assessment frameworks, if they were to receive the desired and publicly accredited demonstration of their continuing education. To this end, the programme is driven by a technical interest.

Processes of assessment engage the technical interests of the MBA, and the accreditation of manager's continuing education occurs against the backdrop of the economic, political and social conditions that initiated the growth of management education programmes in the UK. Despite its location within an overall Action Learning framework that is based on aspirations of student autonomy, the organisation of assessment as it was employed on the MBA studied, conformed to a conventional model. Educators retained authority to judge and decide the standard individuals' learning had reached. Performed in the technical interest, in the Habermasian sense, continuous assessment processes are based on the assumption that marks motivate students to increase their efforts, and encourages them to seek cues (Miller and Parlett, 1973) as to how they might increase marks on subsequent pieces of assessed work. For example, after receiving the mark for his first assignment Huw speaks of how he sought guidance from tutors' comments:

> So, on the second one I did a hell of a lot more work, reading around the subjects, based on the comments fed back from the first one I did.

Political responses

The contradictions inherent to the MBA's various pedagogical practices elicited over time three main responses: accommodation, resistance and ambivalence; each response impacting on the students' identities as managers and learners. Briefly, whilst in the early stages the managers (as students) were prepared to submit to educators' requirements and accommodate their learning approach accordingly, by the time they had reached the halfway stage, they had become more questioning of the feasibility of the methods used to facilitate learning (e.g. the Action Learning sets), and the use of assignments as a way to assess their MBA learning. The case-study-based examinations threw into sharp relief the tensions between the participatory nature of the Action Learning approach, against the individualised nature of assessment. So whilst students worked together to prepare for the open book examinations, they wrote the exam scripts individually. The examinations were therefore illustrative of the different cognitive interests that shape many HRD interventions. On the one hand pedagogic practices are employed that have an emancipatory intent, whilst on the other the assessment of learning has a technical interest of control.

Concluding thoughts

We conclude from our discussion that HRD pedagogical practices are inevitably both political and identity-shaping. We have, therefore, made a case for developers to be cognisant when designing such programmes of the inherent ambiguities that are inevitably present in them. Both programmes designed and delivered 'in-house' as well as those run externally by business schools or training companies are frequently confused in the messages they contain regarding the implicit identities of the manager or leader around which a programme has been designed. The concept of career and self on which the notion of lifelong learning has been based and the contradictions within programmes which at the same time try to both emancipate and assess have been highlighted as contributing to participants' sense of confusion, and to identity-related tensions.

One important issue raised questions whether HRD should be in the identity-shaping business to the extent that it takes responsibility for an employee making a life-changing decision to change her/his career trajectory, or should it avoid such engagement? It is arguable that the moment that we start to engage with a person's work identity in any form, it is inevitable that this will have effects on their home and social identities that we neither see nor understand.

This places a heavy burden of responsibility and care on HRD practitioners designing such programmes. Not to take such impact into account when considering the impact of the design on participants may be challenged morally and practically. We are not arguing for a cessation of people development that impacts on identity, but instead for a greater attention by those involved in the design and delivery of HRD programmes to consider the immediate and longer term political impact of such programmes on other facets of their lives.

Much HRD discourse would claim to have a major influence on the planning and development of managerial and professional careers. Recent research, however, (e.g. Watson and Harris, 1999; Lord, 2003) has proposed the alternative view that career trajectories are accidental and emergent, rather than deliberately planned. Many identity-based assumptions and political processes are inherent in our practices concerning career development, the assessment and development of individual potential and the needs of the organisation.

Identity and careers are tightly knit and mutually reinforcing. In the cases described earlier career aspirations were clearly connected to managerial identity. In the first case, the managers had all achieved success in their careers as manifested by the senior grade that they had achieved. Without exception, they demonstrated awareness that this success had been brought about through demonstrating an identity which had previously been rewarded and revered as appropriate to success in this engineering industry. The nature of the programme required them to 'cast off' their former 'macho' identity and to 'take on' a softer, more empowering one. Inevitable tensions followed. In the second case, the leaders were nearing the end of their careers, were afraid of the consequences of relinquishing their leadership roles, and many of them were unable to conceive of a new identity for themselves beyond their current roles. These emotions were particularly poignant, given that they had seen a number of their colleagues removed from office as a result of low attainment against government agendas and targets. In the final case, the managers, as students, had sought to develop their careers by undertaking a programme of management education, ostensibly politically neutral, but which employed practices which engaged different interests. These, in turn, elicited a variety of responses that had repercussions for their relationship with the MBA, and also their managerial identities.

We have argued in this chapter that an understanding of such socio-political processes is vital for understanding and influencing HRD's role in the future. Whilst we acknowledge that there are many factors at play influencing the future of HRD, we hope that in raising attention to these issues we will be able to influence the debate further. We hope to ensure that the ethical implications of the work that we do in HRD are not removed from the agenda by the enthusiasm of those who seek to maintain the reputation and status of HRD by responding to global business, economic and technological trends. In our view, it is possible for HRD to take account of such trends, at the same time as remaining conscious of its role as critical reflector and moral conscience. Reflexive examination of our own pedagogic methods is both a crucial and moral imperative if we are to safeguard the future of HRD as playing a leading role in organisational life.

We propose, therefore, to work towards a pedagogy that makes explicit the power relations inherent within it as a basis for HRD-participant exploration of asymmetries of power at a broader social level, and which exposes and questions the implicit identity-shaping roles contained within any design.

Note

1 The growth of management education provision in HEIs, as well as the development of National Vocational Qualifications (NVQs) in management, arose from concerns expressed about managers' performance. NVQs were created through the twin drives of Constable and McCormick's, and Handy's reports, and a 1981 report of the then Manpower Services Commission that spoke of the lack of 'an educated, trained and flexible labour force' (Stead and Lee, 1996). Managers who worked towards gaining an NVQ predominantly did so whilst remaining within their organisations. However, both the rise of NVQs, and the growth of accredited management education programmes in Universities, can be seen as parallel lines of a track intended to lead to the 'professionalisation' of managers (Elliott, 2004).

References

Alvesson, M. and Willmott, H. (1996) *Making Sense of Management: A Critical Introduction*, London: Sage.

Bagnall, R.G. (2000) 'Lifelong learning and the limitations of economic determinism', *International Journal of Lifelong Education*, 19, 1: 20–35.

Bing, J.W., Kehrhahn, M. and Short, D. (2003) 'Challenges to the field of Human Resource Development', *Advances in Developing Human Resources*, 5, 3: 342–51.

Casey, C. (1995) *Work, Self, and Society. After Industrialism*, London: Routledge.

Cervero, R.M. (2001) 'Continuing professional education in transition, 1981–2000', *International Journal of Lifelong Education*, 20, 1/2: 16–30.

Chermack, T., Lynham, S. and Ruona, W. (2003) 'Critical uncertainties confronting Human Resource Development', *Advances in Developing Human Resources*, 5, 3: 257–71.

Edwards, R. (1991) 'The politics of meeting learner needs: power, subject, subjection', *Studies in the Education of Adults*, 23, 1: 85–98.

Elliott, C. (2004) *Critical Theory and Management Education. Pedagogic Practices and the Student Experience. The Case of a Part-Time MBA Programme*, unpublished PhD thesis, Lancaster University.

Elliott, C. and Turnbull, S. (2003) 'Reconciling autonomy and community: the paradoxical role of HRD', *Human Resource Development International*, 6, 4: 457–74.

Ellsworth, E. (1989) 'Why doesn't this feel empowering? Working through the repressive myths of critical pedagogy', *Harvard Educational Review*, 59: 297–324.

Fairclough, N. and Hardy, G. (1997) 'Management learning as discourse', in J. Burgoyne and M. Reynolds (eds) *Management Learning: Integrating Perspectives In Theory and Practice*, London: Sage.

Gosling, D. (2000) 'Using Habermas to evaluate two approaches to negotiated assessment', *Assessment and Evaluation in Higher Education*, 25, 3: 293–304.

Harrison, R. (2000) 'Learner managed learning: managing to learn or learning to manage?', *International Journal of Lifelong Education*, 19, 4: 312–21.

Kunda, G. (1992) *Engineering Culture, Control and Commitment in a High Tech Corporation*, Philadelphia, PA: Templeton University Press.

Lord, L. (2003) 'Women doing Leadership', *Proceedings of 2nd Annual International Conference on Leadership Research*, Lancaster University, 15–16 December.

Mabey, C. (2003) 'Reframing Human Resource Development', *Human Resource Development Review*, 2, 4: 430–52.

Miller, C. and Parlett, M. (1973) 'Up to the mark: a research report on assessment', Occasional Paper 13, University of Edinburgh: Centre for Research in the Education Sciences.

Ottman, H. (1982) 'Cognitive interests and self-reflection', in J.B. Thompson and D. Held (eds) *Habermas. Critical Debates*, London: Macmillan.

Perriton, L. and Reynolds, M. (2004) 'Critical management education: from pedagogy of possibility to pedagogy of refusal?', *Management Learning*, 35, 1: 61–77.

Reynolds, M. (1997) 'Towards a critical management pedagogy', in J. Burgoyne and M. Reynolds (eds) *Management Learning. Integrating Perspectives in Theory and Practice*, London: Sage.

Rose, N. (1989) *Governing the Soul: The Shaping of the Private Self*, New York: Routledge.

Russ-Eft, D. and Hatcher, T. (2003) 'The issue of international values and beliefs', *Advances in Developing Human Resources*, 5, 3: 296–307.

Sennett, R. (1998) *The Corrosion of Character*, New York: W.W. Norton.

Stead, V. and Lee, M. (1996) 'Intercultural perspectives on HRD', in J. Stewart and J. McGoldrick (eds) *Human Resource Development. Perspectives, Strategies and Practice*, London: Pitman.

Swanson, R.A. (2001) 'Human Resource Development and its underlying theory', *Human Resource Development International*, 4, 3: 299–312.

Thomas, R. and Linstead, A. (2002) 'Losing the plot? Middle managers and identity', *Organization Articles*, 9, 1: 71–93.

Turnbull, S. (1999) 'Emotional labour in corporate change programmes – the effect of organizational feeling rules on middle managers', *Human Resource Development International*, 2, 2: 125–146.

Usher, R., Bryant, I. and Johnston, R. (1996) *Adult Education and the Postmodern Challenge. Learning Beyond the Limits*. London: Routledge.

Vince, R., (1996) 'Experiential management education and the practice of change', in R. French and C. Grey (eds) *Rethinking Management Education*, London: Sage.

Wain, K. (2000) 'The learning society: postmodern politics', *International Journal of Lifelong Education*, 19, 1: 36–53.

Wajcman, J. and Martin, B. (2002) 'Narratives of identity in modern management: the corrosion of gender difference', *Sociology*, 36, 4: 985–1002.

Watson, T.J. (1994) *In Search of Management*, London: Routledge.

Watson, T.J. and Harris, P. (1999) *The Emergent Manager*, London: Sage.

Welton, M.R. (1995) 'In defense of the lifeworld in Habermasian approach to adult learning', in M.R. Welton (ed.) *In Defense of the Lifeworld: Critical Perspectives on Adult Learning*, New York: State University of New York.

Willmott, H. (2003) 'Organization theory as a critical science? Forms of analysis and "New Organizational Forms"', in C. Knudsen and H. Tsoukas (eds) *Handbook of Organization Theory*, Oxford: Oxford University Press.

Index

Lightning Source UK Ltd.
Milton Keynes UK
13 November 2009

146241UK00002B/46/P